Merry Christmas

love

Manuela + Don

FURY

OTHER BOOKS BY ANDREW H. MALCOLM

Unknown America (1975)

The Canadians (1985)

Final Harvest: An American Tragedy (1986)

This Far and No More (1987)

Someday (1990)

The Land and People of Canada (1991)

U.S. 1: America's Original Main Street (with photographs
by Roger Straus III) (1991)

Huddle: Fathers, Sons and Football (1992)

Mississippi Currents: Journeys Through Time and a Valley
(with photographs by Roger Straus III) (1996)

FURY

Inside the Life of Theoren Fleury

Andrew H. Malcolm

Canadian Cataloguing in Publication Data

Malcolm, Andrew H., 1943-
Fury: inside the life of Theoren Fleury

Includes index.
ISBN 0-7710-5655-9

1. Fleury, Theoren.   2. Calgary Flames (Hockey team).
3. Hockey players – Canada – Biography.   I. Title.

GV848.5.F56M34 1997   796.962'092   C97-931667-7

The publisher acknowledges the support of the Canada Council for
the Arts and the Ontario Arts Council for their publishing program.

Set in Sabon by M&S, Toronto
Printed and bound in Canada

McClelland & Stewart Inc.
The Canadian Publishers
481 University Avenue
Toronto, Ontario
M5G 2E9

1 2 3 4 5 6   02 01 00 99 98 97

Contents

To Connie, who booked those first seats right down by the glass

Preface

Despite my Canadian heritage, longtime residency, and a mother who bled blue for her Toronto Maple Leafs, I come late to a love of and fascination with hockey. One evening a few years ago out of another blue my youngest son, Keddy, who then was still wearing toddler-sized clothes, announced that he wanted to play ockey.

"You mean hockey," I said.

"That's what I said," he said, "ockey."

"And why do you want to play ockey?"

"Because," the four-year-old said, "in ockey you can go ka-pow!"

As a child, I helped change the tone of more than one chum's birthday party by turning musical chairs into a contact sport. So I have long felt that ka-pow is as good a reason as any to be attracted to a sport. I played baseball, football, and learned humility through wrestling. Our children have played football, lacrosse, wrestling, soccer, basketball, roller hockey, ice hockey, some at the collegiate level. Sports participation has been a requisite for each. Each chose a different one. But each had a sport – to play, to study, to practise, to improve at, to train for, to win at, to lose in, to dream about, to be watched doing, to remember doing, but especially to try hard in and thereby learn the rules of life, especially the rule about getting back up when you've fallen or experienced ka-pow. Life, after all, is not musical chairs.

Like most parents, I relish watching my children in sports. Since the decline of the frontier and the rise of public schools, our children do so much of their learning out of our sight. We see the report cards later. We hear the evaluation at parents' night. But the moments we can actively witness the actual progress of our offspring are preciously few, painfully brief, and eternally cherished.

Like most North Americans, I did not know much about hockey, except that Canadians and a growing number of Scandinavians, Russians, East Europeans, and now many thousands more Americans played it well, especially those in northern states and New England. I thought I knew, too, that every breathing Canadian followed hockey avidly and from October through June could be found on Saturday nights attending televised religious services at "Hockey Night in Canada."

I saw my very own reserved Canadian mother go berserk one night at a hockey game when she was the sole person in the arena to spot an obvious trip of one of her beloved Maple Leafs. My mother was born and raised in Toronto, the daughter of a hat-maker who lost his shirt in the Depression and took up farming. My father was born in Calgary and raised on the Canadian prairies by a dairy farmer and a one-room-schoolhouse teacher whose ideas about teaching and corporal punishment sprang from the Inquisition School of Education. As a Western Canadian, Dad felt compelled to cheer against any team from Eastern or Central Canada. Wherever we lived, the Great Canadian Divide ran across the middle of our family table.

Both my parents encouraged, facilitated, and, most importantly, bore witness to the ardent participation of their son in sports. "Minus to a plus," my father told me repeatedly; anyone could turn a loss in sports into a victory in life if they learned one lasting lesson from each loss.

So it was only natural that I did the same many years later. As a dutiful modern father and a pro-football fan drifting into disillusionment and apathy by the evening of that ockey conversation, I was ripe for plucking by a new athletic avocation. I went out the next weekend and purchased a guidebook to watching hockey. I began investing the occasional evening watching a National Hockey League game on cable TV, checking my guidebook, and learning the names of players and penalties.

"You know," I told my wife on about the second evening, "this is a pretty good game." She needed no convincing, having grown up in a family of New York Rangers fans and worked for years in Toronto. We then attended a few games and, like millions of others now, discovered that hockey is much more than a pretty good game. It is a great game of beauty and brutality. Let me admit right now, I am delightfully addicted.

And then one night I saw him for the first time. He looked remarkably small, almost tiny, even on television, a Cycloptic medium that chronically lacks perspective and, as a result, can easily make anyone look like Hercules. But this little guy was everywhere, darting in and out, getting knocked down, bouncing back up, annoying opponents to no end, frequently scoring, challenging players far larger and, as often as not, scoring again. I knew nothing about him except that I liked him very much.

Now, I am a normal North American. I love stories about valiant attempts. I wore out my book about Br'er Rabbit and Br'er Fox. I feel for Wile E. Coyote. I saw each *Rocky* movie at least three times. I admire underdogs. That's strange in a way for someone who spent his formative years growing up and absorbing the often conflicting values between the historically uncertain second-largest country in the world and the smaller but more populous United States next door which instinctively, though not always accurately, feels the spotlight of destiny on its back.

I was raised in an era before video games, "Sesame Street," and Barney. I learned the alphabet from letters cut out of wood by Dad. For growing up my media were radio, which incited my imagination, the welcoming lap of a bosomy Canadian grand-mother, which made me feel loved no matter what, and the worldly-wise, accidental edicts of a taciturn Canadian prairie father who came equipped with the required moustache and no apparent hard feelings that he had nothing ever given to him; you earned your bounty or you did without, in his book. Oh, yes, and I also had books.

Perhaps, in the absence of siblings, books are more important for a youngster learning the patterns and rules of life. Books always have loomed large for me, even when they were small. I particularly remember thin books touting the exploits of the Little Engine That Could, a railroad steam engine that pulled an immense load on the tracks up a huge hill through determina-tion and the rhythmic mantra "I think I can, I think I can." And there was a book about a minor tugboat named Little Toot that despite the initial disdain of far larger tugs turned out to be fully capable of moving giant ocean liners and, indeed, saving one from disaster, merely through pluck and determination.

"You can do anything you set your mind to," my father said. And so, not perceiving the possibility of failure, this teenager from a small rural town in Ohio set out to become a foreign correspondent in the big leagues for the great *New York Times*. Grit, determination, pluck, stick-to-it-iveness were all character-istics my father collected into an admirable classification called "Heart." Underdogs could never lose in our eyes because simply by trying hard against impossible odds, they made themselves victors. Never mind the final score. Vince Lombardi wouldn't understand.

Now there, before my eyes regularly on that television screen, was a living Little Toot. His name was Fleury. He played for the Calgary Flames. I started to watch for Fleury and the Flames. And I was mightily impressed.

I still am.

A friend asked me recently how I came to write a book about a little guy in the big leagues. I said it was the usual way those things happen – I grew up in small farm towns in Ohio and Ontario, the only child of two only children, raised four children of my own, spent twenty-six years wandering North America and the world as a reporter, correspondent, editor, and columnist for the *New York Times*, authored nine other books, at the age of fifty leaped across the continent into a new adventure as an aide to the Governor of Montana to see how government works from inside, took an eight-year-old son to a summer hockey school in Calgary, and fell in fascination with a young man from Manitoba the same age as my oldest son. Isn't that the usual way?

I have always been blessed – or cursed – with a keen sense of curiosity. Why do things happen or people act the way they do? That curiosity drove my parents crazy on long car trips. Relentless curiosity served me quite well in journalism, less so in government. Perhaps curiosity is part of the intellectual legacy of the son of an engineer. I can remember a seminal lesson one Saturday as a pre-teen when I was fully prepared to bash into mangled submission a lawnmower which stubbornly defied my threats and attempts to start its engine. My father quietly suggested a less ka-pow approach, which produced the information that the gas tank was bone-dry. There is, it seemed, usually more to any situation than is readily apparent.

Not only was I keenly curious about the life of any highly successful professional athlete. I was keenly curious about the life of *this* highly successful professional athlete. What was in his gas tank? How does a boy, this boy, from a poor prairie family succeed despite his size, when so many other larger players fail despite their size? How did he get so good? What's it like to be so good at what you do? To stay so good? To live on the road with the team? To be the idol of countless thousands? To be recognized everywhere? To earn more money in any one year than most of us will see in a lifetime? How do you live with fame? How does someone like this fit into a larger team, even a smaller-city sports franchise that must itself fight its own struggle up a huge hill against teams with far larger audiences and finances and the skilled resources they can send into battle on the ice?

All of my professional storyteller's instincts, honed over a half-century from a grandmother's lap to the war zones of Asia, told me there was a whole lot more to this person, to this sport, to this business, to this team, to its members' individual and collective lives, and to the unknown details of their human stories than anyone could possibly spot from the outside, despite all the bright lights, TV cameras, and crowds' eyes watching in the arenas. All of my instincts told me there were fascinating details to be learned when the team leaves the bright ice, steps beyond the boards onto the rubber mats, and walks stiffly down the dark ramp beneath the stands. So I walked down the ramp, too, and inside the life of a hockey team and a hockey star.

All of my instincts were correct. This book is what I found out inside.

Andrew H. Malcolm
Helena, Montana

FURY

It sits on the corner of Crerar Street and Third near the northern edge of a tiny Manitoba prairie town called Binscarth, a dark, brooding metal hulk that houses a hallowed homemade glacier where silence rules the long night's darkness and the air on a midwinter's midnight is colder inside than out.

A hooded figure, probably a strong athletic body though stooped now, and limping, crunches through the pale light and lonely snow towards the old building. He has already worked twelve hours in a potash mine, four days on, four days off, according to the efficiently choreographed schedules of modern industry. He lost his real dream to a bad knee. It's a familiar story in this world. And the collision with that other knee may not have been an accident, which is another pain to endure.

But Dave Chartier still savours every moment of his brief time in the big league. He talks about it with ease and warmth. And he smiles when he thinks about another local boy who first skated in this same structure and then, against all odds, took his skills to faraway ice rinks where fame and fate waited.

Dave Chartier removes one frayed glove, fumbles for a key, and unlocks the frigid padlock to this aging, rundown temple of ice where so many dreams of glory are still born. Dave flicks on the switches to eighteen bare bulbs across a vast room. Most of the bulbs still work. Instantly, the ghosts of players past and games gone by evaporate into the disappearing darkness. Dave's warm breath hangs in a minor indoor cloud while the ice seems to glow strangely. Dave will spend the next two hours in rubber boots pulling a leaking barrel of water on a sled back and forth across the mammoth indoor sheet of ice, adding yet another quarter-inch of frozen water to the dirt floor.

Tomorrow afternoon, after school, Dave will again tutor his seven-year-old son, Nick, in the hockey skills and attitudes that are shaping the dreams and talents of thousands of new athletic adherents across North America these days. But hockey across Canada in general and the Canadian prairies specifically is nothing new. It is more than a way of life; it is an integral part of life, a pastime that becomes a controlling passion and pervades the non-summer lives of players and families alike with the comfortable regularity of the three seasons it spans. Hockey even invades Canada's vocabulary outside sports. In some countries political debates are called debates; in Canada, they are faceoffs.

The dreams and expectations, the thrills and pains, and, importantly, the stories that the game of hockey produces regardless of the score unite generation after generation in a seamless series of shared experiences that expand and grow in the embellished retellings over the years, while the aging bodies themselves may expand in different directions. Hockey with its physical artistry is a perfect reflection of the no-nonsense rural culture that spawned it – originally outdoors, no time for empty talk, instinctive, tied to the seasons. It is also a legalized form of aggression and has become the focus of unquantifiable civic pride as players on each town's teams from the age of six to beyond forty venture out to confront similar opponents in regular contests, not unlike medieval jousting tournaments, that become the fodder for endless café chatter long after the scoreboard goes dark.

The youngsters are raised watching their fathers and siblings play hockey and watching their mothers, their brothers and sisters, their schoolmates, even their childless neighbours, watch them play hockey. They see the pictures in the weekly newspaper enshrined on the refrigerator doors at home. And they see the framed photos lining the walls at the rink. Pictures celebrating a band of kids who came together briefly one season years ago with a couple of dads as volunteer coaches, who practised together, travelled together, laughed and sang and maybe even cried together, and who became, for one brief, shining moment, a Hockey Team – a group of disparate youths who discovered the natural narcotic that they could be more together than they were apart. Perhaps even more than they would ever be later as grownups.

Their hair is all tousled and sweaty in the yellowing photos where many hold up one forefinger. Their pains are forgotten, their bonds invisible but more powerful and lasting than any epoxy. Their victory smiles are frozen in time like the blind, innocent, and unwrinkled hope of children. Life might be hard and unfair most of the time for most of the rest of it. Simply enduring then could be their victory. But no individual adversity could ever erase those victorious moments frozen in frames. These boys were winners once. And they will always have their trophy to prove it.

Playing hockey becomes a given for most, something automatic and beyond decision that most boys, and now not a few girls, assume they will do through much of childhood and, if they are good and lucky, perhaps for some time beyond. Up they go through the complicated layers of skills, ages, and letters that divide the sport – Novice, Atom, Mite, Peewee, Bantam, Midget A, Junior B, Junior A. If they are lucky and very good, or the reverse, and if they stay healthy, they might turn pro and be paid to play for one of the teams that come and go in the leagues with names like the Colonial, United, East Coast, Western Pro, Central, American, or the I, the International Hockey League. More teams have sprung up across the continent in recent years to serve as partial farm teams for the top level, the National Hockey League, and to tap into the sports hunger, leisure time, and wallets of North Americans seeking entertainment, diversion, and some kind of winner to invest their local loyalty in and to wear the logo of on their shirts, hats, jackets, and cars.

For those teams hockey can be a marginal business. It is no less risky for the players, who come and go like gunfighters or cowhands for hire, as determined by their skills, luck, health, and owners. Some players progress. Some come and stay. Others survive but briefly before heading home to play in local recreational leagues with neighbours and old schoolmates and, of course, to share the hockey stories they have collected like scars.

But for many players, in addition to a dream and, for the chosen few, a career, this old game – like most games actually – can also be a blessed escape from anything worth fleeing: disappointment at home, failure in school, a bleak future at work, personal burdens. Hockey can also be an escape from the crushing predictability and limits of life within certain strata of Canadian society, especially in the small communities that dot the vast Canadian countryside like specks of sand on the floor of some vast freezer with the sky for a ceiling. They may not know what they are getting into, these youngsters who still labour for love of the game, but they do know what they are getting out of. For them, hockey represents an escape route, probably *the* escape route from the feared future. For a very few, it is. And the rink, The Rink, is where it all starts.

Binscarth's rink is one of thousands across the continent, some modern and new, complete with concession stands and even massage rooms, some ancient and still aging with discomfort, where the smell of competing bodies accumulates for years and the coats of paint are so numerous they may actually strengthen the old walls. Other rinks are eagerly constructed outdoors early each winter on ponds where bonfires burn by the shore to warm the hands during breaks and keep the shoes from freezing for a few hours. Or the rinks are minuscule backyard affairs of frozen water produced by fathers in the incongruous but heartwarming midnight sight of parka-clad men repeatedly hosing down the lawn in seriously sub-zero weather. If you build it, they will skate. And they do, and they do for uncounted hours. The memory of these healthy heroics will warm the heart and mind for years after, despite the actual temperatures right now.

❖

On this very same patch of ice in Binscarth, beneath the same bare beams and forever-rusting metal roof, about a quarter-century ago another little boy stared out on the same alluring pale-blue frozen water. A shy kindergartener, he mixed well with classmates, when he chose to. But he often opted instead to stand apart, watching closely though perhaps pretending not to.

The boy looked smaller than he was, but he exuded an intense, quiet charm. Adults who knew him always suspected there was much more going on in that mind and little life than met the eye. He loved music and singing but didn't mind fighting. And when he talked, when asked, the boy spoke with a startling openness despite his size and with an insight, almost an unprovoked defiance, that intrigued adults and, later, many others who would watch him and wonder what fuelled and sustained the intensity of such an athletic dynamo.

Almost as a fluke one short winter's afternoon – there are so many of them surrounding the brief, glorious months of summer sun on these northern plains – Greg Slywchuk, a friend and fellow kindergartener, had invited this little boy to go skating after school. It was one of those dim days of childhood that pile on top of each other unnoticed. Only later, with the wisdom of hindsight, did that one day come to stick out from all the others as particularly fateful. And one neighbour had snapped a photo. Had the little boy been ill that day, would Greg or someone else have issued the invitation another day? Would the little boy have ventured to the rink by himself some other afternoon? Skating had not occurred to the youngster. But that day he ran home and asked his mother if the family owned skates.

They did not own much of value. Changing jobs and moving yourself twice in five years from one labourer's job in one province to another in another tends to minimize the acquisition of material possessions. But deep in a cluttered closet – and there were many of them in that household – the boy's mother had found a rusty pair. She bundled her oldest son up in a family hand-me-down snowsuit and boots and sent him off before the gathering darkness down a row of towering spruces, along snow-covered Thacker Street to Third, altogether a half-mile of curb-less streets to the crumbling old rink. The battered skates were stashed in a torn pillowcase slung over his frail little shoulders.

From the back, toddling off in the snow, little Theo looked like an elf. He had no idea what lay ahead that afternoon at The Rink – he remembers a lot of wobbling that first time – or the many afternoons and nights and mornings ahead at so many other rinks for so many years that they became a blur and he had to remind himself now and then of what he had. Now and then.

But he had sat on that same worn wooden bench in that very same dusky rink, watching the other boys closely without speaking, as younger boys do so astutely when they need to learn without revealing ignorance. For the first of what would become many thousands of times, the boy pulled on his hand-me-down skates without socks, left foot first, as it happened and as it would happen forever more. He laced up these strange boots, as he saw the others doing. And then with a searing intensity that was to impress many and frighten a few, he glided off beneath the same lights into a remarkable, fame-filled, lucrative, controversial, all-star career despite all the obstacles of injury, disease, prejudice, and size.

He was – and is – Theoren Fleury, indisputably the smallest player and arguably the largest inspiration in the National Hockey League. Fleury is the Little Engine That Could in the world's fastest-growing professional sport. You can't stop watching him, such big actions, big goals, and big attitude from such a little package. You hate him when you play against him, until he's on your team. And even then, there might be times . . .

◆

Nearly seven hundred miles, several worlds, and one lifetime to the west, Mike Duben and Keith Thomson arrive for work in another hulking metal edifice. This one, too, has snowdrifts on the roof. But it is much, much larger than Binscarth's. It is shiny, almost garishly coloured, sprawling over several city blocks like a silver saddle in the afternoon shadow of downtown Calgary, one of those bustling Western can-do kind of cities where most everyone seems to come from somewhere else.

Like Dave Chartier with his rusty old barrel, Mike and Keith make ice, only they do it with powerful engines that glide across the ice on rubber wheels, skimming off the old frost, and laying down a glassy-smooth surface for flashing skates that have never known rust, and never will.

The television trucks are in place now. The cameras are warming up. And the time is booked on the satellite hovering 21,300 miles overhead to carry this athletic confrontation to millions of people far away who have scheduled their dinners and politely dodged competing social obligations to avoid missing one minute of this compelling competition as it unfolds with intriguing immediacy before their eyes. That is one of the most important, least noticed appeals of professional sports: there will be an ending to this contest, most likely a decisive one. The score will probably provide a clear winner and a clear loser. There is none of the incompleteness of so much of the rest of their increasingly complex lives, when success and learning and rewards, even justice, can take forever to arrive, if they ever do.

Upstairs, Peter Maher is sipping a cup of hot tea laced with honey and not talking. He, too, is a long way from his upbringing. Co-workers know to avoid idle chatter in the pregame hours when Peter studies his notes and saves his voice. For more than three hours tonight in a nonstop staccato account that mirrors the rapidfire action on the ice far below him, Peter's mellow voice and urgent descriptions will carry the game's action to thousands of hockey fans across parts of three provinces and one state.

Peter's competitors in the newspaper business are gathering to feed off the event, too. No matter who wins or loses, if they can make their written accounts exciting enough or different enough or full enough of unusual or unexpected conflict tonight, they will be briefly praised by superiors, read by thousands, and admired by colleagues, they believe. And they know for certain which player's quotes sell the most papers.

At the Saddledome's front door Robbie Forand is answering yet another call from a Flames fan almost incoherently irate that the team is underachieving despite the immense salaries of its overpaid professional players, some of whom are barely old enough to legally buy beer. In the locker room, the windowless world that becomes a home for the team for most of each year, Bobby Stewart has arranged dozens of sticks and twenty uniforms in just the way that each player prefers. Across the hall Gary Taylor mans five satellite dishes and fourteen VCRs, taping the games played by upcoming opponents. Al Coates, the gregarious general manager, and Pierre Page, the bug-eyed, French-speaking veteran who sometimes sounds more like a professor than a head coach, are huddling behind closed doors debating the call-up of a minor-league player and deciding the fate of two veterans who have not been producing.

Ron Bremner, the newer, responsive, hands-on president of the Calgary Flames Hockey Club, is patrolling the concourse eavesdropping for customer comments, watching for poor service, and randomly handing out certificates for free food to unsuspecting fans wearing Flames garb. The team president is pumped on this game day, as usual. On the way in, as usual, he told Eddie, the parking-lot attendant, that he expected a big game from him. "Yes, Mr. Bremner," said Eddie, as usual.

Across town Stella Gendron has invited one of her grown sons to her apartment. It is always good to see Alan, of course. He remains a good boy in his mother's eyes; he played hockey, too, you know. Full of feistiness and aggression, he was, though he never has been a large man. And Alan was a pretty good skater also. As a boy, he loved – oh my, how he loved – the Chicago Blackhawks and Bobby Hull, which is okay, liking an American hockey team, as long as it was one of the original six NHL teams.

But more importantly on this evening, Stella wants Alan to program her VCR to tape The Game. More accurately, she wants to record the athletic exploits of her favourite player to watch over and over again. The widow has never met him. But her kitchen and refrigerator are plastered with his photos. She has a radio in the kitchen and another in her bedroom and a television in the living room so, wherever she walks during a game, she won't miss a second.

She knows she loves him like another son, just from the determined, creative moves he makes on the ice, from the obstacles she knows he has overcome on the ice and off, from the joy of shared success he has unknowingly brought into her life, and from that youthful exuberance and gaptoothed grin he shows when he scores yet another goal and falls to his knees on the ice, looking up at the heavens in open-armed appreciation. "Don't you just love him?" Stella will ask friends, expecting no answer.

Liz Ripak is a high-school guidance counsellor and a fan, too. Forty-one times every winter Liz sets aside her personal life and professional worries to work for minimum wage in the green coat of an usher so she can see the Calgary Flames in general and one player in particular.

Matthew Naylor will be there too, this night. He is eight. He plays hockey. And he has a shirt just like that of his favourite player. Several times a year he goes to a Flames game with his father. Someday, if chance proves charitable, Matthew will talk with him again, a close encounter of the fame kind, and this time he will be able to speak.

Except for its ice-free cleanliness, the pickup truck pulling into the Saddledome parking lot looks like all the rest of the pickup trucks that seem to outnumber cars on the streets of western North America. It moves slowly, deliberately, towards its familiar parking spot while country music seeps around the darkly tinted windows, firmly closed against the cold. The Alberta licence plate says TV1, so the gate guard waves it on through. She, too, is a fan and nods to the familiar though unseen driver within.

When he steps from his expensive truck into the snowy parking lot as dusk begins to fall, the young man in the leather jacket and battered baseball cap is intentionally unaware of it all. On the street this Huck Finn of hockey seems unassuming enough, belying the financial fact that every seven months he will earn many times more than most people or most team-mates make. Indeed, his wispy goatee and shy visage suggest to some a quiet youth poking his booted toe in the dust rather than the aggressive, savvy, feisty twenty-nine-year-old multimillion-aire captain of a professional hockey team who has played and succeeded in – and survived – more than six hundred pro-hockey games in one of the world's most brutal and beautiful sports.

He is no towering physical presence, which has misled many over the years. Those legs may be short. But they reach all the way to the ice. And when they get to churning atop skates, when the ice chips start flying off the razor-sharp edges of those steel blades, as the heavily muscled body gains speed and weaves an inert rubber disk past defenders towards the enemy's goal with lightning moves and a physical intuition given by God and honed by loneliness and determination, thousands of followers this night will be pulled from their seats as one. They will find themselves screaming uncontrollably in anticipation and appreciation, as if they, too, are on the ice in the battle below reaching for fame and glory with their hero. And he will hear them too, as he always does, always has, even as he shifts his shoulders ever so slightly to one side trying to lure the goalie to open that sliver of vulnerable space just another inch. And he will bask in the intense warmth of the crowd's fragile appreciation. There are several aspects to life as a Famous Person. This is the fun part of fame.

The man's hat is pulled way down over his ears. His shoulders, though hunched against the cold, are surprisingly thick, like his scarred arms. His hands are stuffed into coat pockets. His upper lip seems stuck in place to cover the large gap of missing teeth that has become something of an accidental trademark. And there may be a plug of chewing tobacco in there somewhere. His eyes, surrounded by round wire glasses, shift about his surroundings trying to mask the vulnerability but missing nothing, which is the way he plays as well. When he meets people, he looks them straight in the eye. Why not, right? When he shakes hands, as fans always want to do to confirm their presence in his presence, his grip is impressively firm, though half his right hand feels nothing. Which is no big deal, because he says so.

He is receding into his own private world now, the world of the Game, when everything he knows, or has ever learned, over twenty-five years first in the game and now in the business is focused on the next lightning-like move. Every care or concern should be gone now. Every moment of childhood hunger when he was hundreds of miles from home amid angry opponents, a few admiring strangers, and surrogate parents, every game with teammates who both admired and resented him sometimes at the same time, every moment of fear before the drunken father and dazed mother, every fight in school, every endless restless night on the junior-hockey bus wandering hundreds of miles across darkened prairies likely to lose again, every boo and bruise, every cheer and goal, every dashed hope and cut, the hand-me-down equipment and the racial insults about his Métis heritage, all of the blood and pain and stitches, the fearsome smell of the operating room, the sudden, uncontrolled shock on the doctor's face, every intoxicating victory and every gut-wrenching loss are forgotten.

All that matters is right now. This game. This moment. Soon, he will be free, unleashed. He can be himself again within the walls of this small patch of bright ice in his own private world despite all the peering onlookers. Intense. In this world, he is admired for what he is, not judged for what he is not. Just reacting. Just doing. Just being himself, one of the best hockey players in the world.

In about two hours, according to the clock counting down over the locker-room door, he will be back home on the shiny ice where he has rarely failed and where his fans have even more rarely failed him. He will fiddle with a new hockey stick like a violinist stringing a bow. He will don his gear exactly the same way he has some fifteen thousand times since that first dusk with Greg in the Binscarth rink, left side first. Then, with his stick stuck in his gladiator's gloves like a weightless twig, he will skate onto the ice the same way he always does with that same broad stance his father taught him and the same gentle rolling gait. He looks casual, which is what he wants. His eyes will search the filling stands for a familiar face or two. When he catches their eyes from among the many also beseeching his gaze through the thick glass, he will raise his stick in a quiet appreciative salute, which makes them feel warm and welcome, which, of course, he knows.

Every game is a fresh opportunity. Ritually, without touching any of the painted lines – for that would be bad luck – he will skate those familiar broad lazy loops around Calgary's end of the ice. Slowly, amid teammates also going through their own private pregame rituals, he will gain speed. Faster and faster. And faster. And even faster. As if he seeks to outrun something. And faster still. Until the arena's well-lit adjacent world of colour and noise and hope and fear and beer is a blur. Until there is no time to think. No way to remember. There is only time to do.

And not much of that either.

Here he is, Theoren Fleury, at 66 inches and 160 pounds the most minute player in the National Hockey League and the most famous kindergartener ever to play on the Binscarth rink. "We're all just kids in this business," he says, scrunching his baseball cap around on his close-cropped head. "And we always will be kids as long as we get to play the game."

It may be hard for anyone who isn't a National Hockey League player – and everyone in the world save 640 people are not National Hockey League players – to think of these immense icons as kids. Their average height now is six-foot-one, before skates and helmet. That's fully two inches taller than twenty-five years ago.

The average player's weight is creeping past 200 pounds, an increase of about two pounds every year. And that is before the nearly twenty pieces of gear they wear. Many players, of course, are larger, some up near 240 pounds. Some prospects moving towards the big time are six-six; one is six-eight. So large are the players getting, even discounting the constant media attention that seems to exaggerate the size of anything within its gaze, that the league recently had to increase the legal length of the stick.

At the same time the average player's age is down slightly, to about twenty-six. So they are younger and larger. And more of them are not coming from Canada. In the late 1960s, nearly 97 per cent of National Hockey League players were Canadian. Today, six of ten NHL players are Canadian, dropping one or two percentage points every year. Seventeen per cent are American and about 23 per cent are non–North American.

For decades, some Canadians mumbled disappointment that the world in general failed to realize what a great game their national pastime is. Now that the best athletes of more countries are choosing to compete in hockey, some Canadians are mumbling that they are encroaching on Canada's national game. Even Japan has created a team for international competition, and hired a Canadian adviser. The worst blow to national pride was when an inspired U.S. team came from behind to defeat the Canadian team, including a determined Fleury, for the 1996 World Cup. Theoren's brother Ted was videotaping that game for his sibling. When the Americans scored the winning goal, he broke the cassette over his good knee.

For its part, Fleury's team in Calgary averages slightly shorter, lighter, and younger than the league norm. That's not surprising, as the Flames progress through a youth movement, which head coach Pierre Page preferred to call a "refurbishing" not a rebuilding. The Flames are also slightly more Canadian (two-thirds) than the league average.

Frankly, Fleury is somewhat tired of hearing about his diminutive size, though out of politeness he doesn't complain publicly. He has always been small, even as a baby. He has never known big, so he has nothing to compare to small. In the euphoric locker room within the late Montreal Forum in 1989, the Flames were celebrating their first Stanley Cup championship, also the first and last ever taken from the Montreal Canadiens on that home ice. Standing on a bench for an interview, a baby-faced Fleury ending his first NHL season couldn't believe his own excitement at winning his first Stanley Cup. "It's something you dream of since you're just this high," he yelled over the noise. Then, he paused. "Of course, I've always been just this high."

A young woman saw that game on TV with her father. It would mean something only years later.

Fleury says he suffered from "small man's syndrome" throughout childhood, which helps explain the invisible chip on his shoulder in playground scraps and on the ice. As Fleury's reputation as a player spread across Manitoba, even before his tenth birthday, people who had never heard of his home town of Russell flocked to tournaments to see "that little guy." Indeed, in the eyes of coaches, scouts, and fans, his impressive skills may well have been magnified over the years by his small size. Less was expected of a small player, so more was seen.

To this day youngsters are drawn to him. Fleury's face, though more scarred and less baby-like than when he entered the league for good in 1989, is still young-looking and memorable because of the missing teeth, as if his new ones have yet to grow in. His enthusiasm is more mature now but still youthful and apparent – and engaging. Although every hockey player is happy to score a goal, Fleury is ecstatic. Before being swallowed within a celebrating crowd of much taller teammates, Fleury might fall down on his knees in joy. Sometimes he skates around on one foot strumming his stick like a guitar. Or if the goal occurs in

San Jose or some other city where the fans are particularly vocal in their dislike of him, Fleury might skate close to the glass for a few moments, firing his stick like a machine gun into the crowd. They hate him. He loves it. To show his appreciation, he may score another goal.

These antics incense the enemy crowd, as they are intended to do, and bring smiles and chuckles to Fleury's fans, including some former teammates watching via satellite back in Manitoba. "That's Theo!" they'll say. His exuberance annoys, even infuriates, his much larger opponents, who have become accustomed to society's deference to their physical size and prowess. What they say about Fleury is not quoted in family newspapers. But they aren't chuckling when they say it.

Fleury's clear and intended uppitiness, of course, gets their mind off their game and has helped him score so many goals and draw so many penalties from opponents over the years. They get so busy looking for him and being annoyed at him, and maybe even trying to trip him, that they forget someone else on Fleury's team or they are tripped or slashed by that disrespectful little ant. They retaliate. The retaliation draws a penalty and Fleury calmly skates away to join the power play with one less larger fellow to get in his way. Those opponents remaining on the ice, and their incensed supporters in the stands, are focused on Fleury, which pleases Fleury no end.

Ask Fleury how he lost his front teeth. "Well, the first time," he says, "was in Junior. This guy stuck the blade of his stick in my mouth like this." Listeners wince. "Yeah," Fleury said, and then shrugged before breaking into a gaptoothed smile, "but I scored the game-winner on the power play."

Fleury also got to spend nine hours that night on the team bus back to Moose Jaw holding his upper lip over the new gap and the newly exposed nerve. That's just part of the price he paid along the way.

The youngsters at the Theoren Fleury Hockey School hang on their idol's every word. Plenty of time later for autographs. Right now, the hockey god is standing right there next to them in a school jacket with another beaten baseball cap crumpled on his head. He looks more, well, human in person. His hockey-gloved hands are cupped atop his stick holding up his chin. The teeth are still missing. His skates are untied. His eyes search the eager throng of eighteen youngsters.

Every one of them there wants to be in the National Hockey League someday. Every one of them there wants to know how it is done. Every one of them there is eight years old.

"Listen," says the NHL veteran, who has his own nine-year-old son plus a new toddler. "There are, what, three hundred of you in this summer hockey school. If we're lucky, maybe one of you will make a living at hockey. That's a fact. But every one of us can make hockey a great game in our lives. We can have a lot of fun. Watch this."

The all-star athlete proceeds to skate to the far end of the ice. He leans into an ice-spraying turn. His thick legs start driving his blades to dig into the ice. Quickly, he gains speed. He seems to be flying now and some youngsters instinctively step backwards. He weaves slightly, just as each of his eager students has seen him carrying the puck towards the opposition's net in a riveting game of chicken called the breakaway. But this time two-thirds of the way down the ice Fleury suddenly stands straight up. He swings his hockey stick between his legs and squats down on it like a witch on her broom. The youngsters start to chuckle. Fleury digs one blade into the ice and begins whirling in wild circles, seemingly out of control. Actually, it is a game Fleury learned a long time ago in a place far, far away.

In moments, the eighteen hockey-star wannabes are all racing around the ice like witches on brooms, practising ice-skating balance without knowing it. A few minutes later, they reassemble at centre ice around the main man. "Any questions?" he asks.

"Hey, Theo," says one youngster full of enthusiasm and slightly void of breath. "How can you play in the NHL with all those big guys when you're so small?"

Suddenly, Fleury is smiling no more. He is deadly serious. The childish laughter dies quickly. Have the students offended the professor? Silence sweeps the ice as Fleury leans down, not too far down, to look the now wide-eyed boy in the face.

"Because," Fleury says very slowly, turning his head towards everyone, "I don't *think* of myself as small."

There is a pause while these eight words are processed by each tiny mind. Slowly, a flicker of recognition moves invisibly from youngster to youngster, for whom physical smallness is a daily fact of life. They look at each other to confirm their mutual amazement. They smile. And every one of the little helmets begins to nod. They, too, have now been empowered.

Everything on Canada's prairies is bigger than the people – the landscape, the seasons, the weather, and the unseen economic forces far away that set the world price for what is grown and mined and shipped away, including the young people who play out their ambitions on distant stages that are smaller but more populous and lucrative. These prairies were born in cold, which explains the furs that were the initial attraction for the outsiders who came. Millions of years ago immense tongues of ice began accumulating to the north and slowly sliding down in icy waves to change the face of North America for thousands of years.

So huge were these moving mountains that locked up billions of tons of water that the world's oceans fell some three hundred feet. And as they moved across the land in slow motion

– sometimes eight inches a year, sometimes eight feet – these glaciers a mile or more thick changed the course of rivers – and history – and scoured the countryside of everything in their path, everything but hope. Hopelessness is the one thing that cannot survive on this large land where so little was made by the hand of man.

Living on these prairies now or travelling across them, one can easily understand why early voyagers thought the world was flat. For some generations, simple survival there was considered a success. Getting by was good enough. The brief summer sun is brutal on skin but good for the grains. And the long winter whiteness when the fields are sleeping is the same. Winter does not so much come to these northern plains as it seizes and inhabits them like an occupying force. It also inhabits the minds and the cultures of their people with numbing but somehow comforting regularity.

So harsh and seemingly uninviting were North America's northernmost prairies that a century ago the Canadian government offered free land to any families who would – or could – live there for five winters in homes and huts where bedtime heat came from bricks lifted by steel tongs from a glowing wood-burning stove. The young people have been leaving ever since, or dreaming of it. They grow up there and later leave the countryside, portaging with them that prairie pluck and determination to succeed elsewhere. Some gather in modest towns, tightknit commercial hubs of sturdy spirit where the stoic people still suspect the best of each other and still know they need each other. They reaffirm this community spirit at their hockey games, where the ice is hard, the local glory enduring, and the stoicism melts.

Prairie life teaches four qualities very well – hardiness, humility, realism, and determination. Wally Fleury remembers his Grandpa Leclair teaching him about hockey. "I used to help him haul wood on his sleigh to sell in town," Wally remembers. "He had a team of huge horses. One day he takes me out on the Assiniboine River. It was frozen solid all the time. He hitches his horses up to some two-by-tens and drags the snow off a big space. He says, 'There. That's all I'm going to do for you. If you want to play hockey, you need to learn.' I had some skates Grandpa bought for a dollar from some guy in town who needed a drink. I wore three pairs of socks, the skates were so big. I kept falling down. Grandpa says, 'Get up.'

"I said, 'Grandpa, how will I know when I'm good?' Grandpa says, 'When you don't fall.'"

They used willow rods for sticks and frozen horse droppings for pucks. Brothers and neighbours played for countless hours out there in the wind and the cold. Bonfires on the banks kept their shoes and hands from freezing. And they got good at hockey, in Wally's case very good.

He got so good that he could peddle his hockey services to teams in towns all over. His teammates and opponents remember him as a very smooth skater and an excellent puck-handler. "He wasn't as aggressive as his boy is," recalls Bearcat Murray, who would come to know them both well over the years. "Wally had real good eye-hand co-ordination. He loved the game and had a lot of heart, more heart than you expected in someone that size. Does any of that sound familiar?"

Those teams would play a lot back in the 1950s and '60s, usually two or three times every week from early December until April. They played in dank little town rinks across eastern Saskatchewan and western Manitoba where the wind blew the snow through cracks in the wall, leaving narrow drifts indoors. "We'd be so cold and drinking cold beer," Bearcat recalls, "and we'd say, 'What the hell are we doing here?' Then we'd go out and play another period. It was great."

For equipment, some had beat-up shoulder pads. They used rolled Eaton's catalogues for shin pads, tying them snugly in place with baling twine. Helmets were unheard-of. Wally's regional reputation grew. One day an offer came from Yorkton, Saskatchewan: two hundred dollars a month plus room and board. It seemed like the big time. Wally's dad, a bridge and railroad worker who couldn't play hockey because he'd lost his thumb between two freight cars, put him on the train to his future up the line in Yorkton. He gave him ten dollars and a new pair of skates, or at least they were new to Wally. He remembers his father looking him in the eye at the station. All he said was, "Go hard, son."

So Wally did. And he got noticed. In 1963 his big break came, actually two of them. First, the Portland Junior team invited him to a tryout that fall. The Western Hockey League is the big time for small-town boys. With teams scattered from Brandon, Manitoba, to Portland, Oregon, the travel schedule is brutal; only recently did teams even consider travelling by plane. Bus travel is as rugged as the style of play. A player's ability to endure it is a good indicator of his toughness to NHL scouts, who use the Western Hockey League to weed out the weak.

Wally's second break was a bad one. It came in the summer just weeks before his Portland tryout. Some of the guys went to play baseball on one of those delightfully endless northern summer evenings. It was July 20. Wally was a catcher, a very determined catcher. Anyone scoring on him would have to go through him. One opponent did, shattering Wally's left leg. It was very bad. He was in the hospital for many weeks. The leg eventually healed, thanks to a lot of home cooking and his mother's dedicated nursing and rehabilitation therapy, which included standing her son in a barrel of soothing, supportive rainwater while he did leg exercises for hours on end.

But the dream of a pro hockey career stayed shattered forever. That may have been when the serious drinking began. In a year or two Wally could get back on the ice. So he did. He was a determined fellow. Everyone said that about him then. No injury was going to keep a Fleury down for long. His hands and eyes were still good, still better than most, in fact. But his speed wasn't the same. And the drinking made him louder. He got a job as a bartender. But as time went on he spent more time at curling as well as bowling. He got good at that, too. "All it takes is determination," he says.

That's when Donna saw him the first time, at a bowling alley. Her father was a cattle farmer in Saskatchewan. She was a waitress, in her twenties, short and shy. Wally was handsome, a good athlete, and lots of fun. At five-foot-eight, he was six inches taller than Donna. They were married in 1967 but could not afford a honeymoon; that would have to wait twenty-nine years. The next year, on June 29, 1968, the first of their three sons was born near Donna's family farm in Oxbow, Saskatchewan. Donna was nervous about the birth. She was frequently nervous about many things, even the ordinary events of everyday life that caused others to shrug. But despite all of her worries, the birth went well and Donna named the baby Theoren, a distinctive name she recalled from a character in a favourite movie, *Old Yeller*.

Soon after, family tragedy struck. The son of Donna's sister drowned in Williams Lake, British Columbia. Donna and Wally and their infant son drove west for the funeral. Everything they owned was in their car.

Wally had been a lot of things in his life, but one of them was not reticent, especially when it came to playing sports or talking about them. He had been known to take over a locker room with his talking, even when he was not on the team, holding forth on the subject of hockey and games he had seen and played.

When the civic fathers of Williams Lake discovered they had a serious hockey talent in their midst, they offered Wally a job as a town electrician if he would stay and play. He would and did – for four years. He enjoyed every shift of every period, though he concedes now that due to his consumption of beer, he was unable at times to remember much about the games.

The Fleurys' second son, Ted, was born in the fall of 1970. By the next spring Wally's drinking problem had grown more serious. Theoren and Donna had both gotten pneumonia in the wetter B.C. climate. And Donna missed her family and the prairies. So the Fleurys packed up again and returned to what Theoren now calls "the Manitoba tropics" close to Saskatchewan, first to Binscarth and then to nearby Russell, where Travis was born in 1973.

Wally did finish grade six in school. But he had no dream or ambition now beyond getting by, comfortably if possible, and playing hockey at every opportunity, regardless of any pain. Wally saw – and still sees – little if any sense in worrying much. Worrying can get you off your game. And worrying was what Donna did. So well, too. True, for Wally the arrival of springtime, when the sleeping fields surrounding town began to wake and fill with new life and growth, did mean the end of another hockey season. But springtime also meant the beginning of golf. And one rule of life could not change: the next weekend could never be more than five days away.

Wally drove a cement truck at first, and then Russell, three times larger and twelve miles north of little Binscarth, hired him to drive the town garbage truck and maintain the modern civic ice rink, as well as to continue his hockey career as a member of its team. It wasn't the NHL, or even the WHL, for sure. But like a downhill skier, Wally still got that same open rush from accelerating on ice, weaving back and forth seemingly without effort, feeling the cold air on his face, and physically challenging any opponent beneath those bright lights. Skating is the closest thing to freedom some people find. On the ice what matters is what you can do, not what you say. There is that powerful camaraderie with other men. And Wally could still hear the home fans cheering.

Wally may have been at work the first afternoon his eldest son skated in Binscarth. To Theoren and his family, that afternoon seemed like any other at first. Only later, when his parents saw how it affected the boy, how alive he suddenly seemed, did that brief afternoon become etched in family lore and the minds of everyone who knew about it or said they did. As usual, Theoren did not talk much about it; he did not need to.

Linda Baker, his kindergarten teacher in Binscarth, remembers a lot about little Theoren. He has that effect on adults, who can spot spunk and enjoy instructing a child who soaks up what they try to teach. Linda herself grew up in Binscarth and lived her youth desperate to leave the curbless town of 550 that seemed even smaller. She went away to college. She returned temporarily as a substitute teacher. Now, thirty years later, she is principal of an eleven-grade world of 115 Binscarth children, loves her work, and can't imagine ever emigrating from that community.

Farmers live in Binscarth when they are not caring for the cattle, the barley and wheat, even the ostriches and bison recently, or the pregnant mares whose urine is a major source of natural estrogen used for human birth-control pills. Retired farmers live there after they've sold the land to strangers because their sons or daughters or both went off to raise their own families in Winnipeg, Regina, Calgary, or some other place where you lock your car in your own driveway and no longer know most passersby. Farmers who make extra money in the potash mine also live in Binscarth's aging homes tucked in among towering, protective spruces that were not planted last spring. Most of them have stood the test of time, like the personal relationships that silently stitch such communities together without contracts written by lawyers who wear wool suits and use five-dollar words.

Some of the structures, like the ice rink, may well be the result of neighbours coming together for a time to lend their hands to raising a homemade home. Nothing too showy, mind you. What others think still matters. And it doesn't take long for word to get around town about anything, good or bad.

Binscarth is a Scottish name. Like most Canadian communities, its population is a polyglot reflection of the ethnic diversities that have washed across this landscape since Asian hunters chased their prey eastward across the Bering Strait so their families could eat, and westbound French and British trappers chasing profit began ambushing the continent's abundant furbearing creatures so humans in Europe could don a fashionable, slightly used second skin. Later, Canadian immigration officers were dispatched to northern and central Europe to hunt down their quota of skilled worker recruits seeking a new life – Poles, Irish, Icelanders, Russians, Scandinavians, Hungarians, Scots, of course, Czechs, and, later with the railway crews, a smattering of Chinese.

Over the decades they came by the thousands on the boats and the trains with their battered luggage and pregnant dreams, their children with wide wondering eyes, their music, their favourite foods and inherited religions, their holidays and customs, even their prejudices. Over time they intermarried with each other and with the native Americans already on hand. They made new lives and new babies. Talk of the "old country" faded. And parents' memories of what they had known back there became children's tales of what they had heard over here.

What these newcomers had in common initially was a desire to leave somewhere else and a hardy spirit that enabled them to endure in northern North America, a vision that enabled them to look out across more than a thousand miles of flat land with scruffy bushes, early winters, and late springs and still see a future on the horizon. But whatever their ethnic background, the residents still live up to the Scots' reputation for careful use of resources, especially financial resources. One thing certain about rural prairie life, even before the Great Depression's lasting lesson of fatalism, is that life is uncertain. Hang on to what you've got because you or someone in the family may well need it again later. "There are a lot of hand-me-downs in Binscarth," says

Linda Baker, who sees the same clothing on different children over the years. "People make things last in Binscarth."

It wasn't the clothing that made Theoren Fleury stick out in Linda Baker's eyes. He was good-natured, outgoing at times, got along with other children. That wasn't different; prairie children have little reason not to get along with each other, fear not being a part of the early social curriculum as it is in some cities.

Like many five-year-old boys Theoren liked physical activity, almost any physical activity. He wasn't aggressive, created no disciplinary problems, and could be entertaining if the audience seemed obviously enthusiastic; he had a shy air about him, though, somehow seeming quieter than he was.

Motion was good to Theoren. Almost any motion. And phys. ed. was his favourite class. "Theoren was not much for sitting quietly in class," Linda recalls with an affectionate smile. "He had an incredible amount of energy and almost every day, too. I'd be working with one child and I'd notice Theoren was up and strolling around the class. He wasn't disruptive at all. He just wanted to be moving. Sometimes it was like he could hear music that no one else could."

But it was Theoren's almost palpable core of determination, even at age five, that jumped out at adults. It was virtually visible. It intrigued them. It attracted them. Investing time in teaching Theoren seemed to pay off in progress, at least at first. He did not ask for help, ever. But if a teacher or coach or parent quietly offered instruction, Theoren gobbled it up like a starving student.

Most kindergarteners are shy. They're even shy about being shy, averting their eyes, refusing to try something new for fear of looking silly, even refusing to admit something is new to them. For them, silence is safer. They do not want to stick out.

Not Theoren.

He might be quiet. But his eyes were never down. Many children habitually cast their eyes down; their vision and attention land briefly on objects of passing interest and then move on without apparent pattern or purpose like butterflies in a garden. But Theoren's eyes were intense, like lasers. And their beam was magnified by their unusual colour; they were green, bright green. He did not look so much as he aimed those green eyes. He would rivet his eyes on something or someone and keep them there for longer than some teachers or coaches expected or perhaps preferred.

Over the years some adults found that habit disconcerting, maybe threatening. Theoren would fix his green eyes on them and keep them there, making the boy appear to be at least cheeky, almost defiant, possibly demanding. It was an unspoken communication but nonetheless intense. And it seemed nondeferential, somehow inappropriate for a youth, especially one so physically small. A few adults, though, actually became fond of that look; when they captured Fleury's gaze, they knew the mind behind it was paying attention, even if Theoren's subsequent actions at times seemed to indicate a disregard for the lessons or advice just offered.

Over the years Theoren, like many people who learn to live in and with fame, would unconsciously come to use that gaze more gracefully with great power and effect. Even in a noisy arena crammed with thousands of people, Theoren's searching eyes can spot a beseeching, familiar face and lock on with warmth. In more intimate surroundings, even on the sidewalk, casting those eyes on strangers young and old can seem to invite the introduction and the blessing of his attention that the strangers so desperately seek. The eye contact opens the door to a coveted encounter that lasts only a few heady moments in reality but vividly lives on for years in glorified memory.

Sticking out did not seem to bother young Fleury at all, especially if it came as a result of his physical activity. He was also lefthanded. Lefties spend their entire lives having to adapt, since virtually everything from school desks and child-sized scissors to automobile gearshifts are designed for the right-handed.

Adapting becomes second nature over time, but at age five it takes an extra mental step to translate most actions to the other side. Over the years Theoren's teachers saw him watching them closely and then copying their motions with his own physical adjustments.

Linda Baker remembers one day spotting Theoren quietly labouring over some writing exercises. Writing upside down with his left hand, he was having difficulty differentiating the o's and e's in his name. He had not raised his hand for help, as usual. But she squatted down by his seat without asking and wrote out his name several times using her left hand. Awkward was not a word she associated with Theoren Fleury, even at age five. But it was, indeed, quite awkward writing upside down. "You can do it," she said. He copied her motions and had no trouble thereafter. Now, every time Linda Baker sees Theoren Fleury on television, she affectionately recalls that handwriting lesson and quietly credits herself with playing a role in the star's ability to sign that big contract.

But it was a kindergarten gym class one day that still stands out so vividly in her memory, though for the life of her now Linda cannot explain why; there were other days like it. It was just one of those minor moments that tickle the mind like the foreshadowing in a good book that comes to carry meaning only some time later, especially in the eyes of an astute teacher watching each year for signals from each of her as-yet-inarticulate charges.

Most children like gym, as it seems merely to involve lots of running and jumping around, no sitting still, and few rules and boring lessons. Theoren had quickly discovered that he was good at gym, being well co-ordinated even at the tender age of sixty-some months. Most people like what they are good at. But the very young have yet to discover or develop much that they are good at; there has been insufficient time to learn skills or excuses. And Linda's experience over seven years of teaching had taught her that when many children that age encountered a physical challenge, they instinctively sought a detour. They chose to move on. Plenty of time to attempt the impossible later, maybe, unless they could avoid it.

On that day, one by one, all of the children were to walk along the balance beam. It is not the easiest exercise; nor is it the most difficult. But it does pose a mental challenge. Ask someone, even an adult, to walk along a line on the floor three or four inches wide and few will have problems. Raise that line three or four feet off the floor and few will not find it more difficult. Linda has always felt she was teaching her young charges to develop confidence at least as much as any single skill. So she told the children if they had trouble keeping their balance long enough to walk the entire length of the beam, they should not worry. Such skills would come to them eventually.

Actually, few youngsters made it all the way across. They would step out, take two or three uncertain tiny steps, lose their balance, start to fall, jump off on to the floor pads, and be ready to move on to the next exercise.

Not Theoren. He took one step. He fell off. He climbed back up. He fell off. He climbed back up. He fell off. He climbed back up. He took one step and paused. Then, he fell off. He climbed back up. He took two steps. He fell off. After repeated unsuccessful attempts to traverse the entire length of the beam, Theoren was still climbing back up and trying again. He was not speaking. He was not even muttering. He was just focused, very focused, on climbing back up, on stepping out, on pausing, on regaining his balance, on stepping again, on landing, on trying again. And again. And again. And again. Slowly, right before his teacher's eyes, this boy was progressing mentally and physically step by step, try after try. And the teacher was learning a little lesson about juvenile determination, at least this juvenile's determination.

But something strange happened. At some point Linda realized she had stopped being a teacher. The other children had stopped being pupils. They had all forgotten everything else at that moment. This spontaneous demonstration of Theoren Fleury's determination in that little gym in that little town had turned teacher and classmates into an audience, a minor crowd of non-paying spectators silently watching in accidental admiration of so much human spirit packed into such a tiny package overcoming an obstacle.

With a start and some guilt, Linda Baker came to. She rushed over to the balance beam. She reached out her hand, offering to steady Theoren. "No!" the five-year-old said firmly, without removing his eyes from the beam below. "I'll do it myself."

And he did.

Whether he was in Binscarth or Russell, after that first day on the ice Theoren went skating at every opportunity, every single opportunity – after school, after dinner, before school, even before dawn. At five a.m. every morning Theoren would hear his father stirring for work at the rink. Like magic, the youngster would simply appear in the kitchen, sleepy-eyed but fully dressed in the first clothes his grasping hands happened to find piled somewhere in the dark, hair uncombed but skates and stick in hand. No time to waste on breakfast. The pair would trundle the cold mile or so from the Fleurys' government-subsidized rental home through several still-slumbering neighbourhoods into the empty business district to open the rink together.

Theoren sensed no ghosts there. Even before the lights were fully up, he was on the ice. His father would invest some moments in dispensing a quick tip or two: Spread your legs farther apart, like you're riding a horse; it gives you stronger balance. Bend your knees more and push out this way. Keep your head up.

But in a very short time Theoren was off wheeling about the ice on his own, trying all kinds of moves with his skates and with the puck and then putting them together. He might cut too sharply and fall. But he would bounce right back up and try it again and again and again, until he got that move right. Then he would try another and another and another. Over and over, around and around. Then he tried all three moves together. Day after day, hour after hour, he played these imaginary games. He seemed to play them with special intensity if his father was watching. "Skating was born in Theoren," says his mother. "And determination. You could never tell that boy he couldn't do something. That was the challenge then."

Even when Wally drove the Zamboni onto the ice to remove the overnight frost for the rink's first formal activity of the day, the six a.m. figure-skating classes, Theoren would skate wherever the Zamboni was not. He might assign himself to do laps, 125 laps around this way and then 125 laps around the other way, some laps fast, others slower. To rest, he might water-ski on a rope behind the Zamboni, waving to the nonexistent crowd and trying to skate on one leg. He could hear his father's laughter even above the motor.

If the figure skaters did not use the entire rink for their jumps or whirls, Theoren would inhabit the other end or even just one of the rounded corners. Parents dropping off their daughters would see this scruffy-looking youngster in the beat-up skates shifting the puck back and forth, shooting it against the boards time after time after time.

For those who cared to know, he was "Fleury's kid." At first, they watched him only accidentally and casually. Fleury did have wonderful co-ordination for a little guy. He would skate at the net, quickly dart around it, move the puck swiftly beyond an invisible poke check, and stuff the puck past the equally nonexistent goalie. He might also celebrate the achievement briefly to himself. But soon he was back at it from the other side. And then he was shooting at the net from every conceivable angle, until it was time to go home and maybe grab a quick nap before school.

◆

Wally Fleury walks into the Russell Memorial Arena now, acknowledges the familiar greetings of everyone, takes a deep breath while looking around, and remembers. "Welcome to my home," he says. "I spent a lotta hours here."

When Russell, Manitoba, began to congeal around its present site in the 1880s, school was an activity that took second place to the daily and seasonal rhythm of farm chores, which explains the traditional North American calendar of long summer school closures. Heat came from burning split wood or dried animal droppings. Winter wash basins wore ice coverings come morning. And being a neighbour meant more than simply living next door to someone, which explains barn-raisings, threshing parties, volunteer fire departments, and midwives. School classes were informal occasional affairs offered in various homes in the town, which got its name from Lindsay Russell, a nineteenth-century surveyor. Agricultural services were the town's primary economic activity, which explains why the Hudson's Bay Company built a store there before anyone put up a church.

About a century ago the mail still came every two weeks, often by horsedrawn wagon, and farm families felt the need to keep loaded weapons on hand against the perceived possibility of an insurrection by the bands of native people who still tried to lead a nomadic life despite the growing number of homesteads and fences dotting the landscape. Trust between natives and whites was scarce; stereotypes ran rampant. And trade between them was limited to simple exchanges such as milk for tanned animal hides.

Today, Russell has lost its Bay store and a grain elevator but remains a tidy commercial community of almost 1,700 souls. The town map marks *the* bank machine, this newfangled idea called recycling is struggling to catch on, and the noon radio news is preceded by "Chapel Notes," announcements of the latest deaths and funerals, thoughtfully sponsored by the funeral home. Like many rural communities, Russell owes its location to the proximity of water and the railway, although many of the lines have now been abandoned and, in fact, are being torn up for scrap or use in other areas.

Major Pratt School is the focus of Russell's education efforts from kindergarten through high school and Trojan teams are the focus of considerable local interest and pride. School sports are major community social activities. Indeed, hockey games regularly attract more fans than the school's 640 students; even road games three hours away cause car caravans containing hundreds of Russell fans. And youth teams are no less organized, providing a regular draw for enthusiastic spectators and a training ground and feeder system of prospects for the high school.

Before dawn on weekday mornings large yellow buses waddle scores of miles along the narrow icy roads through the flat countryside to collect students from the homemade huts that provide shelter from the wind at the end of long driveways and deliver them to town for their daily dose of education. At dusk the process is reversed. Outside the school, town children's bicycles obediently await their riders, unchained and safe. The parking lot is not crammed with students' cars. And much of the school's stable teaching corps invests its entire career in several generations of pupils who pass through that one building.

Outside the office of Principal Eldon Montgomery stands the Major Pratt Wall of Fame listing famous alumni such as Cathy Burton, the golfer; Irwin Driedger, the jockey; Mark Buleziuk, World Cup auctioneer; and Theoren Fleury, the hockey player.

But only Fleury has his name attached to the town sign out on the highway: RUSSELL, it says, HOME OF THEOREN FLEURY. In case one passerby might not know of this favourite son, the town also painted on the flaming-C Calgary Flames logo.

It may be a minor thing to the rest of the world, which is so full of famous people that it needs entire magazines and television shows to keep them straight and chronicle their turbulent lives, but just about every single hockey publication and record book mistakenly lists Fleury as being from Oxbow, Saskatchewan. Saskatchewan is nice and all, and Theo was born there and had his diapers changed there for a very few weeks. But in his own mind, which he regularly volunteers to interviewers, and in the minds of everyone in his real home town, Theoren is "from" Russell. The tall sign in Russell, which treasures its few famous people, is going to do its part to correct the official record about precisely what community really produced Theoren Fleury and where he chooses to return some summers to play charity games of baseball and hockey for the youth leagues.

"I remember walking into the rink one day," Eldon Montgomery remembers about the mid-1970s, "and here comes this kid – I didn't know him then – full-steam down the ice. He kicks the puck onto the blade of his stick and without breaking stride carries it – carries it! – around the defender. He threw it in the net, literally threw it. The kid was maybe eight years old. I said to myself, 'Who the hell is that?'"

Like most area residents, Eldon knows a little about hockey, having played throughout his childhood over in Saskatchewan where every winter Saturday his parents took him to town, muffled in blankets, in a sleigh with a footwarming firebox. His parents would shop and socialize all day while he exhausted himself playing hockey nonstop on the pond with friends. None of them noticed the sub-zero weather, which Eldon regards as a wonderful conditioner for life.

"A lot of poor people live on the prairies," says the principal. "They don't get much given to them – by the land, by the weather, by anyone. They don't expect to be given much. They have to take what they can. Taking makes for stronger people. Stronger people make better hockey players. Taking is good training for hockey because hockey is a taking sport."

Len Peltz was another teacher who saw the same kid in school during lunch-hour monitor duty. A half-dozen grade-three or -four boys were playing ping-pong. To make it more competitive they were playing it round-robin with each boy changing ends after each shot. One of the boys – Len did not know him by name – was a very good player. He had such quick, accurate hands. The little crowd of boys was cheering for and against each other, as boys do. They weren't really misbehaving, but the noise level was getting up there and Len, who is a fairly large man, thought he'd head off any trouble.

"All right, boys," he said, "let's tone it down a bit."

Instantly, the crowd of boys grew silent. Equally instantly, this little kid stepped forward. He was somewhat scruffy – patched jeans, faded brown shirt, messy hair. He was polite, not quite brazen. The boy wanted to know what they had been doing wrong.

Len explained they had not actually been doing anything wrong. But he thought they were getting close. He said they could continue the game, just do it more quietly. The game continued. The little kid beat everyone.

But the encounter stuck in Len's mind. Later in the teachers' room, he asked his colleagues who the cheeky little boy in the scruffy clothes was. They knew who he meant right away. "He's Fleury's kid," they replied.

"Wally's boy?" said Len. That made eminent sense. Len knew of Fleury from his exploits in senior hockey. "Wally was real smooth," everyone recalls. Wally smoked three packs of cigarettes a day. But he was also developing another reputation – for excessive drinking.

Reputations do not take long to grow in small towns, especially if they are negative. Wally was not quite considered *the* town drunk, but he was seen in the bar of the Queens Hotel very frequently and walking out uncertainly often enough that when his name came up, eyes would roll. For some, a drinking problem was not surprising for an Indian. Technically, the Fleurys are not Indian; they are Métis, the product of long-ago liaisons between French trappers and native women and now an officially recognized indigenous people.

Although education and social progress in modern times have made it more difficult and distasteful to publicly categorize people's behaviour by their race, such thinking stubbornly sticks in the minds of some and is whispered in a confidential tone. Wally, on the other hand, is typically up front. "I grew up Métis-Cree French," he says. "That's not the good French. We're Western Canadian French. My dad's family made their own booze." What's audibly left of that heritage is the slightest French-Canadian accent, as in the concise capsulization of his aborted attempt to have his own career playing hockey: "I went dere and I gave her my best and dat's fer sure."

The same people who would shake their heads knowingly over Wally's drinking might well be found at the rink some night cheering themselves red in the face over his son's athletic exploits on the ice in the name of the Russell team. And with the growth of Theoren Fleury's reputation, locally and beyond, as the little hockey player who frequently brought victory to little Russell, the talk and looks about Wally's drinking were submerged.

Wally was hard to miss at times. He would probably be at the rink for the start of most of Theoren's youth hockey games at home. But he would soon disappear next door to the Queens Hotel, only to emerge at game's end and stumble his way into the arena. "You should have seen your boy today, Wally," some parents would say. "He scored five goals. The last one was a real beauty."

Wally would make his way downstairs, enter the locker room where Theoren's team was celebrating, and give the happy players and their parents a loud rambling lecture about how good his boy was, how he'd told him to score for sure, and how this team would never win without him. It was important, Wally thought at the time, that they know this, though afterward he barely remembered any of it. And Theoren acted as if he, too, had forgotten those times.

In fact, Theoren's team was very good. "You'd look at the score of the games," Principal Montgomery recalls, "and it would be Visitors 2, Fleury 6. Still, much of the credit belongs to Coach Fowler."

The son of a Saskatchewan car dealer and now slightly more than a half-century old, Doug Fowler played hockey past his thirty-seventh birthday. He loves the game that much. He's been a teacher now for more than thirty years and runs his own autumn evening hockey camps to this day. When his son Kent turned four, Doug took him on the ice. First, of course, came skating skills. With a doting and skilled father, they came quickly. Other boys began to congregate around them. Little puck-passing practices broke out. One thing led to another and by the time Kent was five, Doug Fowler found himself coaching a formal team. Jim Petz, whose son Ted also played, became assistant coach. Together, these men coached the same boys through childhood and into their teens.

Oh, the times they shared together! They played all over the province and, literally, put Russell on the map in terms of youth hockey. Russell, like many rural prairie communities, takes a perverse pride in feeling small, insignificant, and ignored by larger, seemingly more important communities. When strangers arrive in town, people thoughtfully, almost hopefully, ask: "Did you have any trouble finding Russell?" As Canada often feels slighted, overlooked, and ignored by the more populous United States, Russell feels inconsequential next to Winnipeg, Brandon, or Portage la Prairie.

All of that changed with the partnership of Fowler–Petz–Fleury and the dozen or so other boys – Michael Gratton, Bruce Coulter, John Adolphe, Mike Derkach, George Parobec, Dion Deschamps, Dan Spurway, Mark Pettitt, the perennial goalie, and one of the Morriseau boys, Warren, from down the street. From the mid-1970s through the mid-1980s they brought their combined skills, their ambition, and their juvenile inattentiveness and poured them into the group identity of one team for nearly a decade of wins and losses, mostly the former. They grew and matured, had pains and squabbles, and long hours of travel in crowded cars to anonymous motel rooms crammed with boys to save money. They even celebrated the boys' birthdays on the road and the photos preserved the memory of the homemade cake that was brought along.

The scrapbook photos, carefully assembled by the official archivist of most prairie families, Mom, show the boys on the ice after yet another tournament victory grinning wildly, looking the wrong way, shoving each other playfully. There's Coach Fowler in his tuque caught in mid-reach trying to calm his excited athletic gang members. Often the boys would sign the program or photo in disorganized, slanted, cramped rows of names, and parents fondly note how the writing matured with the hockey seasons. For one thing the tail on the y in Fleury began to grow longer and longer. Twenty years later, when his autograph was desperately sought by another generation of Peewee players, the tail on the Fleury y was encircling his entire name and number.

The next week's *Russell Banner* would enshrine the latest tournament news: "The Russell Kinsmen Pee-Wee team travelled to Langenburg last weekend and brought home the 'A' side trophy for the sixth time this year out of nine tournaments. In the first game Saturday Russell blasted Saltcoats 11–1. Theoren Fleury led the scoring with six goals. . . . On Sunday, Russell met a tough, fast-skating team from Kamsack, Sask., but managed to score three times in the last eight minutes to win 9–6. Theoren Fleury had four goals. . . . In the final, Russell squared off with their longtime rival Langenburg. The boys were short-handed as Dan Spurway came down with the flu and Tim Kiliwnik had broken a skate. Russell had to work very hard for their 7–5 victory. . . . Theoren Fleury had three goals."

Eventually, even at away games spectators started coming to see the Russell team – the Green Machine – and its little shooter, who wore number 9 then and for all of his youth hockey career. Mike Rolling remembers his father, a Mountie, taking him to see a tournament game one day specifically to see this one Russell player. "There was this real little guy, number 9," Mike recalls. "He was always yapping at everybody and skating all over fast as lightning. I thought he was a real hot dog. But, man, was he good." Mike was impressed that his father was impressed. Little did Mike know he was destined to come to know Fleury much better on another day.

"We practised one hour two or three times a week," Coach Fowler remembers. "In all those years I never once cancelled a practice. Whoever showed up, played. If you skipped practice, you sat out the game. As they grew, we practised more, travelled more, played more. At first, we played maybe thirty games a year. Then, after twelve, we played fifty games plus playoffs. Sometimes we'd drive four hours to play three to five games on a weekend. It was grand."

Coach Fowler remembers from his own playing days how games seemed the most fun while practices could seem like drudgery. Still, he believes most learning occurs at practice. So he worked hard at keeping practices fun for the boys. He turned drills into games. One of his favourites was having the boys race around the rink with their hockey sticks between their legs like witch's brooms. "They didn't know it," he says, "but they were practising balance and bending their legs enough to skate stronger."

The coach smiles warmly. "From his first year on my team," he says, "Theo was far superior to any other kid. He was by far the best player I ever coached. I had faster ones and bigger ones, for sure. But Theo was the whole package – quick, perceptive, great co-ordination, tough physically, and even tougher mentally. He flat-out always wanted to be the best. He had the determination of an I-don't-know-what, but whatever it was, it was made of steel. Even when he was six, you'd stand behind the bench and watch him go and go and scrap and scrap. Jim and I would just look at each other and shrug. You simply had to marvel at his will. And he had great endurance. We were always catching Theo assigning himself extra shifts.

"Hockey, well, hockey was his life."

Some days – Coach Fowler knew of the troubles at the Fleury household – he'd find some excuse to drive down Augusta Street and drop by just to check on things. "I never once failed to find Theo playing road hockey," he says. "All kinds of weather, he and his brothers would be out there shooting and yelling and arguing. All his free time went into hockey. Theo would say, 'Watch this, coach.' And he'd try some hot-dog trick. And I'd say, 'You do that in a game, Theo, and I'll kill you.' But he knew I was kidding.

"I remember one time – I think we were at a tournament up in Thompson – Theo held the puck for his entire shift, skating around everyone, even his own teammates. No one could take the puck from him. We didn't know what he was doing. Then, just before he came off, he took a shot. Understandably, that performance didn't go over too well with the other team and coaches. But Theo just wanted to see if he could keep the puck an entire shift."

The way his coaches and teammates remember those years, Theo was the most determined person they had ever seen. "Theo was different," Ted Petz remembers. "A lot of us talked about wanting to play in the NHL someday. We'd pretend we were this star or that star. We were dreaming about getting to the NHL. Theo, he was driven. He said simply he *would* play in the NHL. And you know what? We didn't argue. It made sense to us."

Sometimes that determination became so intense it got him in trouble. "He had this uncanny vision," Coach Fowler says. "They'd chop him. They'd slash him. They'd trip him. He'd get angry, retaliate, take a stupid penalty. You don't try to shape that kind of talent. You can't control talent like that and you don't want to squash that fiery character; that's what made him so good. You just try to steer it, help him to harness that drive. We worked on that a lot. It took time. I'd say, 'Theo, why help the other team by taking a dumb penalty? Let them get frustrated with you and take a penalty.' I said, 'Look, we all know you can take the puck from end to end and probably score. Great. But if you share with your teammates, we'll do better as a team, a Team. And your teammates will like you better, too.'

"I remember one game against Deloraine. They had three guys on him. On one rush Theo kept going to the outside, going to the outside. I thought, that's strange, he usually goes right up the middle. They followed him and followed, slashing and shoving. And then suddenly, bam, the puck comes flying out to centre. There's Ted Petz wide open. And he buries it in the net. The other team was stunned. I think Theo was happier with the assist than Ted was with the goal."

Things changed after that. Theo got very good at passing and became a better team player. "Passing is hard to teach," Coach Fowler adds. "But he worked at passing and worked at it. And there he is passing, passing, passing all the time now. I said, 'Theo, you can shoot now and then, too.' He knew just how long to keep it and just when to pass it. Sometimes I'd catch myself standing behind the bench, watching him and just marvelling. I'm the coach and it's like I'm sitting in the stands watching this kid."

◈

The Saddledome looks weird when it's empty. The scoreboard is dark. The floor is clean. The cooks aren't in yet. Gary Taylor is down by the locker room videotaping one of the East Coast games off the satellite. Only a few of the powerful halide lights illuminate the ice, an effort to hold down the Saddledome's $325,000 annual electric bill. With 18,888 empty seats, every sound, even a cough, echoes all around. What's even more weird is seeing Theoren Fleury up in the stands, where he has never watched a Flames game. "I couldn't stand to sit up here for a game," he says. With an unguarded openness and no humour intended, he adds, "It's dangerous up here. Geez, pucks flying all over and everything. You could get really hurt up here."

But there he is climbing the steps in the empty Saddledome after another of life's endless practices, thousands over the years in his quarter-century of hockey, to plop himself down in a seat and, with a late-morning sigh, survey his hockey domain.

He leans back and spreads his arms across the adjacent seat-backs, revealing surprisingly thick muscles from weightlifting and, under his upper right arm, an immense jagged scar, now aged to purple. "Welcome to my home," says Theo, smiling that smile. "I spend a lotta hours in this place."

"It's funny," he adds. "I wake up in my nice house, get in my truck, and drive down here to my home. It's a demanding life. But you have everything here you could ever need or want – good friends, carpeted rooms, food and drinks. You can walk around in your underwear, exercise, play ping-pong, watch game tapes on a huge TV, take a hot tub, a shower. I get paid a huge sum of money to do what I love to do, what I do best in my whole life. When I'm in this building, I don't have to think about anything else. Everything is right here in my home. No worries. Just hockey. I love hockey and skating, the whole deal.

"I love it here. I really do. Sometimes I think I'm the luckiest person in the world to be doing all this. It was almost like destiny, me getting here, like I could will myself to be here, if I just worked hard enough and wanted it bad enough."

He pauses for a moment, looking out and back. "I think about those days sometimes. Sometimes they seem like a long time ago. Coach Fowler taught me a lot, a lot about discipline and being part of a team. I was willing to do anything to play hockey. I needed motivation for school; I didn't get much of that at home for school. But I didn't need any motivation for hockey. That's all I wanted to do. Hockey was my escape. I wanted to try everything in hockey."

Theoren smiles and remembers a tournament in Thompson. "I told my linemates, 'Watch me next shift. I'm going to do something special.' I took the faceoff and kept the puck the entire shift. I skated all around taking breakaways. I'd come in on the goalie, deke him. He'd go down. But I wouldn't shoot. I'd go behind the net and back out of the zone and then take it back in myself and fake a shot again. One guy tried to run me. I deked him. He hit the boards. I had the puck the entire shift."

Why did you do that, Theo?

"To see if I could do it. I suppose some people saw that as hot-dogging. But I wasn't thinking about the crowd. I just wanted to see if I could do it. And I did it."

Just then, George Greenwood shuffles out on the ice down below and waves to the crowd of two. Despite his upbringing in British Columbia, he is a fan of Fleury's and one of nearly a thousand little-known individuals in the behind-the-scenes cast necessary nowadays to stage an NHL game. Hockey games don't just happen. Gentle George takes care of Theoren's "home." George is the good-natured, soft-spoken, and demanding operations manager of the Saddledome. He has invested thirty-one of his fifty-one years in the business of making and keeping ice indoors.

On game days George arrives at work by seven a.m. The Flames have forty-one home games every year, not counting any playoffs. But that's the least of running this immense structure, which cost $72.5 million to complete in 1983, back when Fleury was in junior hockey dreaming of the big time, and another $37 million to renovate in 1995 when Canadian Airlines began paying $1 million a year to add its name to the building and its logo to the roof. The Olympic Saddledome (the initial name came from 735 entries in a public contest with season tickets as the prize) was built on the site of the old Victoria Arena (named for the mother of Princess Alberta) and became the site for the 1988 Olympic hockey and figure-skating competitions. It is one of the few North American arenas capable of expansion from the 200-by-85-foot NHL-sized rink to the 200-by-100-foot Olympic size.

Although the saddle-shaped Saddledome fits nicely with Calgary's western image and the Calgary Stampede next door, there are four other arenas like it in the world – in Arizona, Maryland, Bulgaria, and Greece. There is a mundane energy-efficient reason behind the sleepy-U design: the graceful dip in the roof greatly reduces the inside building volume that must be heated, cooled, and lit. The steep slope of the concrete roof, which weighs 3,030 tons, with its special rubber coating, also helps shed Calgary's ample snowfall and eases the load on the thirty-two columns and seventy-two miles of supporting cable.

The Saddledome is the site of almost one hundred other events annually, everything from tractor-pulls and the circus to rock concerts and curling championships, which are scheduled years in advance. So complex has the scheduling become for the NHL's twenty-six (soon to be thirty) teams in their busy arenas in two countries with different holidays, traditions, and commercial needs that it takes the league's computer several days to design each year's regular-season schedule. Calgary's Major Junior hockey team plays its home games in the Saddledome, which Flames management has also been promoting as a conference meeting site. A small-city Canadian hockey franchise must seek all possible sources of revenue these days in order to compete for income to compete for players against the multinational conglomerates with their vast financial resources that control franchises elsewhere.

But George Greenwood and his twenty-one full-time workers are thinking strictly hockey on this day, and hockey means ice. Making ice for professional hockey is considerably more complex than the backyard garden-hose variety. Indeed, the quality of the league's frozen water has become such a point of grumbling among skill players like Fleury and of controversy in some locales – bad ice can slow the skaters on fast teams and perhaps benefit slower home teams – the league has dispatched a consultant to seek ice standardization. The surface of Anaheim's Pond, for example, is known as Velcro ice.

The physical challenge of making good ice is complicated by the widespread commercial drive to pack every moment of a hockey-game experience with entertainment for the fans. Now, even the intermissions between periods must be filled with on-ice activity: youngsters playing hockey, lucky ticket-holders shooting pucks, and the like. The Zamboni or Olympia machines preparing the ice for the next period sometimes seem almost an afterthought. The new ice hardly has time to freeze before the faceoff for the next period.

While most fans think of ice as something to spread salt on or to drop into drinks, for George Greenwood and his counterparts throughout the league, ice-making is a science requiring course study and long experience. The wet-blanket-like humidity of new Southern franchise cities like Miami requires the addition of powerful dehumidifiers to the NHL's ice-making arsenal. Even in Calgary's colder, drier climate, the collective breathing, eating, and body temperatures of a sellout Saddledome crowd will raise the arena's air temperature three degrees above the ideal 65 degrees Fahrenheit during a game. All of this can affect the ice – and the score.

The son of a sheet-metal worker, George began his career in ice in Vancouver as a member of the lowest rung of ice management, the rink rat, the folks on skates who move the net for the Zamboni or Olympia, follow behind hurriedly patching, and push rubber squeegees around to even out the excess water, even as the rested players begin returning to the ice. This is the most obvious form of ice-making. The 350-horsepower machines scrape off the top eighth of an inch of ice and lay down a new layer of hot water – usually 180 degrees – that fills in the scrapes and cracks before freezing in fifteen to twenty minutes. (Although Canada is officially on the metric system, hockey and ice-making, like football fields, continue to use feet and inches, and the Fahrenheit scale.) To combat frost build-up, during the hockey season the Saddledome's ice is scraped and resurfaced every eight hours or so, game day or not.

It takes about twenty-four hours, sixteen layers of ice, and seven thousand gallons of water to prepare the Saddledome's seventeen thousand square feet of ice for hockey (figure-skating ice is two inches thick, twice the depth of hockey ice, so that takes longer to prepare). And another thousand gallons of water go back on during the resurfacings of each hockey game.

First, a desktop computer deep in the Saddledome's basement instructs three huge compressors to flush ammonia brine refrigerant through a tight network of five miles of pipes buried an inch and a half inside the arena floor. That lowers the floor's temperature to five degrees. Another network of pipes six inches deeper carries hot water to confine the cold to the immediate arena floor and prevent deeper penetration that would cause costly frost heave. With such care, modern arena floors can last twenty-five years.

Crews use a fire hose to spread the initial thin layer of water on the rink's smooth chilled cement. Once frozen, that first thin layer is whitewashed with a special ice paint, another layer of ice is added, followed by handpainting of all the ads and logos. After that, the Zamboni adds layer upon layer of water specially filtered to remove oxygen. The less oxygen in water, the faster and harder it freezes.

Because ice, like humans, gets fragile with age and crumbles, warm liquid is pumped through the pipes to thaw the floor several times each season. The lower ice layers melt. The other layers are cracked. Small bulldozers shove the ice sheets towards nearby drains. And an entirely new rink of ice is made.

By the time Theoren steps from the bench for his ritual pregame warmup, Mike Duben and Keith Thomson have parked their twin Olympias and are dumping out the melting dirty ice. The mustachioed George Greenwood is anonymous again, patrolling the halls for problems. And the temperature of the arena floor where all the action will soon take place is back to two degrees above zero.

❖

"I put on a face on the ice," Fleury admits. "I want to put out every ounce of energy and intensity I possibly can. On the ice I have only one gear, fifth. I look at some game tapes and I can't believe some of the stuff I do out there. I say to myself, 'Did I really do that? Really?' It's like you can be two different people – one on the ice in your gear and the other one at home in regular clothes. But, hey, that's hockey. It's a very emotional game. That's what I love about it. Sometimes you do stuff out there or you have stuff done to you and someone gets in big trouble for

53

it. Hey, that's fair enough, eh? Off the ice, though, I'm a pretty laid-back guy."

Indeed, up close off the ice, Theoren Fleury, who has a league-wide on-ice reputation for yapping at opponents and worse, seems downright reticent. He infrequently initiates conversation, though his actions and responses indicate he listens intently. There was a time recently, however, when Fleury himself and others wondered if he'd be laid out instead of laid back.

It started in the early 1990s. Theo would feel a powerful wave of nausea building in his intestines. He would suspect the flu. It couldn't possibly be nerves; while some players grow nervous before games, especially big games, Theo can't wait to play in them. He'd feel sick, then sicker, and sicker still. He'd be sick, very sick. Then the sickness would seem to go away. And Theo could forget about it with the same kind of steely determination he aimed at becoming an NHL player or he can still aim at ignoring pain.

"I firmly believe you can will almost anything," he says. "Lots of things will hurt if you let them. I don't let them."

In fact, Theoren always has worn a reputation for durability. Team trainers become accustomed to regular, even predictable pleas for assistance from certain players for ailments or injuries, most of them real. Not from Theoren.

Terry Kane is the experienced physical therapist with the Flames. He calls himself a physical fireman. "I try to put out injuries as fast as possible." Fans regularly see him run on the ice in street shoes during games to tend to injured Flames players. He says he's amazed at how infrequently he is aware Fleury is injured. "Theo's a throwback," says Terry. "He has a very high pain tolerance. He just blocks it out. I think he wills it. Some players are high-maintenance. You have to talk to them and treat them a lot. Three things are bred out of professional hockey players – to take responsibility for their actions, to have good communications skills, and to be accountable. They are trained from childhood just to become hockey players. Nothing else matters and most everything is excused. Theo doesn't blame his skates, his stick, the ice, his teammates. He doesn't hide. He steps up. He takes responsibility and moves on. He's the most unique player I've ever met in all these years."

Terry remembers one game when Fleury badly twisted his ankle. "It was a serious sprain," Terry recalls. "I mean serious. Theo has built up immensely strong ankles. It's like they're reinforced inside with something extra. But I told the coaches that night we had lost Theo for at least two games, maybe more. The next day he couldn't get his skate on, it was so swollen. The next night in Edmonton he taped it up. He not only played, he was first star. Theo's one tough little dude. He'll put trainers out of business."

Through his first nine NHL seasons Fleury missed a total of seven games out of more than seven hundred. That's less than a 1-per-cent absence rate. And two of those seven games were due to an off-ice injury – a puck hit Theo in the eye when he was sitting on the bench.

But Theo could not will away the nausea, which grew much worse in 1995, right after his big five-year contract was settled. Every five minutes it seemed Theo would feel a spasm coming on. Or as he puts it, "I'd get this terrible pain like someone was stabbing me in the stomach. Then I'd puke my guts out several times a day."

Fleury went to the then-trainer, the crusty, grandfatherly Bearcat Murray, who had played with and against Fleury's father for years. "I said, 'Hey, Bear, something's wrong, something's really wrong here.'" It was.

Bearcat knew there was a serious problem if Theoren was seeking help. At first, doctors suspected appendicitis, which would have been better than the final diagnosis: Crohn's disease. That's a chronic, debilitating disturbance of the intestine that causes weight loss and prevents proper digestion of food.

Theoren underwent lengthy treatments. At one point he had to down six pills every day, which did not please him. For Theo, routines like taking medicines at set times are constricting, like wearing tight clothes. He even hates to take cold pills. But nausea is a powerful incentive. To ease the burden on his restless stomach, Theo even gave up his beloved chewing tobacco, at least for a while. Those treatments, plus some herbal medicine suggested by a herbalist he visited in a shopping mall, seemed to get the disease under control, and Fleury has decided he is no longer bothered by it. He has, however, done some charity work for a Crohn's foundation.

Fleury's smaller body has always taken a beating in hockey. Over his career various teammates have been assigned or assigned themselves to protect him; in Junior, it was the hard-nosed, red-haired Mike Keane, more recently a regular adversary of Fleury's on the Colorado Avalanche and then the New York Rangers, or Steve Chiasson, a tall, droll defenceman who rolls his eyes every time he hears of another Fleury flap. During the infamous Junior World Championship of 1987 in Piestani, Czechoslovakia, the entire Canadian and Soviet teams were ejected from the tournament for an on-ice brawl that did not end until the arena lights were extinguished and armed guards with dogs brought in.

Fleury is famous among teammates for instigating on-ice scrapes which they are then compelled to enter either for the sake of hockey honour or their top scorer or both. Someone takes a run at Theo. He retaliates or maybe they retaliate for something he did. Suddenly, there's a scrum of immense players enveloping Fleury. His teammates jump in. Fleury squirts out the side, usually unharmed.

Was Fleury responsible for the brawl at Piastani? "What I'll say," he says, "is I was on the ice at the time. In fact, Chiasson saved my ass. I was getting thumped in the dark by some huge Soviet defencemen. Hey, that's hockey, right?"

Binscarth, Manitoba: Theoren Fleury heads off for his first ice-skate.

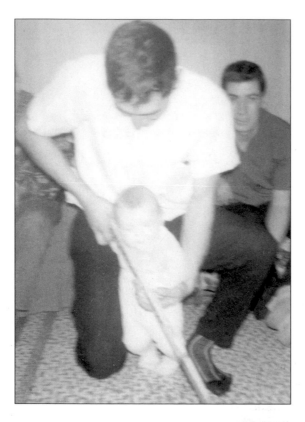

Above: Fleury, unable to stand, gets his first hockey lesson from father, Wally. Right: Fleury, age seven.

Grade three.

Vanier High School, graduation photo.

Midget hockey, Winnipeg.

Left: Second year of Junior with Moose Jaw Warriors. Below: Fleury scores trick goal with stick between his legs for Moose Jaw against Regina Pats.

Celebrating 1989 Stanley Cup championship – with the Stanley Cup.

The Fleury family, left to right: Theoren, Ted, Donna, Travis, Wally.

There is a powerful fraternity in this sport which is apparent when the twists and turns of each player's own career intersect the twists and turns of former teammates who become current opponents, later, teammates again – and vice versa. Chiasson, for instance, was Fleury's teammate in the Worlds, his opponent when Chiasson was in Detroit with the Red Wings, and a teammate in Calgary. That brotherly relationship, which involved their wives, sharing rides to work, droll jokes, cans of smokeless tobacco, and waking up in the same row of uncomfortable airline or bus seats, ended with five minutes' notice in the winter of 1997 when Chiasson boarded the Flames' charter flight after their game against the Whalers in Hartford, grabbed his bag, and announced that he was suddenly a member of the team he had just been competing against. In Chiasson's seat instead sat Glen Featherstone, a lanky, goateed Whaler defenceman and former Ranger who an hour before had been hassling and hating Fleury on the Hartford ice. "There's no time to get sentimental in this business," Fleury said. "Things happen so quickly, on the ice and off."

Mike Vernon, the Calgary goalie, went to Detroit in the previous trade for Chiasson and now Fleury regularly shoots on him. In the same season – in fact, in the same week – Jamie Huscroft, a scrappy Calgary defenceman with a mischievous sense of humour, went from being a teammate and popular Flames locker-room jokester on Monday to an opponent in the visitors' dressing room just down the basement hall on Friday, as a player for the Tampa Bay Lightning and coach Terry Crisp, who used to coach the Flames. Lyle Odelein of the Montreal Canadiens and then the New Jersey Devils and Mike Keane of the New York Rangers were Fleury's teammates on the Moose Jaw Warriors. Now, Odelein is a New Jersey teammate of Doug Gilmour, who was a teammate of Fleury's on the Flames' Stanley Cup team in 1989 before being traded to the Toronto Maple Leafs. Keane, who as a Warrior linemate used to protect Fleury in the rugged Western Hockey League, used to confront Fleury in the NHL's Western Conference as a teammate of Joe Sakic, who tied Fleury for the WHL's scoring title in 1987–88 as a member of the Swift Current Broncos and later became a co-owner of the shortlived Calgary Hitmen Junior team with Fleury.

"It's not hard to play against your old teammates," says Fleury. "That's what so great about hockey. We fight for each other and then we go out and try to knock the snot out of each other. They expect it of me and I expect it of them. We wouldn't respect each other if we didn't. Then we go have dinner together after a game."

Eating meals together is a powerful ritual in professional hockey, as it is in most strong families, the sharing of the same food and table providing an opportunity for social intercourse and common routine that forges strong bonds for later times when members are apart or under stress. On that evening long ago, for instance, it was the Last Supper they held. And the disciples did not tuck their knees beneath their own individual TV tables, as the senior Fleurys have done for years of meals.

Calgary coach Pierre Page is a big believer in the power of shared activities, having experienced so many as a child. The oldest of two boys and one girl in the family of a hardworking Depression-era carpenter in Lachute, Quebec, Pierre did not have a lot of material things when he was growing up. His father earned twelve dollars a month, sixteen in summer. Those grim economic times, like winter, lasted somewhat longer in Canada than in other places. As products of the Depression, his parents were forever preparing for the worst; that pessimistic attitude seemed to bring them real peace. Even in their eighties, his proud parents – the quiet, reticent father and the more emotional mother – had yet to borrow money or own a credit card. But though the times may have been tough, the Pages always ate well. Pierre's father promised his family that. Meals were important. And the family always had each other at all times, which is even more important as nutrition for their spirit.

And outside the Page home, over the years, Pierre had his athletic families. He and his pals played every year for a variety of amateur sports teams sponsored by Lowe Brothers Dairies, a local family-owned company famous for its milk, ice cream, and a hockey-playing son named Kevin, whose long professional career involved winning Stanley Cups for the fabled Edmonton Oilers dynasty and the New York Rangers. "From age seven to twenty we played hockey for the Lowe Brothers in winter," Page remembers with a fond smile, "and baseball for the Lowe Brothers in summer and we worked for them after school each year. And we played tennis together. We were together so much. They had dinners for the teams and parties for the teams, all the time. It was a very close-knit family and we had pretty good teams."

Among Page's fondest memories of his own upbringing were the Christmas mornings when several generations of his mother's family gathered without fail in the country home of his Grandma Kingsbury. The rule was everyone had to arrive before dawn on Christmas morning. And all those children and parents and grandparents would have Christmas breakfast together and watch the sun come up, sharing the food and the moment and building memories to treasure later in faraway places. In Pierre's mind, the Christmas presents were nice but not really necessary to bronze those mornings in his memory.

A major part of Page's reputation within the NHL concerns his ability to carefully construct successful teams, annual families of players whose disparate skills, emotional strengths and needs, and personalities play off and to each other. He has built his teams technically, patiently, and studiously, which is not always the standard approach of modern professional athletes, or impatient owners, who look at the win column and see $$ instead of W's.

But Page did his rebuilding successfully. As coach of the Minnesota North Stars he built them and took them to the

Stanley Cup finals. As coach and general manager in Quebec City, he began the slow reconstruction phase of the Nordiques, including the famous Eric Lindros trade, before the team moved to Colorado and won the Cup. In 1995 the Flames turned to him for the same approach with the Calgary franchise, which since the 1989 Cup win had frittered away all of its star talent – in fact, every player from that team – except Fleury.

So it should not have been surprising as Page and his assistant coaches struggled to assemble a victorious new Flames franchise from a sprinkling of veterans and a large cadre of young, new, lower-cost players that Page turned back to the Lowe Dairy's low-cost but effective family strategy for team-building. He arranged for a variety of non-hockey activities for the players to share and, he hoped, bond through.

There are a surprising variety of forces working against the forging of strong emotional bonds on professional teams these days, especially when the teams are at home. There is an invisible caste system among players based on salary, with some stars earning as much in a dozen games as their teammates do all year. Usually, that is also well more than earned by the coach, the alleged boss.

This dollar disparity is magnified by the amazing ability, when you think about it, of some stars who live in Canada and play for Canadian teams to demand that their salaries be paid in a foreign currency (U.S. dollars), which is, in effect, a 30-percent raise. That is like Albert Belle or Brett Favre demanding, and receiving, their multimillion-dollar salaries in German marks or Japanese yen. That salary disparity is invisible in the locker room but palpable.

There is also free-agency, which enables the best veteran players to try to sell their services to the highest bidder with varying degrees of compensation to the old team. The result is that few stars spend their entire career in the same dressing room any more. The allegiance is usually given more to the money than the team you have grown up and matured with. And the fans, who do the cheering and buy the tickets and their hero's jersey but cannot sell their allegiance to a higher bidder, are left behind, suddenly idol-free. Fellow players are quick, maybe too quick, to volunteer that such self-interested behaviour is understandable and acceptable given every player's need to look out for number one regardless of his uniform number, and the precarious lifespan of a professional athlete whose career could end in the next shift, as Dave Chartier's did one day so suddenly.

The players come to the rink in their expensive cars. They practise. They lift weights. They shower. They shave with their individually numbered disposable razor. They sign a pennant for someone's child in hospital. They go home to their family, to lunch with their agent, or to meetings for their other business interests. If they are single, they may linger in the locker room and mingle, taking on each other in intense games of ping-pong or cards or Scrabble or any of the other myriad forms of competition that seem destined to break out even in their off-ice lives. They know each other well as co-workers but not really like a full-time family that has shared pre-dawn Christmas mornings since childhood.

It is on the road, away from the demanding distractions of wives, girlfriends, children, adoring local fans, and chequebooks and investments, that the team ties can be bound: shared meals, airplane journeys, practical jokes, bus rides, gruelling practices, on-ice battles, running gags, lectures – or praise – from the coaches.

Road trips, however, can also provide temptations for men with no shortage of testosterone, and opportunities for wives with fertile imaginations. Frequent, long absences can put additional strains on already fragile relationships, as can fame. Few other professions virtually require that wives sit and watch their men every minute at work. It takes a very secure woman to put up with forever sharing her spouse with an always adoring, ever-demanding, and often thoughtless public that gets first dibs on the player's attention while she is sitting in a restaurant or even a darkened movie theatre, shopping for groceries, in the family car at a stoplight, or, in her imagination, in foreign arenas in faraway cities where the team plays half of its games. Just outside the team locker room, even after a devastating loss or an injury, a player must wade through an insistent throng of adoring fans to reach his wife. Often, a wave or nod must suffice for ten or fifteen minutes while the wife waits, sometimes patiently.

Of course, gender differences virtually guarantee that many married males who may be physically present in their own kitchen are actually still on a virtual road trip emotionally. One of the most striking aspects of life inside a professional hockey team is the intensity of everything – the physical action, the intimidation, the emotional highs, the emotional lows, the anger, the physical pain, the distractions, the strengths, the fellowship, the noise, the financial stakes, the lights, the speed – and most of it is all right there in the public eye for everyone to see and to judge and to talk about, though few of these self-appointed experts possess 30 per cent of the skills they are assessing. And the player is not expected to argue.

The challenge of separating work and home is not confined to hockey. But it seems more difficult in hockey than in many professions. It is all packed into one televised three-hour span, timed to the tenth of a second, and many more people are watching and judging. Take, for instance, a player struggling to build his career or perhaps preserve it. He has sat out several games. He has not scored in weeks. The newspapers have noted this many times. The stories speculate that his career is over. One reporter divides the player's large salary by his small number of goals; they become very expensive goals.

For days, even weeks, the player prepares himself to play. He eats right, practises right, sleeps right, studies right, thinks right. And he wears his old lucky shirt. Each time, he sits out. Then, one night he gets a chance to play. Numerous shifts on the ice produce much activity but no points. Then, with just seconds left in the game, with his team losing by a goal and needing a point to make the playoffs, opportunity kicks in the door. From out of nowhere that little black piece of rubber squirts right in front of him. Unbelievable! Instinctively, he swats at it. Silence sweeps the stands. He feels the sting of a stick on his back. The puck slams into the post. It ricochets the wrong way. The horn blows.

Within minutes the player is in the silent locker room, sweaty, smelly, thirsty. No one talks to him. The coach walks by, silently. No one talks to anyone. He is totally exhausted. His back is beginning to hurt. He is naked. A pack of reporters with notebooks or huge video cameras rushes through the door, aimed straight at him. They know a good story for tomorrow's breakfast entertainment. They swarm his stall. They stick a half-dozen little tape recorders just beneath his nose. Tiny red lights blink on the machines. "This has been a tough year for you," the little reporter says. "You had a chance there at the end to tie it up for your team. But you didn't. How'd that feel?"

To be sure, some professional athletes are just as good husbands and fathers as those in any other profession, albeit far better known than most. And the Flames make regular good-faith efforts to help, like sending each wife a bouquet of appreciation if the team is away on an important family holiday.

Yes, the salaries can be great. But the demands can be great as well. When Steve Chiasson was abruptly traded to Hartford just as he was boarding the Flames' charter plane one winter's night, all of his team family and some of their wives knew about it long before Steve's own wife, Susan, who was two time zones away back in Calgary and very pregnant. Days later, Chiasson's new team announced that it was trading cities, leaving Hartford for somewhere unknown. Weeks later, after the birth, the

Chiassons discovered with the rest of the sports world that the team was relocating to Raleigh, North Carolina.

Divorces have resulted from such strains, frictions, and misunderstandings. More surely will follow. Brian Patafie was married once. He has spent much of the past eighteen winters on the road as a trainer and assistant with the Flames and its former International Hockey League affiliate in Salt Lake City, the Golden Eagles. "Something happens among people who travel together," he says from experience. "You wake up in the morning and it's your linemate you need to decide about eating breakfast with." With a sly smile, Brian talks about hockey players who spend long hours of quality time with the most important people in their lives and then go home to their families.

When the competing ice-time needs of and income from the National Curling Championship Brier forced the Flames out of the Saddledome one March and onto the road for two weeks, many muttered about the fatigue and boredom of a long road trip. Given the vast scale of their region, Western Conference teams, by definition, spend more season days on the road than their Eastern Conference colleagues, who can bus to away games and still be back home in their own bed that same night.

Coach Page instead sees a possible advantage to this regional reality, if only he could more frequently overcome management's cost-conscious proclivity to avoid charter flights. Charters are more expensive, but they virtually eliminate long airport waits and tiring transfers. According to the veteran coach's calculations, one hour of air travel is as physically demanding as twenty minutes of a game. So eliminating one two-hour layover and shortening a flight by another hour through chartering saves the beating of one game on his charges. And, he reasons, charters should not be too hard to arrange for a team with Canadian Airlines as an arena sponsor.

More importantly in the coach's book, shorter travel time opens up more time for practice, which is when a player really works and progresses. "Western teams travel more and practise less," he says. "That catches up to you after a while in a long season." The coaches can see it in the players' legs. Page calls it "jump." "They didn't have any jump this morning," he says.

But while the NHL's organizers officially could place Toronto and Detroit in the Western Conference for years, nothing is going to change the geographic location of Calgary and its distance from Los Angeles, Phoenix, and Dallas. Long road trips are inevitable and they do bring Flames players together as one group for longer, in this case fifteen days. The coach arranged for a variety of non-hockey activities for everyone to do together. They saw movies together. They ate together. They went to Broadway shows and comedy clubs together. And, not coincidentally, the team produced a good record.

Not only that but the players felt such a sense of companionship and synergy that, even when they returned home, they arranged similar outings; they went to a warehouse and had a paintball war, veterans against the rookies. The coaches were not invited. The coaches were delighted.

Fleury loved the paintball battle. But in a long season of many shots missed and many games lost by a single goal, Fleury no longer loved practices. "Maybe I've been doing them so long," he shrugged.

Coach Page regards practices as the most important part of a pro's life in hockey. "Practice is the ticket to getting better," he says. "Of course, you have to eat well, sleep well, train well, all of that. In the games you see the players who are good. Everyone wants to play in the games. But in practice you see the players who want to get better, who are willing to pay the price of working hard and learning, no matter how good they already are. Working hard in practice is very important."

Practice is part of the underbelly of a professional hockey player's existence that few people know about. The world sees these pros skate into the glaring spotlight on the white ice and into our consciousness in their colourful uniforms exactly thirty-five minutes before a game. The unspoken and inaccurate assumption is that they come to work like everyone else goes to work and they do their thing and then go home until the next game. But in a regular hockey season of about 200 days, not counting a possible extra 60 for the playoffs and 30 more for training camp, there are 82 games. On the great majority of the 120 other days, there is a crucial practice.

In the perpetual construction and reconstruction of the skills and personal chemistry of each pro team, there is a steady string of lessons and strategies being taught and, perhaps, learned. Those who learn quickest and make the fewest mistakes, regardless of innate skill, tend to stay. Those who don't learn don't stay. Practices are the classroom. And the ensuing tests are very public. In fact, they sell tickets to them eighty-two times a year.

Practices usually are closed to the public, save for a very few spectators or sponsors with special permission and a handful of beat reporters less interested in the on-ice workout than grabbing an interview or two for an upcoming story. Practice times vary but on non-game days usually occur in late morning, giving the coaches time to meet beforehand and watch edited videotapes of other teams' games from the previous night or the Flames' own game.

Al Coates, the Flames' savvy general manager, uses practices to silently judge every Flames player. It is the reputation earned at those times that lingers in the general manager's mind and in consultation with the head coach and his assistants shapes the player's future. Coates, the former longtime Flames public-relations manager who seems to joke around less since he assumed overall management responsibility in 1995, rarely misses a practice, if he's not travelling to evaluate talent elsewhere.

Coates prefers to sit in some darkened luxury box and quietly watch the activities on ice from on high. He especially watches how hard each man works. "You can see a lot from here," he says, not taking his eyes off the ice. "You watch for little things – who's hustling, who's not, who's improving, who's not, who's encouraging his teammates with words and little taps, who's listening and who's daydreaming. I like to have a personal feel.

"We want our players to have some bite to them, some consistent bite. We are trying to develop a particular Flames culture, players with bite and character who are good and want to feed off each other and get better. You need a balance of young players and veterans and those veterans play an important teaching role for the youngsters about what is acceptable in terms of effort and attitude. Coaches can only talk so much. These guys communicate with each other by example. So you can't keep a bad seed. It becomes more mental than physical much of the time. These guys are for the most part very well-conditioned, strong athletes. It's their mental approach to the team and game that keeps them here or weeds them out."

Each player has been in the building at least an hour already, sipping coffee, water, or Gatorade, stretching, riding a stationary bike, chatting with teammates, watching a tape of a hockey game or golf match on the big-screen TV. On such days Fleury regularly rises at about nine in his custom-built lakeside home in southeast Calgary. He throws on casual clothes, hugs and kisses his wife, Veronica, pats his dogs, Hat Trick and Ditto, and steps into another frosty Calgary morning. He jumps up into his white Ford pickup where the country-music station comes on automatically.

"Ever since I was a kid," he says, "I've never been much of a breakfast person." So he stops at a nearby Tim Hortons donut shop for a cup of coffee with cream and sugar. When he goes to pay with a twenty-dollar bill, the young female clerk says, "It's on me, Theo. Good luck tomorrow."

"Hey, thanks a lot," he says to the gesture of generosity that has become a persistent feature of his daily life. "Part of the perks of fame, I guess," he says. The commute to his hockey home takes about twenty minutes. En route, two drivers and one pedestrian recognize either him or the truck and wave. Mornings are not Fleury's favourite time to smile. But he does and waves back. Does he ever leave his house and not get recognized by someone who wants such a connection or autograph?

"Nope."

At the Saddledome he strips, showers, and sits for ten minutes in the hot tub to wake up and warm up. Like many hockey players, his body carries not only the scars of games and battles gone by, but a tattoo – a large Indian chief's head – on his upper arm, a souvenir of his Junior days on the Moose Jaw Warriors. Fleury dons his red and grey hockey underwear along with a battered Detroit Vipers baseball cap that a fan tossed on the ice after a Fleury hat trick months before. "It's a good hat," he says, taking it off to re-admire it. "I think it was the only one that night."

Fleury joins a half-dozen barefoot teammates on a couch watching a distant golf match. A loud cheer erupts over one beautiful drive. Goalie Trevor Kidd and Tommy Albelin begin an aggressive ping-pong game. "Prepare to die, Tommy," says the goalie. "In your dreams," says Albelin.

But soon coach Page is wiping off the green blackboard. The TV is doused. First comes a pep talk about effort from Kevin Constantine, an assistant coach who usually gives the motivational offerings. One of the few Americans in the organization, Constantine is former head coach of the San Jose Sharks. He is followed by Page, who goes over strategies and patterns of attack he has noted employed by their next opponent, the Vancouver Canucks. The team meeting is over in thirteen minutes.

Then comes a brisk suiting up. Fleury has already installed his contact lenses. "I couldn't find the rink without them," he says. In fact, Fleury rarely bothers to change them. "Whatever," he says. First, the underwear goes on, then the jockstrap outside the underwear, Velcro garter belt, two shin pads, two stockings stretched to hook to the belt and taped round and round, two elbow pads, red, yellow, and black breezers, skates, shoulder pads, helmet, gloves. For reasons that matter only in habit, Fleury always puts the left item on first. It's familiar. Then, they each grab two sticks and walk like stiltmen down the rubber carpet beneath the grandstands to the bright lights and the chilly rink.

Practice begins with a casual warmup skate, the players shifting from one leg to the other like drunken sailors swaggering in slow motion. Even shuffling, they glide around the rink faster than most people could race. The players wear different coloured practice jerseys – yellow, black, white, according to their line. Red denotes injured players prohibited from contact but not from the ribbing that comes with such special treatment.

Somewhere a whistle chirps softly. Everyone breaks into a sudden sprint, two complete laps, more than nine hundred feet, at full speed. Automatically, they slow for a lap. Then, full speed again. Another whistle. They do the same thing backwards. Then they change direction. The sharp scraping sound of steel blades, driven hard against the ice, echoes in the empty Saddledome. It is a wordless warmup and conditioning routine each player has done thousands of times. It is a complicated athletic choreography refined over the years on various teams. They know it by heart.

On television or from the cheap seats the movements of hockey players seem natural and impressively smooth. But up close, the speed and grace are what impress. Most players weigh a tenth of a ton. Beneath their baggy shirts sit muscles honed by forty-nine weeks a year of conditioning and weight-training. They can run into each other like trucks colliding. Or they can knife through the smallest space without touching and shoot the puck blindly and accurately to a linemate they simply sense is charging up just behind. It is strangely balletic.

As soon as Billy Hughes, an assistant coach, dumps two buckets of pucks on the ice, everyone grabs one with their stick and skates around. Quickly, deftly, they move the seven-ounce piece of rubber back and forth, like kittens batting a ball. Soon they form into rows facing each goalie, Trevor Kidd at one end and Dwayne Roloson at the other. One by one across the row and back again they fire puck after puck at the human targets. Their faces are serious. Soft oomphs seep out of straining bodies as they shoot with full force.

The head coach calls a quick team meeting by the penalty box. He draws plays on a plastic board stuck to the glass. They adjourn to practise. Then on another unseen signal they break into a series of drills – two attackers against one defenceman and the goalie. "C'mon! C'mon! C'mon!" Two half-ice scrimmages break out. "Buckle D! Buckle D!" In the hockey world everything on the ice, it seems, must be said at least twice. "Take the middle! Take the middle! Okay. Play it! Play it!"

The coaches stand around watching closely, their gloved hands atop their own sticks. "Work it! Work it!" The players practise dumping the puck into the offensive zone and chasing it. A particularly nice move draws a spontaneous round of hockey applause – sticks banged on the ice – from players awaiting their turn at the drill. A minor scuffle breaks out. Fleury leaps in to join the fray. He skates back to the end of the line and grabs a water bottle for a short drink. On his white helmet the M in FLAMES is nicked from a past encounter with something sharp. The sweat is dripping off his slightly goateed chin in a steady stream. No more sleepy eyes. He's into it now. He takes a quick squirt of water. "I ain't getting any younger," he says, smiling that smile and not caring. Then, he winks.

When he was younger, Theoren Fleury lived for sports, most any sports. Russell has no football. But it does have hockey and baseball. "I never had much trouble with the boys," Donna Fleury remembers quietly. "They were so much into sports. And what I remember about Theoren especially is him shooting the puck. It seemed like that's all he did. Day and night, there's Theoren. And there's the puck. He'd close the door and shoot the puck against it, time after time after time. Ka-bang. Ka-bang. Ka-bang. He'd go on for hours. One time I wasn't feeling good and I got after him. But that was a real passion with him. We were always replacing the linoleum."

Not surprisingly, Theoren's little brothers, Ted and Travis, became involved in hockey, too, though after some hard falls early on Travis postponed his serious playing until he was eight. They'd play mini-games in the basement with mini-sticks and the goalie could use a tennis racquet. Even when Theoren was not home, which seemed to be often, he took the basement mini-game idea with him to friends' homes. "We had to replace some basement tiles," Ann Petz says. "Ted and Theo would go at it for hours down there. Every once in a while, you'd hear a crash and a pause and then the game would resume. We never minded. They could have been getting into trouble somewhere else."

Outdoors, the Fleury boys would make a net out of blocks of snow and water it down to freeze overnight. A couple of winters Wally flooded the backyard and hung a light bulb on the clothesline. For a break the boys would play bumper skiing, which involved crouching down and grabbing the bumpers of passing cars and skiing behind the unsuspecting vehicles as far as possible along the icy streets. One time Theoren went three blocks without falling. "It's a wonder any of them survived," says Carmen Fleury, Ted's wife. "The stories these guys tell are fantastic."

In the summer the Fleury boys would play road hockey with a puck or tennis ball. Each brother got five shots in an endless series of sudden-death shootouts. Theo was very good at aiming his shots even at painful places if the competition became heated. Typically, Travis would get hurt and run in the house crying while Ted and Theo battled outside over who was responsible.

Theoren's teachers do not remember him as a poor student. But he remembers putting up with school to get to hockey. There were some fights; Theoren says now he cannot remember what they were about. Schoolmates say they usually involved derogatory comments about Theo's size or native heritage. "Theo was always the smallest," recalls one buddy. "But he took no crap from anybody."

Even on the ice Theo was known for being aggressive. Neither the size of his opponent nor friendship seemed to matter once the puck was dropped. Greg Slywchuk, Theo's kindergarten friend who invited him to that first skate, played on the Binscarth team until he moved to Russell several years after Theo. "I remember I got the puck at the point one time. Theo took my feet right out from under me. He skated right through me and stole the puck. He was always very intense, but I didn't care for him too much after that."

Now, Greg is an electrician in Winnipeg. But one of his most vivid memories is the one time Binscarth beat Russell. "We must have played Russell, oh, maybe forty times over the years," he says. "We never could beat them or Theo. But one time we did. Theo was hurt. Some accident to his eye at home. So he didn't play. And we barely won, 2–1. Our goalie stood on his head. It was great. We finally beat Russell and Fleury. We thought we'd won the Stanley Cup."

As soon as school was out each afternoon, Theo would race home down Russell's snow-packed streets with the bare trees past the blue water tower and the Manitoba Wheat Pool elevator to Augusta. After a hot snack, he'd shoot pucks or play some road hockey until it was time for practice at the rink. After Coach Fowler dismissed his boys, Theo would usually try to stay and practise with the next team. He'd go home, often late, gobble down dinner and go back outside to play. Donna Fleury remembers coaxing him inside sometimes as late as eleven.

Donna admits now, sadly, that she has few memories about her boys' childhood; facing reality is part of her therapy. "My mind was so fuzzy much of the time for so long, it's hard to remember much," she says. Donna has always been a nervous person, intensely shy, and often subject to depression, even back in her teens. She has overcome much of it now and even volunteers to help around town sometimes. But years ago just the thought of going into downtown Russell for groceries was terrifying. Donna would stay at home and endlessly prepare meals, often cabbage rolls, which Theoren loved. His youthful appetite far exceeded his size, according to family legend, although the cabbage gave him cramps when he played hockey soon after. Housekeeping was often too much for Donna to face. Or she would go to bed for long periods during the day. She also took Valium, a lot of Valium.

A doctor first prescribed Valium to calm Donna's nervousness and depression when she was sixteen. Over the years there was always a refill available or another doctor who would write yet another prescription, thinking it would help this nervous housewife. After a while Donna became so dependent on the little pills that she stashed them all over the house and in every purse so she would never be without them or far from them. "I was addicted," she says. "I regret now my problems from before. Theo and I are closer now. I think he understands. We didn't get to many of his games. But when we did, we'd wave and wave and wave until we were sure he saw us. He'd smile and say, 'Now, I can play.'"

Most nights Wally Fleury was not there to help at home either. He'd be home right after work to eat something, maybe watch a little TV. If his oldest son had a hockey game, Wally would tape Theo's sticks and give him a little pep talk. "I'd tell him, 'These sticks are taped good now. You get some damn goals tonight, boy.'" Then, Wally would be gone until the family heard him stumble in after midnight.

"I think booze was Dad's escape," Theoren says now. "And hockey was mine. But he's not a bad guy."

"When I was drinking," says Wally, who has been mostly sober fifteen years now, "I didn't know what I was doing. I knew I didn't make the NHL. But my son did. That's for sure. I wanted to win the Stanley Cup. And my son did that. That's for sure, too."

These days, driving around town revisiting some old haunts in his Buick LeSabre with the climate control and the Calgary Flames licence plate, Wally wants to add something: "I feel bad about what I did, all the drinking and all. I feel real bad. But I'm sober now. We move on and I'm there for him now. I don't know how good a dad or a player I could have been. But Theoren has been a very good son to us."

Indeed, every two weeks when Fleury's Flames paycheque arrives in Winnipeg at the office of his agent, Don Baizley, a portion goes to pay for his parents' housing and utilities, according to Theo's instructions. In September 1996, when Theoren was playing for Canada in the World Cup, he flew his parents to watch him in Philadelphia, Toronto, and Ottawa. For years now thousands of spectators watch every game he plays in person, at times millions of others are there via television and radio. But whenever possible, Theoren Fleury arranges for someone he actually knows to be in the stands – family, friends, former teammates. He buys the tickets. He knows where they will sit. When he skates out for the pregame warmup, Theoren Fleury – team captain and all-star – looks for his personal audience. He gives that person a little salute with his stick. And if, at some point during the game, number 14 thinks his special guest is not paying full attention, he might skate up and tap the nearby glass with his stick.

Theo also thought it was a nice touch, the Fleurys' oldest son paying for his parents' long-delayed honeymoon twenty-nine years after the September 9 wedding day. Theo has always been more comfortable giving gifts than receiving them.

Donna had overcome her fear of flying. Despite the frightening crowds, Donna went to all of her son's World Cup games, of course, though she was very quiet. "I still don't understand everything about the game," she explains. So her cheers and responses lag slightly behind the play. But Wally understands it all immediately, sometimes even before immediately. He can see a play developing. He loves every minute. And he doesn't mind sharing his delight and opinions with everyone within earshot, including the referees. Wally saw, for instance, some penalties committed against his son that should have been called. And he thought that his son's successful line should have played a good deal more. And in that opinion Wally was not alone. "When I see Theoren play," Wally says, "I feel great. It's like a part of me is out there playing like an all-star. And when Theo plays, he says, 'This is the way Dad played.'"

The only time Wally fell silent on that trip was when he arrived at one of hockey's holy shrines, Toronto's Maple Leaf Gardens. It was the first time in person, though he had been there hundreds of times on the radio. "I swear I could hear Foster Hewitt's voice," Wally says in a reverential whisper.

Theoren was taking his father to lunch after practice. Wally, who had dreamed of playing in the big time and scoring in places like the Gardens, stepped out of the car his son had hired to bring him from the hotel. Wally was standing on Carlton Street soaking up the scene and the moment. He was actually in the presence of Maple Leaf Gardens. His heart was pounding. He thought he could hear old-time voices, as he had so many dark nights on the radio on the prairies. As Wally tells it, just then a guard walked right up to him and said, "Mr. Fleury, right this way to watch your son practise. Theo said the locker room is closed, but he'll meet you in the lobby after they're done."

Wally asked the guard how he knew him. And the guard replied, "Your son told me to watch for the man arriving in a limo. You're the only one arriving at the Gardens in a limo today." Wally adds, "I drive up to Maple Leaf Gardens in a limo ordered by my son who's playing for Canada in the World Cup. And the guard recognizes me. Now, how is that for living, eh?"

Wally strode into that old building like the all-star captain he knew he could have been. But now he would watch his grownup son, the one who had worn Wally's wobbly oversized helmet when he skated by himself in the corner of the Russell rink while his father drove the Zamboni before dawn. Now, Wally would watch that same son practise with Wayne Gretzky and Mark Messier and the other modern greats. No drink, not even a double, could ever have matched that kind of high.

Wally also regards himself as a good-luck charm for his son, a fact that Theoren confirmed for a nationwide television audience during the 1996 World Cup. The day after his father arrived, Fleury scored the game-winning goal against Sweden. Against the United States, with his father present, Fleury scored a goal and an assist. Even after the World Cup, with Wally and Donna back in their home in Russell, Theoren checked in with his father.

Following his World Cup success, Theoren was experiencing a serious scoring slump which brought with it something new for Fleury: a fierce frustration that seemed to fester and feed on itself as the goal drought grew. Theoren was not the only one who played superbly in that international competition and then had trouble in the regular NHL season. The media saw a pattern of emotional letdowns and made much of them in the sports pages for days; with the tight playoff race still seventy-some games away, there wasn't much else to write about. A few players said they agreed with the letdown theory. Many said they did not.

Officials of the National Hockey League and the National Hockey League Players' Association demurred. They had seen the powerful exposure that international competition on TV had brought the National Basketball Association. In fact, NHL commissioner Gary Bettman had played a major role in the NBA's international marketing, which was a big plus in the minds of team owners.

The power of television to create fame is already famous. Television is to fame-building as steroids are to muscle-building, with the same potential for longterm destruction of normal functions. Point a TV camera at any section of seats at a CFL or NFL game and just watch what it causes otherwise rational people to do. Some print ads even proclaim "As Advertised on TV," as if being scanned into electrons by a television camera confers some kind of commercial credibility beyond the ability to purchase air-time. Television can both cause and spread fame. And fame can sell most anything. Even athletic infamy sells, as basketball's bad boy Dennis Rodman has proven. Pro football players are now paid thousands of dollars just to wear a particular baseball hat on the sidelines within camera range.

These hockey officials know that people in rural European communities who have never even attended an NBA game and will never be on Chicago's West Madison Street are now buying Bulls caps and jerseys to wear on the weekend. And the marketers of cars and beers and other mass commodities know the irresistible attraction for millions around the world of the spontaneity and pregnant possibilities of excitement within live sports events. The international-minded executives of the growing TV networks were coming to ignore the borders of countries as effectively as their electronic signals falling down from the fleet of satellites in outer space ignored them. They also know their networks' insatiable appetites for inexpensive programs to be televised. One minute of time unsold today is gone forever.

So emotional letdown or not, scoring frustration or not, hockey games on globe-girdling television and the international competitions that attract foreign audiences and the fame that comes with it all are here to stay. Witness the 1998 Winter Olympics.

As usual with Theoren since even before the kindergarten balance-beam episode, he does not volunteer much about what passes for his frustrations. When asked, he tends to speak in short simple sentences. Theoren, when he does talk, comes across with an appealing, even childlike openness. He seems genuinely to be trying to answer the question without spewing out the usual safe, empty player's platitudes and worn clichés about "grinding it out," "going to the net," "paying the price," and "burying the puck." Talk may be valuable or carry weight in some circles – universities and the media, for instance, where it can seem important to show others what you know with words. But the world of the professional athlete is based more on doing; show the people what you can do. Talk is what opponents – or players like Fleury – do to distract and anger you, to get you off your game.

In the physical world of most professional athletes, especially athletes from rural communities, talk by itself never seems to accomplish much. "Excuse me, could I please have that puck so I can score and you can lose?" In fact, talking publicly, usually to a reporter, can get you in real trouble, especially if your talk is candid. There are three things that can happen when you speak publicly and two of them are bad. If they take the quote out of context, you can look dumb or foolish. The opposition can post your quote in their dressing room to incite themselves. Or it can happen that nobody notices you said anything, which is the best you can hope for. Still, the league says you must do it.

Talking to the media is like talking to a woman: it's not so much what you're saying, it's that you're being seen to say something. The real agendas in those communications can be hidden, hard to anticipate, and turn for the worse without warning. An interview can take a player into unknown territory, terra incognita mined with faux pas and peopled by prima donnas, whatever they are. So when it comes to talking with non-team members, the players who on the ice are veritable surgeons with their meticulously taped sticks of curved wood, aluminum, or graphite think of themselves like ducks trying to dance in a ballet. These men who can twitch a shoulder beneath thick pads and a coloured jersey and cause a goalie to fall down too soon think of themselves as incapable of subtlety. These players, who routinely plunge their bodies with awesome gusto into fearsome physical frays, fully expect the team's public-relations people to find out in advance every interview subject.

Watch most young pro athletes walk to the podium at the civic lunches their teams invariably endorse for the public involvement and ticket sale possibilities. These are the players who can command their bodies to do the most graceful things at the fastest speeds in the tightest quarters seemingly unaware of opponents' onrushing bodies and the thousands of judgemental eyes scanning them. These finely tuned young men are standing in front of eager fans prepared to love them, like family watching a young member in a school play. The closest current connection a fan has to the rigorous demands of a pro athlete's life is this morning's sports page and the Ironman model watch he got for Father's Day. Yet there the typical young player stands at the microphone fiddling with his tie or unfolding his scrawled notes and uhm-ing and awh-ing as awkwardly and uncertainly as a professor or reporter might who was suddenly handed a hockey stick and placed at the faceoff circle of the Stanley Cup finals in overtime. Words do little at times like this. Be good or be gone.

Theo talks when he has to and as he has had to. Everything he would say would be true even if, to be truthful, like all savvy people in the public eye, he wouldn't always say everything he knew or was thinking. There's a knack and a protocol required of people speaking publicly these days. The knack, usually acquired through painful experience, is being able to gauge in advance the volume and impact of words spoken between two individuals by the time those words get printed or broadcast to millions. It's like shooting at a moving target, having to gauge distance and velocities to imagine an accurate intersection some time later. This is very difficult, even with experienced eyes.

For example, after practice one day a reporter asks a tired player if he's still got the energy and drive to win, despite a lingering injury. It is not a question that will change the course of history. But it is a reasonable thing to ask of a star player, the kind of question that reporters like to imagine their readers would want answered. In response, the player might like to suggest, perhaps pointedly and certainly proudly, that his long productive record in the league and before suggests he can be counted on. He might like to suggest that he is as human as the questioner and can have an off day too, though his off days are far more public. He might like to point out that pro athletes, unlike reporters, do not have editors to catch their mistakes before anyone sees them. He might like to note that the most important people in his life, his team family and his biological family, not to mention team management, seem to think he is still quite good. And he might like to question what the questioner ever accomplished or earned in sports that qualifies him to judge the skill or effort of a professional who has been playing the game for major money since before the questioner even started classes at his fancy college.

But instead the player responds politely and simply: "I can do it." And he adds a modest shrug that comes with long experience. Those four little words sound eminently plausible and quite reasonable when spoken by a professional athlete to an apparent friend privately in a locker room while sitting on a towel and sipping a mid-morning can of pop.

But now, trumpet those same four words atop page one the next morning in the playoffs in a blaring boldface headline the size of Alberta, maybe add a mean-looking colour photo from training camp, shed the shrug, and insert a little punctuation mark for dramatic effect. And now, you have:

"I CAN DO IT!"

Those four simple little words are now no longer so little or so simple. They have become a papal pronouncement, a virtual declaration of superiority with a real ring of swagger, possibly pomposity, that will strike many as not much like the modest smalltown boy they knew or like to picture. Those words may help sell a lot of newspapers that morning and quench the curiosity of commuters munching on their whole-grain flakes. But those words surely will make the speaker a special target on the ice that night. Worse yet, those words may prompt the player's teammates to mock him in the locker room or, worst of all, silently in the privacy of their minds. Who needs that hassle, eh?

Nowadays, the protocol of speaking in public requires more humility than the speaker might feel and more discretion than necessary for words spoken in, say, a friend's car. There are so many media now to magnify the volume of every word everywhere. Like every player, Theo has seen the league's training-camp videotape that encourages players to co-operate with reporters whose hastily prepared stories then go out to the eager waiting fans who form their opinions about teams and players and then buy – or don't buy – the tickets and the hats. Angry or not at the team and players, they still buy the newspapers.

Fleury knows co-operation with reporters is encouraged, indeed required. And he knows pro athletes do not have the luxury of certain public figures such as Michael Jackson, the singer, whose carefully programmed media reticence comes from the "The less you get it, the more you want it" school of public relations. This theory of modern communications relies on the current need for instant gratification. The more you know what you can't see, the more you simply must see it. By not granting interviews, Jackson and others actually raise the mystery quotient of their public personality and the commercial value of their words when they are finally uttered to a selected representative of a mass audience. Michael Jackson can be celebrated for his seeming secretiveness by the celebrity press. On the other hand, Steve Carlton, the pitcher who refused to grant interviews for years, is portrayed by the sports press as grumpy and unco-operative. And what corporation would want to pay immense sums of money for product endorsements by an individual widely thought to be grumpy and unco-operative?

It does not take long for young professional athletes to learn the PR routine. Theo learned it during his rookie 1989 season by watching veterans like Doug Gilmour and Lanny McDonald field even the dumbest questions without embarrassing the reporter who thought twenty minutes of jogging three times a week was a pretty rigorous workout schedule. The players could joke about the questions later in the showers after the reporter ran off to carry the players' words to the presumably waiting throngs. But out in front of the notebooks, mini-recorders, and cameras, the players would keep a straight face.

So when reporters inevitably asked Theoren about the scoring slump, which was almost every day, he said, well, yes, sure, it was disappointing. And frustrating. No, there was no World Cup jinx. Yes, he was still doing all he could, which was to keep trying, not to press, but just to keep trying. And eventually the goals would come. He got asked about the problem so often that the slump took on a magnified reality that probably made it even harder to shake.

That focus on the negative is an intriguing social phenomenon and, in their daily role as society's instant chronicler, the newspapers and television infotainment industry merely reflect the public's perverse desire for bad news. If there is no real bad news, we'll make it up: that's called gossip and rumour. And gossip and rumour were alive as word-of-mouth delivered by nosy neighbours long before televisions, radios, and cellphones lengthened, broadened, and quickened the reach of half-truths and untruths. With the World Wide Web now, we can make gossip go around the world faster than we can make instant coffee in a microwave. And with the anonymity of electronics, there is little account-ability. We say we don't like bad news. But a choice of competing headlines – "MARRIAGES LASTING LONGER, STUDY SAYS" or "PRINCESS CAUGHT IN 2ND NAKED AFFAIR" – is not much of a choice for most readers. Naked wins every time.

It's not the twenty-two thousand airline flights that landed safely yesterday that make the news; it's the one that didn't. It's not the forty-seven shots the goalie stopped that make the news; it's the three he missed. It's easier to blame the news media than ourselves. Beyond a chronic eagerness to believe the worst and then overstate it just a bit like that nosy neighbour did for a more dramatic telling, the news media's crime is that its editors, reporters, and camerapersons know so well what we secretly want so badly.

Still, few openly accuse reporters of taking perverse pleasure in chronicling bad news. Get them on the ice and it might be a different story. It's not written down anywhere and nobody says it out loud. But publicly accusing the press is bad form. It can sound like whining, which it is sometimes. And complaining gets you burned later. Never argue with people who buy ink by the barrel, goes the public-relations adage.

So in their hunt for more discouraging words the reporters would usually thank Theo for his time; they knew they'd need more of it tomorrow. And they would quietly walk away to gather some more quotes, like miners looking for nuggets, maybe from a sympathetic Fleury teammate or from a coach, whose words about the slump would sound patient and under-standing because being open about their frustrations with the star's slump could only make it worse. Meanwhile, Theo would quietly finish the unusual business of getting dressed in public and go home by himself.

Publicly, Flames coaches and management told the reporters, no, they had not lost confidence in their star. Yes, the Flames did have more rookies this year and that might put more scoring pressure on the veterans. But all players go through these times, they said. They are frustrating for everyone. Theoren would just keep working. They knew that. And one day the slump would end. Everyone was sure of that.

Everyone, that is, but the angry callers who felt that their investment of emotion, allegiance, and occasional ticket money in the Flames entitled them to bend – even burn – the patient ear of Robbie Forand at the front desk about the overpaid babies on the team. "Well, sir," she would say ever so politely, "I'm sure no one here wants to lose. No, sir, he wants to win as much as you do. Well, thank you. . . . Thank you for. . . . Sir, you don't have to. . . . Thank you for calling, sir, and I will pass on your comments. Yes, thank you. . . . Good morning, the Calgary Flames and Canadian Airlines Saddledome."

The Fleurys have caller ID on their phone, so they can screen the calls to their unlisted number. But they can't edit the newspapers that arrive on the front steps or the sports shows off their satellite dish. It is truly amazing how every day just enough news happens to fill every newspaper and news show. And most of that news chronicles failure, corruption, tragedy, or possible failure, potential corruption, near-tragedy, and certain death.

For many years one of the few places in the world that still celebrated successes and heroes was the sports page. In recent years, however, even the sports page seemed to succumb to bad news, providing a growing daily dose of what looks like police-blotter news about the off-ice, off-field exploits of athletes that used to be considered out of bounds.

Most places Theoren Fleury has played he has enjoyed great success, even if his team was terrible. The Russell team won regularly, taking three provincial championships. Most days the Moose Jaw Warriors struggled. But Canada's international teams regularly won with Fleury in the lineup. On the Flames' Salt Lake City farm team, the Golden Eagles, Fleury consistently led team and league scoring, and it won the International Hockey League championship in 1988. Fleury's first partial year in the NHL, the Flames won the Stanley Cup.

But now, sitting at the counter in the morning sipping coffee in the privacy of his own airy and spotlessly white kitchen, Theoren could read the stories of struggle in the newspapers, his struggle. Friends and family were supportive. Teammates were supportive. Even people who said nothing were supportive, their eyes and avoidance of the topic speaking silently of private sympathy for the public slump. It was a strangely isolating experience. On the outside, Theo remained outspokenly determined. But inside Theoren Fleury, now that was a different story.

"You say to yourself, 'You know, I don't need to go through this.' You play in the World Cup and you have so much success playing with and against the greatest players in the world and you come back home and nothing, absolutely nothing good is happening. It's like, oh, God, no matter what you do on the ice – you can work as hard as you possibly can – absolutely nothing is going to go right for you. You take a pass and it hits a chip and skips over your stick. Or you get a real breakaway and beat the goalie and it hits the post. You get in a bad rut. It just happens. And it goes on and on.

"You know what it's like? It's like carrying a huge piano around on your back everywhere you go. Everyone tries to be nice and supportive. And everyone who says anything just reminds you of the problem. And the reporters want to know how you're handling it. That's their job. Your teammates are great. They say, 'C'mon, Theo, we know you're going to break out of this.' And the coaches are supportive and say the same thing. Everybody is pulling for you. It feels like someone keeps piling more stuff on top up there. You press. You try to do too much by yourself, try to beat the whole team by yourself. You don't wait for the puck. You shoot too soon. You just want to get on track so badly that you can taste it. And when you go home, you lie there and ask yourself what else you could possibly do. You're doing the same thing that has always been successful. But now nothing is."

So how does someone who has been famous all of his life for scoring goals stop becoming famous for not scoring goals?

"You score one."

But how do you suddenly score one when you haven't for twelve games or more?

"You just do. It's a fluke. It just happens one night." And he shrugs that trademark shrug that says, "I don't have anything more to say about this."

Actually, according to Wally, there is slightly more to it than that. Theoren called his father on the phone late one night. Theoren knows his father's daily schedule in retirement – up at seven-thirty or eight, a bowl of cereal, over to check on his own father, who is nearing ninety and suffering from emphysema, errands, shoot pool, bowl, curl, or, come summer, at least thirty-six and maybe fifty-four holes of golf. Then comes dinner and watching sports on TV, almost any sports on TV. "If there was a marbles competition on," says Wally, "I'd probably watch it."

Wally has the TV set up in the corner of his living room opposite the couch, beneath the ceiling with the dents from a few grand indoor golf swings, and near all of his bowling trophies and the posed photo of Wally and Theo facing off against each other. Wally also has a collection of videotapes of favourite Flames games and Theo interviews, plus the remote control at hand and a cordless phone, so he won't miss any goals should someone happen to phone at the wrong time. On the table he has a weekly TV-program guide and a Flames schedule with wins, losses, ties, and son's goals and assists properly noted. Of course, Wally watches the sports shows to keep up on the latest scores. Wally says he's much more calm on Theo's game days now. Just before going to bed at around midnight, Wally will again check the late sports news. Who could possibly sleep without knowing the scores of the West Coast games?

As it happens, Wally's son is often watching precisely the same show one time zone and a good ten-hour drive away. One night during a commercial the phone rang in Wally's government bungalow. Wally punched the mute button on his remote. It was Theo on the phone, stuck in his slump and stuck thinking about it. Guys don't usually announce they need to talk; that should be clear from the call. They just start talking.

Wally recalls Theo saying he was really frustrated. Nothing he was doing seemed to work any more. Wally recalls recalling Grandpa Leclair's advice. "Grandpa always told me, 'If you're happy doing what you're doing, everything else will fall into place.'" Wally recalled, as Wally often does, some painful losses in curling championships. The family has pretty much memorized these accounts. "We've had three chances at a championship," Wally says. "We blew 'em all. You can't get nervous out there. You get too serious and you'll never win. If you miss one, you just go out and have fun and everything will come together and take care of itself."

Apparently, that's what Theoren needed to hear. Theo went out the day after they talked and took his father's advice: he simply had fun. The newspapers reported nothing about a hockey player calling his dad or shedding a piano from his back. But they did record that Fleury got four points. And next morning Theo's answering machine recorded a familiar voice. "I told him," Wally said, "he should call his father more often."

◆

Despite all of the fans and the cheering, the teammates and attention, and the local adulation of his youth, Theoren looks back on his years in Russell and one word comes to mind: "Lonely." That would seem to have less to do with the intentions of anyone in Russell; they were, by and large, inclusive, if sometimes that was also for their own advantage.

It did concern Theoren's separateness, his I'll-do-it-myself attitude that Linda Baker saw on the balance beam and others saw elsewhere. Doing it yourself can seem safer and is often admirable. But it also keeps people at a distance. To this day, even in a crowd of admirers lobbing questions and compliments and soaking up every word of his brief, often humorous responses while signing autographs, Fleury seems somehow apart. On the ice in practice he is the initiator of chat; teammates respond warmly, but they wait for his first move. On the road in airplanes, he can joke and laugh with the best of them. But he is also likely to shun the card or board games and trade seats with someone to sit by a window on the left side where he appears to sleep.

Awaiting the team bus at the hotel, Fleury will be leaning against a lobby pillar, silently sipping coffee from a paper cup by himself. Unlike some professional athletes, he does not seem to call attention to himself. The lone piece of jewellery, for instance, is a gold chain with the number 14. And that is tucked inside his shirt. If some fan has eluded hotel security and asks for an autograph, Fleury's inevitable reply is, "Oh, for sure." If the fan has a youngster in tow, Theo will look down and ask, "How ya doin', bud?" Typically, the child is struck speechless, though his eyes never leave Fleury's. The parent's face glows.

When Fleury joined many teammates at a noisy bar on an off evening during a road trip to Los Angeles, he took the stage at one point for an energetic karaoke performance of "Amarillo by Daylight" that teammates still remember fondly. The team and crowd laughed and clapped enthusiastically. Fleury actually has quite a good voice.

But even then, Fleury was alone on the stage.

"There is a deep part of Theoren that no one will ever touch," says a close friend from childhood. "No matter how long you've known him or how well you think you know him. It's part of his mystery, I guess."

Part of it has to do with his diminutive stature that discourages notice, something which he encourages. Part of it has to do with his skill level, which was and is so far above anyone else's that he naturally stood apart. Being so good and so small seemed to create an aura of physical impertinence around Fleury that riled opponents and their fans; it still does. Even his own teammates and their parents got annoyed at times with his blatant excellence, even though it served their ambition to win as well. How dare that little twerp be so good! People in Manitoba and Saskatchewan travelled long distances to see "that Russell kid" not "that Russell team." And while Fleury obviously could not control that, he did not dodge negative recognition. Sometimes he even seemed to seek it.

Len Peltz tells of a game in Russell when he stood by an opposition fan from Regina who verbally pestered Fleury unmercifully for much of the game. When Theo scored a goal, he made a point of skating by that vocal fan and pausing to wave and smile a very annoying smile. To this day, whenever Fleury's name is mentioned on the sound system in San Jose, nearly twenty thousand voices begin to boo, so successful has he been over the years against the Sharks. Fleury responds by holding his stick in the air and waving. "You've got to be good to be booed," says Kevin Constantine, once San Jose's head coach. One time in Calgary, Kevin discovered a surprising whole other side of the Fleury personality, the quieter, more thoughtful, hockey-wise, off-ice side.

Teammates and Fleury himself tell of games when he would turn around on the bench – it happened in the old Chicago Stadium regularly – and start a shouting match with an opposition spectator. "It gets me in the game," Fleury explains. Being hated, it seems, is better than being ignored. With relish, Theo recalls Junior games when his Moose Jaw Warriors would visit Swift Current. As soon as Fleury stepped on the ice, the loud-speaker would play "Pop Goes the Weasel." "They always called me the weasel," he says, smiling that smile.

Part of this Fleury apartness also stems from his posture, which has been unusually aggressive on the ice and strikingly passive off the ice. Part of it also has to do with those eyes of his, which seem to grip the people talking with him. None of those wandering eyes of some public figures that betray boredom, a readiness to move on and greet the next fan, or indifference at being talked to. With Fleury, the eyes have it. Those green eyes rivet you: even when he is tired, they do not leave you while you are speaking, even if you are yet another total stranger in yet another airport.

Those eyes don't always invite an encounter. The first half-hour after a tough loss it's probably best to leave those eyes and their owner alone. But once an encounter is initiated, the eyes don't discourage it either. Terry Kane, the team therapist, recalls watching a very tired Fleury on one postgame commercial flight from Hartford to Chicago. In Theoren's row of seats was a very elderly woman and her young nephew, a hockey fan. All three introduced themselves. The woman had never heard of Fleury, or even the Flames. So the Flames' team captain pulled out the airline magazine map and showed the woman where Calgary and Manitoba are and where Russell would be if it was on the map. He described his job and signed the map for the nephew. Only then did he fall asleep.

Through a combination of fortuitous events no one can quite recall, Theo met Len and Ede Peltz, two of the most important people in his life. For years, they owned the Jolly Lodger Motel out on the south side of Highway 16 in Russell. It's a homey older motel, always quite clean, with paper mats to step onto from the shower and the tiny soap bars that indicate few customers stay more than a night or two. Legions of these independent establishments still dot the North American countryside where they struggle to compete with their personal touches and local reputations against the newer chains with their computer links, satellite dishes, and internationally marketed logos.

Len, of course, was the teacher who had encountered Theo, the cheeky third-grader, at the Russell school's ping-pong table. Ede was something of an informal social worker, a quiet, nurse-like woman who had found herself counselling and comforting Donna Fleury during her assorted attacks of fear. A crucial trait of skilled counsellors is the appearance of acceptance; the good ones are excellent, nonjudgemental listeners. How things are is how things are; let's work with it.

Donna was a doting mother when it came to meals and eventually getting her boys into bed each school night. But in between mealtimes and bedtimes the three boys were pretty much on their own. One day Donna mentioned Theo's inability to attend a hockey banquet because of his ragged clothes. Ede had only heard of Theo's hockey prowess. But she thought seriously patched pants was a pretty flimsy reason for any youngster to miss a big event like a team dinner. So she promptly invited Theo to accompany her to the store to buy a new pair of jeans. He went to the store eagerly. She learned all of his clothes sizes that day for future use. And Theo went to that hockey banquet in new jeans.

Pretty soon, Ede and Len noticed Theo dropping by the Jolly Lodger regularly. Indeed, Theo and his brother Ted became daily visitors to the Peltzes' motel home, which had a ping-pong table and the kind of warm family dining table they did not know on Augusta Street. It got so even Donna Fleury knew where to call first if her boys were not home.

The boys got a second welcoming home and ample food virtually any time they wanted. The Peltzes were eager to hear the daily reports of the boys' doings. The couple even inquired about events at school and checked on homework assignments, something that never happened at the Fleury household. In return, Ede and Len, the parents of two girls, got two surrogate sons. "We were in the right place at the right time," Ede says today. "They needed us and we needed them. Their parents were pretty much nonfunctional at that time. The boys were good boys and we let them know it. Who wouldn't?"

As his birth parents drifted into and out of normal functioning with their drinking and pill problems, Theo also benefited from the several parents and extended families of his hockey team. They provided rides to the team's away games, at least part of a bed in a motel room, occasional meals, and a supportive social unit. They tried to teach some appropriate manners at times; meals in the Fleury household, for instance, were more like refuelling stops conducted free of substantive dialogue with a plate in a lap and a sports show on the TV. Theo did not appear to take offense at these lessons, though he did better with the pleases than the thank yous. An adult might also suggest that Theo veil his candour a little; his sudden observations or opinions at times could sting others, though the observations were often accurate.

From time to time, Len would buy Theo some hockey equipment or other families would donate hand-me-down gear. "We wanted to see him do the most with the talents he had," Len says. Together, the families ensured that the team's star player could take the ice every autumn with the other boys. Indeed, Fleury was sixteen years old before he got his own first pair of new ice skates.

In return, the Russell team got a member who would become probably one of the best youth athletes in the province. And the players were exposed to his unique spirit. It impressed several parents that the quiet, possibly-sullen-though-maybe-not boy they would see around town could become the almost ebullient player on the ice and in their cars. They thought his amazing determination might melt the ice. But they also thought it was a good example for their own boys.

Crowded into the station wagons and well-used family sedans of teammates for the long trips to tournaments and back home late on many dark Sundays, it was always Theo who would suggest group songs. Either that or Theo was quietly solving the Rubik's Cube game again. He and Ted got very good at that. Ann Petz, the mother of Theo's teammate Ted and wife of Jim Petz, the assistant coach, remembers marvelling at Theo's stubborn optimism, an attitude no one expected from a youngster growing up in such an inconsistent home environment.

"There was one tournament the boys were not doing well in," Ann says. "After another defeat, all the boys were terribly down, except Theo. He went around the locker room telling everyone one by one, 'C'mon, we can still get the bronze medal. We can still get the bronze.' And they did."

Len saw Theo's optimism on the golf course. "Theo would be having a terrible round or hole," Len says, "but he'd always say, 'I can still make five.'"

Over time, Len and Ede Peltz's role in caring for Theo often became primary. They arranged for routine medical care, such as the eyeglasses he got in grade seven when he developed serious headaches in school (the contact lenses came later), helped pay for a summer camp, administered haircuts to minimize shagginess, and performed the kind of standard chauffeuring duties that come with modern parenting. Ede was accepting of Theo's frequent tardiness but firm about manners in her home – food was to be eaten, not shovelled in – and about Fleury's attitude towards their daughter Jackie, who was two years older than Theo.

She called him Fluffy. They developed something of a brother-sister relationship, the good and bad sides. One day Jackie was going on about her interest in acting and school plays. "Drama sucks," said Theo, which prompted Ede to yank him into the kitchen.

"You're a visitor in this house," Ede told him. "Yet Jackie not only accepts you as a member, she is there for you, like a sister, at almost all of your games."

Theo looked stunned. "You're right," he said. A few years later when Jackie won a major role in her high-school production of *Hello, Dolly*, Theo travelled hundreds of miles back to Russell to witness her performance. Even later, Theo would host a fancy reception for Jackie after she eloped.

As a new teenager, Theo then took that lesson about kindness a step further. Ede was giving her daughter a permanent one afternoon. As usual, Theo was hanging around. He liked to help Ede run the motel switchboard. Jackie was bemoaning the colour of her hair. "I wish my hair was either blonde or dark," Jackie said, "instead of this blah mousy colour."

Theo was sitting at the opposite end of the table looking at her seriously. He put his hand on Jackie's. "When I have a daughter," Theo said, "I hope she looks exactly like you."

Holding her head quite steady, Jackie smiled a little. "Why, thank you, Fluffy," she said, a little suspiciously. In shock, Ede looked over at Theo, who was looking up at her quite hopefully. Ede's look back said, "Don't lay it on too thick, kid."

At times, even Fleury's birth mother called on Ede to help with Theo. Late one night when Theo was in the seventh grade or so, Donna phoned to say he was not yet home, she was worried, and had no idea where he was. Theo talked to Ede. Ede suspected Theo was at the house of a girl he had a crush on. Ede drove there, knocked on the door, and, sure enough, Theo was in the house watching television. Ede drove him home and delivered a mild scolding that he had no business being out at that hour. She was surprised to sense that Theo not only did not appear to mind her admonition, but actually seemed a little pleased.

Ede could also be staunchly defensive of Theo. When the headlights on one local businessman's car were broken, he sent the police to the Fleury home. Almost immediately, Ede showed up at the businessman's office, demanding proof of his charges. It turned out that he was simply suspicious of native teenagers. And Theoren Fleury was by far the most prominent native teenager in Russell.

The Peltzes were even drawn into helping care for Theo's parents at times. Donna might appear at their motel seeing demons. Ede encouraged Theo to spend most nights at home, but there were times when a frightened Theo would phone Ede late at night. She could hear Wally shouting incoherently in the background. So Ede would pay a post-midnight visit to the Fleury house to calm the situation until several cups of black coffee could take effect on Wally.

There were several unsuccessful attempts to get the adult Fleurys into treatment. And there were countless road trips with the hockey team and, come summer, a baseball team. Theo was an excellent hitter and a sure-handed catcher and second baseman. Above all, he was competitive. Whatever he was playing, no one could ever want to win more than Theo. Len gave Theo some very competitive games of ping-pong. But when Theo talked Ede into playing on the motel table, he volunteered to play on his knees. "I wasn't very good," Ede recalls now fondly. "I'd look down the table and you couldn't see anyone at the other end. Suddenly, this little head would pop up and he'd slam the ball back and then disappear. He'd still beat me on his knees."

And always there was Theo's determination in anything related to hockey. "The first time I saw him play," Ede remembers, "I wasn't sure who he was. There was this little person. His teeth were too big for his head. His head was too big for that little body. His helmet was his dad's and it wobbled all over. And his pants were big and baggy. And here he came, grabbing the puck in his own end and weaving his way down the ice all over towards the net so quickly and gracefully. Then, bang, he'd take that big shot of his and score. That sight still brings chills to my spine when I see him grab the puck and go with those little legs churning so strongly."

Len savours the memory of one time when Theo was at the end of a shift, coming off the ice, all tired. "Suddenly," Len says, "Theo whirled and just took a shot from the blueline. No one expected it, including the goalie. He scored. Theo did stuff like that all the time. You never quite knew what to expect."

Theo came to expect Len and Ede to attend his games. "We had two daughters, Jackie and Kim," says Ede, "so we couldn't be there all the time. But we were there a lot. And when we couldn't go, he always looked so disappointed." But there were many more times when the Peltzes were there in the stands. Theoren would skate out for warmups and spot them. Then, just before the first faceoff, he would raise his stick and give them a little salute.

Ede remembers Theoren as always hungry, whether he was downing six pork chops at their house or on the road. He found chicken disgusting until years later. Spaghetti and meatballs was the favourite. And if Theo was around, Ede and Len simply could never keep ice cream in their freezer, especially vanilla. There was one Saturday morning before she knew Theo well. It was eleven o'clock, after one game and before another. All the other Russell players were consuming substantial breakfasts with their families. Theoren had one dollar, which he was saving for dinner. Ede ordered a huge plate of perogies but feigned an inability to eat them after all. "Could you please help me eat these?" she asked. Theo did her a big favour by downing every morsel. Theo remembers that incident, too. "They were good," he says. "I was always hungry."

Ede found herself thoroughly enjoying simply watching Theo play hockey. "Even before I knew him he stood out on the ice," she says. "Down by four goals or up by four, he was always driving, driving, driving. I just admired his spunk and his eternal optimism. A lot of people, especially if they become

96

famous, don't want you to know they are not perfect. Theo never minded. And he still doesn't. There's a powerful attraction to that. And he accepts our imperfections, too. That's pretty endearing."

The Peltzes imposed the same rules on Theo as they had on their daughters. Every child had chores. Theo was willing, Len recalls, but clueless when it came to things like running a lawn-mower. "He never had any chores at home," Len says, "and his mother was always the one who mowed the lawn. She still is. There's always some game Wally's got to watch on TV. Theo's responsibilities were to attend school and do well in hockey."

And Theoren could be undisciplined. "His focus was sports, especially hockey," Len adds. "Anything else was a distraction. So I'd have him mow our lawn. It was quite large. He'd start out okay. But after twenty minutes or so you'd realize you didn't hear the motor anymore. You'd look outside. There's the lawnmower parked on the unfinished lawn and there's Theoren picking up trash or tossing a ball around. It was kind of annoying. But it was also very Theo. In that sense, he hasn't changed much."

Theo also developed an intriguing and puzzling routine with Ede, something like a ritual verbal touch after every game. Knowing of his pride in his play, after every game Ede would ask Theo how many goals and assists he got. Every time, she recalls, he would say he did not remember. At first, she thought it was Theoren being sensitive to the feelings of his nearby teammates. But he would reply similarly even when no one else was around.

Ede knew Theoren kept close track of his scoring himself; Russell players had to because Coach Fowler did not believe in keeping youth stats. Ede herself kept pretty close track of Theo's on-ice accomplishments. She was Theo's biggest and most faithful fan. And Theo knew that.

In those childhood days Ede wanted to let Theo celebrate the goals with her. Truth be told, she also wanted to celebrate Theo's goals with him. So Theo's consistent refusal to tell his surrogate mother the score always puzzled her.

Still, the exchange became a ritual between them, albeit a ritual that showed her abiding interest and presence and his abiding desire to keep a distance even in her presence. To this day, perhaps sensing this reason, Ede has never asked Theo why he did this. And Fleury, for his part, says he does not remember not remembering.

Then there was Christmas. Actually, there was no Christmas for Theo. Christmas was not a holiday in the Fleury household. No Christmas tree topped with crayoned angels from grade two. No paper chains of green and red paper. No strings of familiar lights shedding their magical glow on the green needles. No letters laboriously written and seemingly dispatched to the North Pole. No holiday greeting cards. No pre-dawn trips to a grandmother's home in the country to share familiar foods, sunrise, gifts, and the familial warmth of being together again on that joyous day. No Santa Claus. No anticipation building to an almost unbearable level. No wrapped presents sitting there mysteriously holding God-knows-what coveted thing. No cameras flashing. No mom opening a parcel adorned with more tape than coloured paper and oohing and aahing over a complicated kitchen doodad she had not known she needed. No dad, still in his pyjamas, poring over incoherent assembly instructions printed in a language resembling English for a toy that did not appear to be unassembled in the dramatic photo on the box. No search of drawers for fresh batteries. No huge holiday dinner with mashed potatoes. No hugs of appreciation and no silent smiles of satisfaction at day's end and, in a week or so, no handwritten thank-you notes.

Christmas morning to Theoren Fleury meant there weren't any other kids outdoors to play street hockey. Christmas meant more shooting pucks by himself or possibly playing with his little brothers. Christmas was the day when all of his neighbour friends appeared outdoors in the afternoon wearing new coats and hats and tugging new sleds. The Fleury children were given no detailed explanation for this void of warm traditions that seemed to permeate every other household on every other street everywhere they looked.

The boys knew they were a poor family; Wally and Donna said that all the time and poverty was the excuse for not doing or not buying anything the boys requested, when they forgot not to request anything.

The real reason that the Christmas spirit never entered the Fleury home was that Donna Fleury is a member of the Jehovah's Witnesses. They do not observe Christmas. And Wally, who is Roman Catholic, did not wish to make an issue of it. Life was so full of everyday challenges that he did not need more trouble every blessed December.

Theoren did, however, seek out religion on his own – for a while. For six years or more he was an altar boy at St. Joseph's Roman Catholic Church in Russell. That struck some rather like Huck Finn becoming a school principal. Theoren is not famous among friends and family for his adherence to schedules or routines. "I've always been more of an ad lib kind of guy," he says matter-of-factly.

Linda Baker was not the only person in Theo's young life to notice his inability to sit still and quiet for long periods. In church he was expected to sit still, then to stand, to sit again, then to kneel, then to stand, and then to recite the same old words at the same time in the same services on the same day every week. Still today, Theoren rarely makes appointments more than a few days in advance; he prefers his schedules loose. He knows that most people will accommodate him now given the many demands on his time and attention and their desire to be part of his famous life somehow. Theo also likes his clothes loose. In fact, he always wears his game jersey untucked exactly the same way to keep his arms free for shooting. And despite repeated facial injuries he now shuns a visor on his helmet. Too confining, he says.

But there Theoren was, even on those dark, wintry weekends in Russell, getting himself up for mass every Sunday and over to the church on time. He remembers enjoying the ritual, even the religious music; some of the rinks he played in had organ music, too. Church services were predictable, comforting, not unlike pregame preparations in hockey.

And, of course, he remembers Father Paul, an energetic middle-aged man who always seemed very accepting and non-judgemental. He was inevitably willing to listen to people, especially young people and especially one determined young boy who was open, eager, and seemed unusually intense. Whenever Theoren showed up, Father Paul would set aside whatever he was doing to talk, or better yet, to listen.

"Father Paul was a helluva guy," Theoren remembers. "A really great guy." Every Sunday morning – sometimes even during the week on non-hockey nights – Theoren would walk into St. Joseph's and there would be Father Paul, happy to see him. A few times Father Paul even came to Theoren's games. Theo saw Father Paul there during the thorough eyeing of the stands that Theoren still does during pregame warmups. The next time Theo saw him, the priest would have something good to say about the boy's play, something that showed he really had watched the game closely. It would make any boy feel good. It could make even Huck Finn go to church.

Then, one snowy Sunday morning when Theoren showed up to help serve mass, Father Paul was not there. People were urgently running around. Women were crying. No one had much time to explain anything to a boy, it seemed. At times like that children can make adults feel uncomfortable. The children don't know what to ask and the adults don't know what to say. But Theoren overheard that Father Paul had been out in front of the church that morning shovelling snow. Everybody shovels snow on the prairies; it's what you do outdoors at home when you don't have to cut grass or rake leaves. Nobody saw what happened. But apparently Father Paul had collapsed on the sidewalk in front of his church. They found him there. He was dead. The man who was always there for their services, their baptisms, and their funerals was himself absent. Suddenly, this friend became a memory. It didn't seem like enough.

"He was gone just like that," Theoren says, still with surprise in his voice so many years later. "I couldn't believe he was dead, just like that."

Theoren walked home that morning very slowly. Suddenly, there didn't seem to be much else to do. There wasn't anything anyone could say. And there certainly wasn't anyone to talk to now, if talking to someone about his feelings ever occurred to Theo.

Theoren Fleury says he never went back to church after that.

Why not? He shrugs that shrug again.

But he did go back to hockey. "When I was a kid," Theoren recalls, smiling, "hockey is all we did, eh? It's all we did. Hockey. Hockey. Hockey. School was secondary. We went there between hockey games. Even in school I was thinking about hockey later. Hockey was our escape. Hockey was life. Hockey is life. I mean, before school I'd go to the rink with my father. After school we'd go to the rink and practise, like around four o'clock. Be on the ice an hour and a half. Go home. Eat supper. And go right back out on the street playing hockey until nine, ten, or eleven o'clock at night every night. I'd only play goalie to get the other guys to play. Goalies are weird. If we had ice, we'd play ice hockey in the backyard. If we didn't, we'd play street hockey. Every day. In summertime it was ball hockey, maybe a little baseball. But always sports. In the winter it was hockey, hockey, hockey. That's all we wanted to do. That's all we did."

It doesn't get dark right after lunch on the wintry Canadian prairies; it just seems that way. So if darkness or bad weather forced the boys indoors, they'd go over to Ted Petz's house and play hockey in the basement with a tape ball and miniature sticks. Usually, it was everyone against Theoren. Usually, Theoren won.

Coach Fowler encouraged such passion. So successful was he in this that today Fleury can recall with Technicolor clarity specific plays in particular games with his teammates of long ago – the time, for instance, that the coach of the other team of seven-year-olds insisted Fleury play goalie half the game and Theo still scored a hat trick. But Theo can have a hard time remembering many of his more than seven hundred more recent pro games. On a shelf in his home Theo still keeps two stainless-steel pucks, his MVP trophies from successive Thompson youth tournaments, right along with the pucks from his number 1, number 100, number 200, and number 300 NHL goals.

"Theo was an exceptionally good practiser," the coach remembers. "To me, practice is when you learn. Games are the tests. In games you have fun and show what you have learned in practice. I've seen a lot of kids who are great, but maybe they don't practise hard. And pretty soon they aren't getting better any more. There are a lot of stars at age twelve. But pretty soon, the others are getting bigger and better and they pass the stars by, and by twelve or thirteen, the 'stars' are just average. Theo was a star all the time and he practised hard all the time. As a result, he was always getting better."

Coach Fowler rode Fleury hard but, he felt, affectionately. The coach demanded more of his smallest player because he knew Theo could deliver more. Fleury did not always sense the affection, but he sure did feel the driving. In the locker room between periods or after a game, if the coach thought the team was playing well, he said so and patted everyone on the head. If the coach thought the team needed to play better, to be more aggressive, and to stop taking stupid penalties, he said that, too. But he looked directly at Theo when he spoke.

At times, that made Fleury feel good and important. At times, that made him feel angry and resentful. One of those times was every year when the coaches announced the team captain. Usually, they named Bruce Coulter to wear the coveted C on his jersey. Sometimes Theoren was named assistant captain. In hockey, it is permissible, when appointed captain, to talk about the honour of being appointed captain. It is not acceptable to talk publicly about not being named captain. "Theo was always the best player," Coach Fowler says firmly. "The best players don't always make the best captains."

But relentlessly the coach tried to steer his star to do better. Theoren almost always responded to firm but affectionate attention. "I tried to channel his frustration from losing or from school or from his home life into hockey," the coach says. "I'd say, 'Let's do better in what you can control, Theo. And what you can control is your game.' So he worked hard. God, how he worked. He even worked on his speed. He had to be the fastest out there. He was always the smallest. So he had to feel in his heart and his head that he was the biggest guy on the ice."

Of course, Theo was not perfect. There were some fights in school. He was an average student. And that playing intensity got him in trouble at times with penalties and with the coaches. There was one hard-fought game that Russell lost. The eleven-year-old Theo was so angry that he stormed off the ice, refusing to shake hands with the other team. Coach Petz went after him. "Theo," he said, "if you don't shake hands, you don't play next game." A half-hour later and Theo might have congratulated the victors, maybe even complimented their goalie. But right after an unnecessary loss he could not compliment anyone about anything. Theo didn't shake hands. So he was suspended for a game.

Theo was angry because he thought his team should have beaten the other team. He also hoped the coaches would relent. They did not. On the next game night later that week Fleury was not allowed to suit up. So with a juvenile arrogance that makes the adult Fleury wince even today, Theo walked into the dressing room of Russell's opponents, Roblin. He announced that he was not playing and he offered the opinion that the visitors would win.

They didn't. Russell beat Roblin 6–5 without Fleury, a final score that pleased his coaches for more reasons than one, though they said nothing more. "It was a good lesson for him," said Jim Petz. Fleury agrees. He returned to the team a wiser boy. "And I never did that again," Theo adds.

Theo was also a star in baseball, his sure hands and eyes making him an excellent batter and ball-handler. Even in baseball, he had his own brand of determination. "He'd get a triple," says Jim Petz, who was also Theo's baseball coach, "and we'd signal him to slide into third. But, no, he'd just keep on running right on through – geez, he was fast – and I'll be darned if he wouldn't score."

Wally Fleury was very proud of Theoren. "He was and is a super skater," Wally says. "And he was and is a super shooter with great hands and good eyes. He's not big now. But he was even smaller back then. I never told him I was a doubter about him and the NHL. No way would I ever tell him that. I told him, 'You've got the skills and you've got the speed and the love of it. Now, if you work hard, if you have a dream, then you follow that damn dream, boy.' If you put your mind to it, there's nothing anyone can't do."

And, between coughs from all the cigarettes he smoked, Wally shared another memory. "I remember one game," he says, "two old ladies were watching and one of them said to the other, 'Here he comes again. That little guy has no chance.' But Theoren scored. And I said to them, 'Ladies, take a good look at him because my boy is going places.'"

One day Jim Petz took his whole family and Theoren into Winnipeg to see an NHL game. The Jets were playing Don

Cherry's Colorado Rockies. It was a meaningless end-of-the-season game with both teams out of playoff contention. But everyone in the Petz party was excited, especially Theoren. It's one thing to play in rinks like Binscarth's, where dads replace broken light bulbs between periods, the bench actually sits on the adjacent curling ice, and the toilet is a bucket in the dressing room. But to drive into the big city and walk down that ramp into a brightly lit professional arena with the crowd and noise and the coloured uniforms was enough to take the breath away. It was an intimidating place to dream about. But Theoren wasn't dreaming. He was planning.

Cathy Petz, Ted's sister, was awed by the spectacle that night. As a result, she was responsible for an unlikely encounter. She was a longtime admirer of Lanny McDonald, the red-haired Hall of Fame player with the career longer even than his drooping moustache, then with the Rockies. But when the moment came after the game to dash down to the bench and actually ask the legendary player for his autograph, Cathy froze. "Oh, I can't," she said.

"Gimme the paper," said Theo. "I'll get it for you." And down he went to wade through the crowd to the front and politely request Mr. McDonald's autograph. Minutes later, Theoren proudly presented the handwritten trophy to Cathy, who has it still as proof that one time, one night, she was in the presence of Fame. Or at least in reasonable proximity to Fame.

Eleven years later that same Lanny McDonald and that same Theoren Fleury were together again, skating around the Montreal Forum as Calgary Flames teammates and handing each other the Stanley Cup to hold over their heads as NHL champions. "Now, what," says Lanny, sitting in his Flames office and touching his still-huge, still-red moustache, "are the odds of that happening?"

Injuries are a part of sports, especially collision sports such as hockey. Fleury has never shied away from physical contact.

"Out there," Fleury says about any hockey rink, "no one is going to give you any space at all. None. You've got to take it for yourself or create it with speed."

At times in his career to make a point, or a reputation, Fleury has actively sought physical confrontations, to the consternation of his coaches and teammates, who then had to back him on the ice. "Sometimes," he says, "you have to make a statement. Sometimes, you lose control a little. That's hockey, eh? Sometimes now I look at videotapes of my games and I can't believe I did some of those things. I say to myself, 'Was that really me out there?'"

Many times Fleury got the worst of the battle, if the fight judges were awarding points for punishment delivered. There was one memorable incident in a Flames game against the Los Angeles Kings. A melee erupted. Fleury was cut on the face and bleeding profusely. According to the on-ice hockey code of honour, at such times players from each team pair off, not necessarily to fight but to keep the odds even for the actual combatants. Fleury could hardly see, he had so much blood streaming down his face. Wayne Gretzky of the Kings paired off with him, firmly grasping Fleury's bloodstained shirt. All eyes focused on the players actually fighting. But anyone could have noticed that, while still holding his opponent's shirt, Gretzky actually was tugging Fleury little by little towards the Calgary bench. There, the Great One unobtrusively delivered the battered Fleury to Flames medical personnel with no further damage done and no loss of honour.

But to Fleury the point of these occasional confrontations is not necessarily to land blows. It is to carve out for himself just a few more cubic inches of space on the ice, another split second of time to shoot or pass, and to plant in the opposition's mind a lingering uncertainty about just when this little guy is likely to explode and what he is likely to do.

The fact is, with his skills and his size, Fleury tends to be the hittee more often than the hitter. He receives more than his share of facial cuts. "I'm down there closer to the ice and the sticks than most players," Theo explains with that gaptoothed smile.

But over the years Theo has used his speed and savvy to avoid collisions. He does a lot of circling and very little parking. Indeed, his daring to dart into an on-ice crowd and his ability to squirt out of the way at the last moment is one of the most annoying aspects of his play for defencemen. Just when they think they have him lined up to knock into next week, he's not there any more. And, of course, with the opposition's attention focused on Fleury, that leaves less attention to be devoted to the Small One's teammates.

As a result, Fleury has known relatively few serious injuries. The ones he has known he has not liked, but not so much for any pain associated with them; he takes pride in ignoring pain with the same kind of mental discipline that has allowed him to ignore all of the knowing remarks over all of the years about his size. Especially in the early days, any injury was career-threatening, because it could keep Theo off the ice, shutting down his antics and heroics and allowing the doubts about his size to spread in the minds of coaches and management. The only thing worse than being a little guy in hockey is being a fragile little guy.

No one likes injuries. They happen, of course, in regular life and in sports. Some hockey old-timers say that today's rising salaries have caused many players to think of their bodies more as valuable business investments, living money-producing machines to be protected, and less as tools to use to win on the ice. So, the suspicions go, today's players sometimes hold back and are more reluctant to pay the physical price that is seen as necessary in hockey.

Most athletes tend to handle most injuries the way office workers handle head colds. They happen. They're treated. They go away. To be sure, in pro sports injuries are sometimes deliberately inflicted, which can remove a star and give the opposition a leg up, so to speak. As in the criminal underworld, inflicting an injury on one side can cause retaliation on the other and re-retaliation and re-re-retaliation. And that all creates the kind of running dramas and bitter rivalries that make for sports pages full of extra conflict and great TV with slow-motion replays that prompt even distant viewers to exclaim, "Ouch!"

But Theo doesn't just dislike injuries. He seems to hate them, to belly up to them defiantly, as he would a defenceman who hooked him down on a breakaway. Fleury hates injuries because each carries the potential to put him in a hospital, those immense impersonal structures with the fearsome smells where life is ruled by the mysterious schedule of others, where strangers can take total control of your life, your meals, your visitors, and your activities, including watching TV. Those white-coated strangers in hospitals don't care who you are. They fully expect patients to be, well, patient.

But, above all, Theo hates injuries because injuries get in his way. They are just so damned confining. As a result, he has not allowed them to exercise much control over his life, applying his steely will to their pain and their healing like a tight tourniquet. One time in Russell he got clipped in the corner of his eye by a stick swung by his mother. "It was my fault," Fleury says. "I was really acting up all day, running around and making too much noise in the house. It was a fluke. I happened to turn just as she was swinging."

Fleury spent a couple of days in the Russell hospital with a blood clot in his eye. He remembers that time not for any physical or emotional pain but because the hospital stay kept him out of a game against his old rink in Binscarth. "We lost, too," Fleury says. "I think it was the only time Binscarth beat us." As a youngster, he found the hospital an antiseptic, confining place.

But there came a day when he had no choice. Everyone in Fleury's life calls it The Injury. They remember its shock vividly, as if it happened only this morning. It scared the hell out of everyone in the rink that day. It marked Theo for life. It also frustrated him and it taught him something important about survival and endurance. It challenged his assumptions about the power of his will and the future of his career. In the end, The Injury became one more obstacle for Theo Fleury to overcome.

It happened in a game in Portage la Prairie, Manitoba, on March 21, 1982. Theoren was thirteen. It was meant to be a friendly competition. To save money, the Russell boys would stay with Portage families. Not long before, little Russell had beaten bigger Portage quite soundly – "thrashed" is how Fleury still gleefully describes it – in a major youth tournament in Minnedosa.

According to memories in Russell, the Portage players and coaches could not believe that a motley bunch of farm kids in hand-me-down gear and green uniforms had actually beaten – twice! – the well-equipped team from a far larger community. So they challenged Russell to a rematch, a non-league, two-game tournament. Pride would be the major prize, along with a small trophy from McDonald's or somewhere. Russell's players readily agreed. Who in their right mind would turn down two more hockey games near the end of another season? Summer can seem to last a very long time when you're waiting for winter.

There were about nine seconds left in the second period. Theoren was skating down the right side, hoping to set up one final successful rush before the buzzer. He could have gone up the middle, his favourite route of attack. But for whatever reason Theo had chosen the right side. It did favour his right-handed shot, which was very quick and very powerful for a thirteen-year-old.

Theo was looking back over his left shoulder expecting a clearing pass from his first skating pal, Greg Slywchuk. Already, Theo's legs were churning away like powerful pistons. The pass was perfect, just like in practice. The puck caught up with Theoren right on the tape. Theo turned and looked ahead to let his developing intuition size up the defence.

Few things frightened Theo on the ice. One of them was not a lone defenceman, even a sizable one, angling towards him. It wasn't the exquisite excitement of a penalty shot, Theoren against the goalie. It was one-on-one, size against speed. Theo could not pass the puck; no teammate had seen the turnover coming as quickly as Theo had, so they were too far behind. Theo sensed that. And Theo couldn't dump the puck in; he knew the clock was running out too rapidly. Still, no big deal.

Theo could have cut back to the left at any time and proceeded up the middle. But he wanted to wait until the last second. The defender, too eager to squeeze Russell's main offensive weapon against the boards and run out the clock, would be overcommitted then. He would take himself out of the play. He would be unable to recover. He would be unable to stop Theo's shot.

The defender was getting closer and closer. Theo's legs were still churning. Closer and closer. Theo tried a head fake to throw off the defender's aim. Maybe it worked. Maybe it didn't. But just as Theo was about to cut sharply to the left and go around him, the defender stumbled. Perhaps his ragged skate blades caught in the ice. Perhaps he simply lost his balance. Either way, he did a complete somersault. His feet came flying up and over right in front of number 9.

Theoren threw his head to the left, dodging the blades slicing through the air. Next thing he knew the arena was filled with an audible gasp. Theo heard Greg scream his name. Theo just stood there, puzzled. There was blood everywhere. Something was bleeding badly. But it was not merely bleeding. It was spewing blood in large, high arcs all over the ice and onto the right arm of Theoren's jersey.

Then, Theoren realized. It was his blood. It was his arm. How could he be bleeding? He didn't hurt anywhere.

Instinctively, Theo headed for the bench, leaving a darkening trail of blood in his path. "Coach?" said the wondering little boy. "Coach!?"

Ann Petz remembers it as the scariest moment in her life. Her husband and Coach Fowler were stunned. What was going on? Quickly, it hit them. Theo was cut. Theo was cut very badly. Buella Fowler, who had been in the stands, blew right past her husband and hurtled the boards to reach Theoren. She ripped off her scarf and stuffed it into the bubbling wound under his upper right arm.

The crowd sat stunned. A few people turned away, unable to watch. John Adolphe's mom fainted. The players who a moment before had been keen competitors were now united in shock and fear, even disgust at having been involved. Some began to cry quietly. Others vomited on the ice. In the flash of a skate probably the province's best youth hockey player had been turned into a badly wounded youngster who could bleed to death within minutes or be crippled for life. How could something as familiar and simple as a friendly hockey game for little boys turn so suddenly into carnage?

At the bench Coach Fowler scooped Theoren up in his arms. The boy looked even tinier than usual. The lad might have weighed eighty-five pounds. The coach and a group of Russell parents and players headed for the parking lot. On the way the Portage coach shouted directions to the hospital, just five minutes' distant. Ted Petz remembers hiding in the backseat, silent and afraid, and still wearing his sweaty hockey gear. He felt cold.

The coaches remember driving very quickly. "Go as fast as you want, Coach," said Theo, who was working very hard not to be afraid. "I'll tell the police I need a hospital." That was the same excuse Theo's grandmother once told him to give a policeman who stopped her for speeding en route to a bingo game.

Ann Petz recalls talking calmly, holding a very white, very small Theo very still, and maintaining the pressure on the wound. After a moment of silence, she remembers Theo thinking his arm was broken and swearing. "Now, I probably won't get to play tomorrow," he said.

Emergency treatment was delayed at the hospital. A scalded baby had just been brought in. And burned babies took medical precedence over teenage boys with a cut arm.

When the doctor arrived, the bleeding had stopped. "This is quite a cut," he said calmly. Theo was relieved the bone was unbroken.

The doctor was prepared to begin stitching. First, he placed his fingers on the inside of Theoren's right wrist to take his pulse. Theo remembers the doctor's face suddenly going blank.

"Does your arm hurt?" the doctor inquired even more calmly than before.

"No," Theo said with relief and absolute honesty. "Nothing hurts." Theo figured the less pain the less serious the injury.

Theo figured wrong.

◈

Injuries have always been a part of professional athletics. With the growing size and speed of modern-day players, today at any given time on a pro-hockey rink there will be in excess of 2,400 pounds of human bodies encased in many additional pounds of leathers, pads, and plastics, carrying long sticks of wood, graphite, or metal, moving at lightning speeds on razor-sharp blades across a surface of glistening ice between walls of unforgiving boards. Injuries are unlikely to disappear.

What's new, however, are the determined, highly scientific, and little-known strategies that have been developed to prevent injuries through better training. Hockey players used to come to training camp in late summer to get in shape. Today, they had better be in fine shape before camp starts or they won't last until the regular season, let alone through it. Coach Pierre Page sees summer training like investing money in a physical savings account, to be available for withdrawal as the regular season wears on.

Tapping into the scientific and university communities for training expertise has become standard procedure for professional as well as national athletic teams. With the ever-escalating costs of acquiring skilled players – and keeping them – and paying them not to play when they are injured, no possible advantage is too small to overlook. The Flames, like several other teams, even hire a psychological consultant to help train players in the power of positive thinking. Recently, he's been working with Flames' veterans to look upon rookies as a healthy challenge to improving their own play instead of as a threat to their careers.

Though emotional, coach Page always has been methodical and fascinated by the mental part of hockey, the meshing, adaptation, and application of an infinite number of perfect plans with an infinite variety of imperfect humans, each with his own personality, skills, attitudes, and emotional chemistry. One of the few times in his life he plunged into something without careful, detailed study was when Page met his wife, Donna, on a blind date at St. Francis Xavier University.

A female college friend said the Homecoming Committee needed one more escort for a princess. Pierre was still learning English at the time. "What's an escort?" he said. Today, Pierre drives Donna crazy with his reading habits. He will purchase book after book, devouring just one or two chapters in each, trying to find another strategy, another motivational technique, another inspirational quote or story, that he can use in his work. "I never read fiction," he says. "I'm too much of a realist to read fiction."

So the Flames' head coach is a big believer in the scientific breakdown of training. His thesis for a master's degree in physical education was titled: "The Bio-Mechanics of Skating." His goal was to determine why some people skate so much better than others. So he broke the actual motion of skating down into identifiable motions and sequences. His conclusion was that a major factor in skating speed, power, and efficiency rests in the angle of the leg at the knee; 90 to 120 degrees provides the most powerful push.

When the new graduate, a mere teacher in junior high school in Nova Scotia and then at Dalhousie, wanted to apply his theories to skating instruction, few would listen. In the 1960s, applying theories of motion to such a physical sport seemed rather esoteric, if not downright silly. Finally, the community of Coal Harbour allowed Page to teach his theories to its hockey teams. Coal Harbour teams became champions. Suddenly, Halifax, Dartmouth, and other places were willing to apply theories to hockey.

Someone else who came calling was Al MacNeil, now a Flames institution but then the coach of Halifax in the farm system of the Montreal Canadiens. He had played ten years in the NHL and in 1971, with Montreal, would become one of a very few men to win the Stanley Cup in his rookie year as a head coach. MacNeil asked Page to evaluate his players' skating and make suggestions for improvement. While Page was doing that, MacNeil was evaluating him. Today, the quiet, white-haired MacNeil is director of hockey operations for the Flames. But first in Atlanta and then after the move to Calgary in 1980, MacNeil was the Flames' head coach. He brought Page in first as an assistant and then, in 1995, he was a major Page supporter for the top coaching job.

Small and medium-sized sports franchises have a major challenge these days. They will likely never have the fan or commercial base to finance the many multimillion-dollar salaries that larger franchises use to buy and keep the star players deemed necessary to produce championships. With recent annual player payrolls running around $16 million (U.S.), the Flames rank twenty-fourth of twenty-six teams in terms of salary totals.

Calgary's payroll, in fact, is about $7 million less than the league average and less than half the sums spent by the New York Rangers ($38 million) and the Pittsburgh Penguins ($35 million). Still, the Flames, which are owned by a consortium of nine local businessmen, missed the playoffs only twice in their first seventeen years in Calgary.

The Flames, like the Cleveland Indians and Montreal Expos in baseball, made a conscious decision to develop their own stars almost from scratch, using a combination of increased scouting, a farm-team coaching philosophy consistent with the parent club's, and a comprehensive conditioning program that looks four years down the road, not four months. It's cheaper to develop your own talent, but it also takes longer.

This is one of the biggest changes in the game that Lanny McDonald has seen since his early days. "In the old days, maybe ten or twelve years ago," he says, "you'd come to the rink for every game and the best team on the ice that night won that game. Now, with all the technology and science, it's not who's best. It's who's best prepared."

So a continuous conditioning regime has become a crucial ingredient in the construction and evaluation of talent for today's players and for tomorrow's, those working up through the Flames' farm system, the so-called Baby Flames of the American Hockey League in Saint John, New Brunswick, and in the WHL franchise the Flames bought in Calgary. Such training is scientifically targeted for each player's strengths and weaknesses. It is all documented by "readouts" – computer printouts of test results. Now, first thing in training camp and throughout the year, teams can test every player and tell instantly who has been working out – and who has not. A crucial factor in the conditioning of the Flames is Rich Hesketh.

Rich played hockey as a youth, but today his slim, taut body screams "track." In fact, he is a successful international decathlete. He has financed his own training in latter years by renting out his expertise and time as a relatively recent phenomenon in affluent societies like Canada and the United States. He is a personal trainer, basically a hired expert, coach, friend, and cheerleader to those willing to invest forty dollars an hour in becoming better conditioned and healthier.

Several years ago Ryan Griffin, one of his clients who also happens to be Fleury's off-ice agent, introduced the two men. Fleury is wise enough to know that physical decline is inevitable with age. He has seen his little baby face age in recent years. He knows nothing can change that. But conditioning, endurance, and strength can postpone the inevitable and help prolong a lucrative career.

Even for a professional, maintaining the off-season training discipline necessary today is difficult, especially alone. The lure of summer sun, the golf course, freedoms and indulgences that can come from possessing large sums of money and free time, even legalized casinos, and the eagerness of most anyone to spend time with a famous person can overpower the knowledge that the body must be prepared for the ten-month beating it will soon take. A personal trainer can provide the guidance and daily routine necessary to stay on track.

So by early summer for the past several years, Fleury has begun his daily 90- to 120-minute workout with Rich. He trains five days a week. On the sixth day Rich prescribes a brisk hour-long cardio workout on a stationary bike or in-line skates. Rich lets Fleury and Fleury's body have the seventh day off.

"Theo is an amazing physical specimen," Rich says. "He's an unusual package of good balance, excellent co-ordination, especially eye-hand. It's probably genetic. He's got a lower centre of gravity, a tight, hard package of human body. It's harder to knock him down. And he's compact, not gangly all over the ice and more subject to injury. So he's quite durable. He's built more like a tank than a sports car. But he's still quite quick. I can't teach him to be a better hockey player. But I can teach him to be a better athlete."

The pair starts together in June. That allows time for mental and physical regeneration. In that time, in fact through much of the summer, Fleury goes nowhere near an ice rink, except to coach at his hockey school on Calgary's south side. The intense workout routines will continue for a little more than three months.

"We train for explosive power," says Rich. "We train his large muscle groups for explosive power, forty-five to fifty seconds of very intense activity, much like a shift on the ice. Theo has an incredible recovery rate. We'll train intensely for a full minute. His heart rate will go up to 185 beats per minute. Then we'll rest. In forty-five seconds his heart rate will be back to 115. For normal people that would take two minutes."

Rich knows pro athletes want direction and plans mixed with variety. So he sets up a shifting daily regimen involving conditioning and lifting. While the goals remain the same – to increase strength and endurance – the routes to that goal – the exercises and physical demands placed on different muscle groups of the body – change almost daily. The idea is to keep the players mentally challenged while keeping their physiology off balance as well, much as it must be in real game situations. So while the exercises change, the strenuousness within them also changes.

"I try to make it as entertaining – and intense – as possible," says Rich. "These guys have enjoyed great success. But they always need new challenges to stay sharp, like Theo wanting to play for Canada in the Olympics. That'll help raise him to a new level. Sometimes when we're working, he's laughing and joking. Sometimes he's serious. Sometimes he's silent and in another zone.

"We always warm up with eight to ten minutes on a stationary bike. Mondays, Wednesdays, and Fridays we'll do general coordinating exercises with some lifting. We work on grass for less impact. Skaters don't have the impact of runners or football players. We'll do all-out running for forty-five to fifty seconds six or eight times with two-minute rests in between. On Tuesdays and Thursdays, we'll do harder strength and endurance work, running up and down hills and then doing some medicine-ball work for forty-five minutes or so. I can make it harder than any shift he'll ever encounter. In the weight room, we'll do power jerks and squats, bench presses, eight to twelve chin-ups. He'll do ab sit-ups to build his lower back and three to five squats with 300 to 350 pounds. Not bad with a body weight under 170."

After five summers of such workouts, usually early in the morning, Rich has noticed a cumulative effect, sometimes a 20 per cent strength increase summer to summer. "It all boosts Theo's confidence," Rich adds. "He knows the better shape he's in, the longer he'll last in this league."

So impressed is the Flames' management that it has hired Rich and consults with the sports-science team at the University of Calgary to develop similar individualized programs for all Flames players, even the ones on the farm team. They figure real progress will show up in four or five years. "That way," says Rich, "every succeeding generation of homegrown Flames will be starting from a higher level. I tell them we can't control what goes on in a game. But we can control how we prepare for a game."

In the end, much of hockey is really about control – control of the puck, control of emotions, control of sticks, control of bodies and skills, control of focus, control of the collective team and its emotions. Through their individual superstitions and private and public rituals, the players even seek to control luck and the fates, or at least to minimize the lack of control they experience in a violent, lightning-fast game.

In this sense, mental conditioning becomes even more important than physical conditioning. One of the striking aspects of life inside a pro hockey team is the often delicate psyche and ego of these immense men who seem so rugged, fearless, and confident on the ice and yet, up close in private, are so childlike in their singular passion for what, when you strip away the trappings of big business, is only a game. Some of these players need stroking. Some need goading. Some need some of both. Some learn to handle sudden fame and money well. Others don't. Some can clearly see the end of their playing days coming, so they prepare. Others do not want to think of being discarded for younger talent, losing their seat on the bus with the guys, and having to move on or grow up, or both. They can soar like comets on some nights. On other nights, they play like amateurs.

Despite all that we do to place them on a pedestal, despite all of the care and feeding that we lavish on them to ease the way to victory, to make money, and to win a moment in the sunshine of their gaze, despite all of the attention that we create and consume about their doings on and off the ice as if they were truly important, in the end each player is merely human after all. In a peculiar and even predictable kind of human alchemy, aided and abetted by a pervasive media desperately hungry for new stories and heroes, we eagerly turn these public people into sidewalk gods. And then when they end up behaving imperfectly, as many of us in the audience might, behaviour at least as pervasively chronicled as the build-up, we are disappointed, even angered.

But this should be no stunning revelation, though we work hard to see what we want to see and not to see what we want to avoid. The Flames have had veterans retire who then sought guidance on how to acquire airline tickets for personal trips. It was always done for them. These athletes, who could do so many things few others can, were unable to do one thing that most everyone else could. Actually, there could be considerable solace instead of disillusionment in the discovery of that reassuring humanity. We made them gods for a time out of our own needs for earthly deities, and paid them well in money and love. But in the end, they stayed human after all.

"These guys," says general manager Al Coates, "are all for the most part very well conditioned athletes. We want them to constantly work on getting stronger and better conditioned, to get just that little extra edge. But in actuality the business of this game becomes more mental than physical. Can they control themselves to work hard every day, to avoid the little mental errors, to learn from last night's loss and then let it go for tonight's game? That's hard to do day to day, and it's even harder to do for an entire season. In the long run, it's the mental approach to the game that keeps them here or weeds them out."

Coaching and controlling the mental approach has become harder in recent times. Hockey always has been an emotional game. But there was a time when coaches coached and players played, by and large, as they were told to play.

Today's players arrive in exceptional condition. After his Kamloops team was eliminated from the 1996 Western Hockey League playoffs, Jarome Iginla arrived at the Saddledome one noon-hour thinking he would sign his NHL contract with the Flames and watch the first-round playoff game between Calgary and Chicago. He was correct about the signing.

Iginla walked into the Saddledome at 12:10. By 12:15, he had signed his previously negotiated contract. By 12:25, Ian McKenzie, a Flames scout and a key person in the life of Fleury as well, was walking Iginla into the locker room to shake hands with his new teammates. "Hey, Iggy," said one of them, Ronnie Stern, "you don't have time for this bull. Get your gear on!"

A half-hour later Iginla was on the ice in his NHL debut. "You could see he was a little nervous, fumbling the puck," Coates recalls. "But we knew he was mentally tough enough to handle it. Pierre put him on a line with Theo and Jarome scored in his second game. We need that toughness, that hunger, and that little spark."

In an effort to control as much of the Flames' future as possible, Coates has an extensive, and growing, scouting system, and he has his Red Book. That is an immense binder containing the constantly updated computerized evaluations by Flames scouts of every player in the NHL. "The Book makes our judgements a little more scientific than just talk," Coates explains.

Every year, every Flames scout evaluates in person every NHL player at least three times, giving each player subjective numerical scores for offensive skills, defensive skills, size, grit, speed, skating ability, and character. "I started this about five or six years ago," Al says. "Back in '91–92 we made a bad trade. We realized if we had had this system we would never have made that mistake. We said, okay, Gretzky, Mario Lemieux, and Grant Fuhr are 10's. Now, everybody else is something less. We've worked on it, adjusted it, worked some more until now we think we have a pretty good system. We can overlay any team's players on ours and see where our boys score better and where theirs do. That can suggest where there might be a winning trade for us. If we follow this book, we should – I say should – not make a mistake in any trades.

"You can get caught up in the moment in this business, let public opinion, media influence, a string of losses get you off track, and make a trade for momentary emotional reasons. It's very easy, even off the ice, to let your emotions cloud your vision. You might be tempted to take a quick fix that would actually get you away from your longterm plans. The numbers are a stop sign. They bring you up short. They remind you that you do not want to trade one of your younger 7.7's for somebody else's older 6.6."

On the amateur level the Flames have four full-time and eight part-time people all over the world, including Russia, Sweden, the Czech Republic, and all across North America. Since the Flames do not possess the financial clout to cherry-pick expensive stars from other teams, the team may even expand the number of scouting staff. Their job is to find the best amateur players and to watch their development. That's how the Flames'

Ian McKenzie, for example, found Brett Hull, who was merely the son of a famous player, and Fleury, who was obviously too small to play in the NHL.

In addition, the Flames have numerous "bird-dogs." "These are guys who just go to games in their local areas and keep their eyes out for you," Coates explains. "They might get a thousand dollars a year and a Flames jacket. They just want to be able to phone somebody and report what they think. A lot of times they give you very valuable information. These are people you meet over the years in this business, maybe a teacher or a city recreational director. Hockey is a big fraternity, you know. You treat people right, they'll treat you right, too. They'll go out and talk to ushers, doctors, trainers, schoolteachers, Sunday-school teachers, police, next-door neighbours. They'll give you some pretty darned good information on potential players that won't ever show up in the stats. You want players with character, not characters who play."

Indeed, the word "character" crops up throughout the Flames organization. "The stakes are so much higher in this business now," says Coates, who has more than twenty-six years in the business of this game. He started with a Detroit farm team wrapping players' knees, selling tickets, shepherding players on road trips, and handling the public-relations job. "You can't afford to have someone on your team whose attitude or character is actually hurting your chances. I am constantly concerned about who the newcomers like Iginla are going to turn to for advice. The general manager and the coaches and the team psychologist and all the fathers and mothers can only talk to young people so much so often. Where they are really going to get their direction from is the guys who've been through it on a year-to-year basis.

"So it is really important to me, in this longterm development blueprint of ours, to ensure that they get the right advice on the ins and outs of the NHL, the rights and wrongs of professional sports, and particularly the rights and wrongs of the Calgary

Flames. We're trying to create a Calgary Flames culture here. And we simply cannot afford any setbacks among our young players who think they can blow off work because they see a veteran do it."

Today's players require a different motivation than past generations. They need more explanation for why they are doing what they are doing. Both Coates and Page see their jobs as at least part-time psychologists. Coates wants to see players who are confident but not comfortable. "They need to carry a sense of urgency with them," he says.

Surprisingly, comfort is regarded as a cancer potentially afflicting modern teams and individual players. The average NHL player's salary is creeping up on the million-dollar mark. That means over an eighty-two-game season young men in their twenties, most of them without a college degree, are earning before taxes slightly more than $4,000 per game-hour, not counting money and free goods and services paid for endorsements or simply for lending their presence to a commercial establishment or function. Such money – and it comes quickly – can buy virtually anything. Those sums can't help but create a sense of comfort.

Additionally, such salaries – and many players, like Fleury, earn much more – can create invisible barriers within a team and even quietly corrode the authority of coaches, few of whom earn as much. Coach Page, for instance, earned $260,000 U.S. a year, about 10 per cent of the salary of his highest-paid player.

Even more potentially deadening to the competitive spirit is the corrosive power of fame. It takes a strong psyche and a supportive family to keep these young men from thinking they are overly important. "People judge fame by where the money is," says Lanny McDonald, one of the most popular Flames ever and, since 1992, a Hockey Hall of Fame member. When he entered the league in 1973, the average NHL salary was $85,000 and the pay of individual players was not published. Though most players likely made more than their friends who worked outside hockey, no one knew that for sure; they all could still go out for beers and burgers together. And the fans were not forever measuring their players and their players' goal production against six- or seven-figure paycheques that sound less like salaries than lottery prizes.

"With the media, the money, the endorsements, the adulation of thousands, and your picture everywhere," adds Lanny, "it's pretty easy for these guys today – and they're pretty young, eh? – to think that they have suddenly become something pretty darned special. I have a wife who brought my head back down when it got a little big and brought my chin back up when it got a little down.

"People think fame is great. And it can be. But it can put incredible pressure on you, not only to produce up to the public's immense expectations of your immense public salary, but up to your own expectations as well. It's hard also just to stay normal. It's very easy to forget you put your pants on the same as everyone else."

Page sees fame, especially quick fame, as breeding complacency. "Fame changes people," he says. "It really does. They need always to have something to strive for. My God, these kids are in their twenties. They can't sit back now. That leaves, what, fifty-five years of sitting back and being comfortable?"

"See," Page says, "young people today think what's important is how fast you get somewhere. When you send someone down to the minors now, they think it's the end of the world. 'Oh, my God, a year in the minors.' A year to them is an eternity. I tell them, 'No. Enjoy yourself there. Make the most of it. We're sending you there to learn as much as you can, like IBM or Xerox sending future managers back to school. If you don't make the most of your time there, then when your time comes up here, you won't be ready. You won't be able to handle it.'

"See, it's not how fast you get to the NHL that's important. It's how long you last. Too many think they are in the minors preparing to *play* in the NHL. No! Wrong! Not true! You're in the minors preparing to *win* in the NHL. There is a very big difference."

Page sees confidence-building as crucial, especially since nearly half of his team in recent times have been rookies. The obvious problem with that is that rookies have so much to learn. What is less obvious is that there is so much for each coach to learn about each rookie. Each player's chemistry, for instance, is different under different conditions. While shouting might produce results at times, it would be counter-productive in another place and time.

"Half of this game is mental anyway," says Page as he draws his trademark precise doodles on a battered legal pad atop his desk in the Saddledome's windowless basement. "You always try to arrange some success for your players. It helps build their confidence. If you ask them to do too much too soon, try to bring them along too quickly in your eagerness to win, they'll experience too much non-success too soon. It can really hurt them – and you – longterm. Right now, our team, I don't know – in my twenty five years of coaching this is as big a challenge as any I've known."

Part of the challenge involves eliminating excuses and combating complacency. "Eliminating excuses is important for success in any life," the coach says. "We're all full of excuses. They pop up everywhere: I wish I had more money, I wish I had a better job, my wife doesn't understand me, my parents are always on me, I feel tired, my boss is too demanding. When we eliminate all the excuses on our team and in our lives, then we can really take off. Then, there are no more reasons not to succeed."

But how do coaches combat complacency among players in the face of so much money, fame, comfort, and the knowledge that they are among the seven hundred or so best hockey players in the world? "Well," says the coach, looking down at his pad again and making a new list, "you remind each one of them what it took for them to get here, to be this successful, to win. Two or three things that happen along the way are that you forget what it took to be so good or maybe you never knew what it took to be so good. The third thing that can happen is you remember what it took and you know what it takes, but you're no longer willing to pay the price to stay there. Hopefully, it's one of the first two. Those you can teach."

❖

The telephone rang in the Fleury home very late that Saturday night of the friendly Portage youth hockey game. As usual, neither parent had made the trip with the team. Donna does not drive. Never has. The Fleurys had two other boys at home. And money was always tight. With Ede Peltz down visiting her sister in the States, the coach had given Theo a ride. Len Peltz was at home running the motel.

Wally answered the phone. The coach's voice had an unusually urgent tone. Wally listened carefully. "Winnipeg?" he asked. "I thought the games were in Portage." He listened further to Coach Fowler. There was no time to be frightened or stunned at the news of Theoren's injury. Hours had passed since the awful event and by then the doctors had figured out what had happened: the defenceman's jagged skate blade had sliced through Theoren's jersey, skin, artery, biceps, and nerves. The severed artery and nerves would explain no pulse and no pain.

Wally had a flashback to the leg he had broken years before in a friendly baseball game. He suspected this latest injury to a Fleury in a friendly game meant the end of Theo's big-time hockey dreams, too. Wally glanced over at Donna. As a Jehovah's Witness, she had religious problems with most medical treatment, though not with medication. "Well," Wally said to the coach without consulting his wife, "you have them do what they have to do." And Wally said quite a few prayers through the night.

What they had to do, if this boy was ever going to regain the use of his arm, was to sew up everything inside, the artery, the muscles, and, of course, the torn skin. But first, they had to build a channel for the nerve to grow back down towards the hand. Nerves don't heal. What's cut is cut. But under ideal conditions with some luck and a lot of care, the good nerve end just might grow back down towards the hand.

It would be a long, slow, and tedious process, both the operation, which would involve four doctors and last almost six hours through most of that Saturday night, and the recovery, which might never quite finish. The long, demanding recovery, if the operation worked, would be subject to failure at any time with the slightest bump or re-injury.

There was a very tired, very frightened Theoren in uncomfortable hospital garb very late at night on the phone to his parents very far away. "I was freaking out totally," he recalls. "All these strange people around. I was thirteen. I was alone. See, my parents never had a whole lot of money for me or for them to travel as well as me. So your road parents were like whoever you went with. Mrs. Petz was there. The doctor in Portage says, 'You're going to Winnipeg.' I didn't know what that meant. It was maybe an hour away. I don't remember. We get to the hospital. It smells funny and is all busy. They had to rebuild everything. I couldn't move my arm. I'm by myself. And the next thing I know I'm talking to my parents on the phone just before going into the operating room. It was like saying goodbye, you know? Freaky."

In Russell, word of the injury spread through the post-midnight darkness like wildfire. As usual, little of the news was good. Little Theoren's hockey-playing days were almost surely over, the reports said. What a loss for him, for the team, for the town. He might even lose the use of his entire arm. The team was devastated.

Then, something strange and spontaneous happened. Actually, it's not unusual in a small rural community, but it can seem strange when the story makes its way into the larger, more impersonal urban centres where most people now live. Len heard about the injury at two o'clock, Sunday morning. Theo had just gone into the operating room. Things did not look good. Hockey was the last thing on Len's mind. A young man needs two good arms to earn a decent living in the country.

Ede was returning from Los Angeles in the morning. Len decided to start on the two- or three-hour drive to the Winnipeg hospital at nine. That would give the road crews a chance to clear snow off the main highways and for Theoren to come out of the anaesthesia. Len called the Fleury house. Would Donna Fleury like to ride with him to see her possibly crippled son in the hospital in the city? Oh, no, she said, she couldn't do that. She was way too distraught.

Len went to bed around three a.m. to catch a few hours of sleep. But he got very little. Throughout the night the motel's front-door buzzer kept ringing. One by one and two by two, townspeople kept driving up to the motel in the blowing snow to deliver a little gift for Len to take to the hospital. "Please give this to Theo," they said. "It's just a little something."

There were cards and candies, small toys, notes, a couple of ten-dollar bills, a new shirt, and a new set of pyjamas. "This was so magical," Len recalls. "No one organized it. It just happened. People, and not all with kids on the team, just felt moved to do something for him."

While her husband and son went to a Winnipeg motel, Ann Petz stayed at the hospital throughout the six-hour operation. When the operating-room door opened as the sun came up, the team of doctors was tired but hopeful. When Theoren was safely sleeping in his room, Ann went to the motel for a nap and a shower. A few hours later she returned and what she did not find seriously frightened her.

Wherever Theoren has gone in life, he has carried with him an aura of the unexpected. On the ice this element of unpredictability is good, exciting. No one, not even Theoren most times, knows what amazing deke he's going to pull off or when he might shoot or pass; in one recent game, with victory almost sealed and criticism mounting about his low goal production, Theoren bore down on an empty net – and passed the puck to his road roommate, Dave Gagner, giving up the easy stat. Why? Did he hear Coach Fowler's urgings from years later? Again, the Fleury shrug.

More importantly, with this unpredictability no one knows when Fleury might explode on the ice. This tension is invisible, but it keeps people watching him. It keeps the eyes of his wife, Veronica, riveted on Theoren during games, even if she's talking to someone. Sports franchises and the media outlets and merchandisers in their orbit desperately want people to want to watch their athletes. So they encourage, even feed, this part of his public persona. Few people are willing to publicly criticize famous people for being late or forgetful, for instance. We make excuses for them before they have to. That seems to be another perk of fame. And like all the other perks, famous people can get used to having excuses made for them before they even try.

Off the ice, however, in the orbit of his friends and family members Theoren's unpredictability, or even occasional undependability, brings a different tension to those relationships. He's definitely more relaxed off the ice, although his brother Ted, the frequent target of Theoren's childhood backyard anger, might dispute that. Around Theoren, family and friends have come to expect the unexpected and to accept it, though not always affectionately. Theoren has learned this, too.

So when Ann Petz walked into that hospital room, she expected to find a groggy Theo determined to let no one know how much his newly rebuilt arm was hurting. What she found instead was no Theoren. He was gone. His bed was empty, the covers thrown back and not even warm. What flashed through her mind was: Now, what has he gone and done? She would not be the last person in Theoren's life to wonder this.

Ann was quite fearful at first. Theo's was a serious operation, requiring quite a delicate recovery. The wound alone took more than forty stitches to close. Inside, the surgeons had painstakingly pieced together his artery and tissues and his muscles; someone said there were nearly five hundred stitches involved there. And the surgeons had set up the severed nerve to regenerate back down the arm. What lay ahead was months of care and therapy for a boy not known for his diligent attention to routine, unless it concerned hockey. And hockey was clearly out for the foreseeable future, possibly forever.

Even if Theoren did everything with great care and conscientiousness, followed all of the doctor's orders as if a mother was watching every moment, there was no guarantee of success. This was real life without clear winners and losers.

Ann looked around Theo's empty room quickly, then rushed out into the hall. There was no Theo in sight. In fact, there was no one in sight. The hall and nurses' station were eerily empty. Theo's disappearance worried Ann more because it had happened on her shift as his surrogate parent. She almost ran down the hall. She could hear voices at the end. Then, she heard laughter and applause. In a children's hospital ward?

A small crowd of nurses and staff was peering through a door into one hospital room. Ann pushed her way through. There was Theoren in a bathrobe sitting in a wheelchair, his right arm in a temporary cast less than four hours old. He was reading storybooks to the other children in the pediatric ward. They had been bored, too. Now, they were enthralled. And Theoren was at centre ice, entertaining the crowd again, still.

"Hi, Mrs. Petz," said Theoren Fleury.

In the end those scary morning moments became an unexpected memory she would cherish for years, privately.

That Sunday afternoon Len and Ede Peltz hurried into the hospital. The Petzes and the Fowlers had to get back to Russell for their families and work the next day. The Peltzes would take the next parenting shift. Len carried the gifts from Theo's hometown admirers. The couple found the youth bright and happy and bubbling, again not what they had expected. The recovery was amazing. Theo's colour was excellent, especially given his blood loss and hours under an anaesthetic. He was alert and jovial. He was wheeling himself with one arm from room to room visiting with every youngster and enjoying immensely being something of a tiny celebrity.

The Peltzes were delighted, too. After a while, they took Theoren back to his room and got him into bed, sitting up. Time for some rest. Len pulled out the bags of presents. Theoren seemed genuinely puzzled at first. His birthday was not for three months. Len explained that spontaneously during the night, while Theo had been asleep in the operating room, many Russell families had delivered these gifts to the motel to be brought to the hospital for Theo. Everyone back home was thinking about him and everyone wanted him to know how much they cared.

Theo just sat there looking at all the gifts spread out on his hospital bed. He didn't open them. He didn't say anything. Expect the unexpected, Ede thought at first. Theoren continued to look sort of perplexed. Then, Ede thought perhaps Theo had fallen asleep. He had closed his eyes and he was not moving. "Theoren?" she said. "Theoren, are you all right?" She moved closer.

Then, she saw it. Was that a tear? First, one. Then another. And another. And another. Until the tears were simply pouring down Theo's face in a steady stream. Ede looked at Len silently, as parents do at such times. Len quietly closed the door of the hospital room. And Ede gave that little boy the biggest, longest hug he'd ever had, just as a mother would.

❖

Allan Beesley loves to say Theoren Fleury's name.

He does it so very well, too, even if in its joy the Saddledome crowd never lets him finish. When Beesley (he prefers one name professionally) is officially announcing from on high yet another goal or assist by Fleury, he will use his mellifluous, radio-trained voice to play with the crowd. He knows what the fans are going to do. And so does every hometown fan in the building.

"Calgary goal scored by number fourrrrr-teeeeen." Big pause. "Thairrrrrr-innnnnnn Flurrrrr-reeeee."

But as soon as Beesley gets the "Thairrrrr–" echoing through the cavernous building, more than eighteen thousand voices drown him out. It's frustrating, as a professional performer, never to get to finish your line. But Beesley understands the crowd's audible affection. He'd like to be cheering, too, because Beesley has become a major Fleury fan himself.

"All of my relatives in B.C. hate Fleury," Beesley says with energy. "They hate everything about him. And our fans adore the guy. That's the way it is with Fleury – you hate him if he's not on your team or you adore him if he is. The guy never quits. He's got a will of steel. My dad – he's in the hospital now – instilled in us never, ever, to give up on anything we did. We could never give up in our house. Fleury hasn't ever given up. I really admire that. I think a lot of fans do. Maybe they wish they had that will, too. And they want to believe that someone, maybe not them but maybe Fleury, can succeed no matter what."

At age thirty-six, tall, and carefully dressed, Beesley has more than fifteen years' experience in radio in B.C. and Calgary. He has one of those remarkably deep voices that reek of authority, which radio loves.

Beesley began doing sports announcing for Kamloops Blazers games. "I'm Canadian," he explains, "so I've always been a hockey fan, big time. I began playing at age five. My dream was to play in the big league. I didn't make it on the ice. But I did make it to the big league on the loudspeaker."

He has also announced the Calgary Stampeders football games. But now he is a diehard Flames fan and even hates the Canucks. Announcing hockey is more of a professional challenge. First of all, it's indoors. Indoor sound systems are trickier. And then hockey teams are hiring so many foreign players now that Beesley must print out both teams' rosters phonetically and rehearse just the names. During a game there is no time to grab a Finnish dictionary and look up Janne Niinimaa. So Beesley's roster for the Flyers includes a player named Yaw-knee Knee-nah-mah.

Beesley says he had a premonition during a recent game. Fleury had scored twice that night. Beesley asked his assistant to check Theo's career records. How many penalty shots had Fleury taken and how many had he scored on? The records showed he was two for two in his career. By the end of that same evening, Fleury was three for three. He scored a hat trick for the night counting a penalty shot against Patrick Roy of the Colorado Avalanche.

Beesley was ready to announce that one – "Calgary goal by number fourteen. His third goal of the night and his third career goal on his third career penalty shot, Thairrrrr "

Beesley put a lot of feeling into that announcement. "Fleury is a prince," he says. "Well, maybe not a prince on the ice but off the ice the guy is a prince. He's really into the community. And have you ever seen him with kids?" That night against Colorado, Beesley had the crowd in a frenzy for Calgary; a lone hat sailed onto the ice. "Imagine," he says, reliving the moment and its sounds, "a hat trick on a penalty shot! I love this Fleury guy. He's got the most incredible concentration, like he's practised every possible move a thousand times."

Perhaps only an announcer and an announcer in Calgary can appreciate how great it is to have a surefire crowd-thundering line like "Thairrrrr-innnnnnn" to ignite Flames fans. Calgary's hometown crowd is renowned as possibly the most somnolent in the entire league, the exact opposite of Chicago's, which tries to drown out the National Anthem and never stops creating noise after that.

Old-timers explain the polite behaviour of Calgary hockey crowds by pointing to the dominance of white-collar fans in the early years after the eight-year-old franchise moved to Calgary from Atlanta on May 21, 1980. While the team changed cities and countries, it kept the name Flames.

As a name, Flames is a priceless (and quickly tiresome) gift to lazy newspaper headline writers: FLAMES GET SMOKED, FLAMES GET BURNED, FLAMES SEASON IN ASHES, and so on. Actually, the name is an historical reference to the conscientious Civil War sacking of Atlanta by Union General William Sherman. His army's determined destruction of everything in sight was a kind of military forechecking that blazed the way in the history of army strategy for the Nazis' blitzkrieg seventy-five years later.

The Flames' first games in both Atlanta and Calgary ended in sizzling ties (1–1 against Buffalo in 1972 and 5–5 against Quebec in 1980), which might help explain an initial lack of fan passion. Whereas Chicago fans tend to be buddies out for a noisy evening of beer and hockey, according to popular thinking in Alberta's business capital, Calgary's fans tended originally to be well-dressed oilmen entertaining potential clients. The need to seek major money from serious investors tends to discourage rowdiness. "Nice neckties tone things down a bit," observes Bearcat

Murray, who now has to wear a tie as a Flames community representative after many years as an open-collared trainer.

"Actually," recalls Ralph Klein, "the Flames and I came in together." Klein was a broadcast journalist who became Calgary's energetic and outspoken mayor about the same time and later took control of Alberta's long-running Conservative political machine to become premier. "The Flames' arrival had a tremendous impact on the city," Klein adds. "It made Calgary feel big-league. We could compete in the big time. It provided the impetus for a new arena and the successful simultaneous bid for the 1988 Winter Olympics."

As mayor of Canada's go-get-'em city, Klein's athletic loyalties were clear. But after he became political leader of the entire province, what happened? He leans back in his office chair with a quick luncheon sandwich in hand and half smiles. "Well," he says, "let's put it this way. If Edmonton is playing anyone other than Calgary, I cheer for Edmonton. If Calgary is playing anyone other than Edmonton, I cheer for Calgary. If Calgary and Edmonton are playing each other, I hope for a tie."

But Premier Klein, himself not overly tall, need not be non-partisan about his enthusiasm for Fleury. "He's a tiger on the ice," says the premier, "and a prominent role model for young people, especially smaller young people, who might think success in hockey – or in life – is determined by size."

Klein may be the only Calgary fan who says he does not cheer for Edmonton's annihilation. Quiet fan behaviour is less of a worry during Flames–Oilers games and, increasingly, during Flames–Canucks games. But, in general, good behaviour and not speaking loudly seem to suit Saddledome crowds quite nicely, thank you. It is all enough to drive the drivers of the Flames' scoreboard crazy. But that doesn't faze Brian Funfer and his associates, who man the Saddledome's Jumbotron.

The twenty-two-ton scoreboard is the electronic focus of the arena, the furnishing centrepiece like the television in most living rooms. And it is the most space-age symbol of the new, changing, and more sophisticated marketing of hockey. If a hockey fan is thinking clearly, the idea of an immense electronic screen hanging over the rink so he and fellow spectators can see on tape cinematic confirmation of what they just witnessed live on the ice might seem redundant at best and quite possibly bizarre.

But in professional sports today, and in hockey in particular, it is no longer just the opportunity to view a hockey game live in person that is being sold. It is a total entertainment experience that includes the opportunity to re-view a play within moments. Management of that experience also involves everything from the colour of the logo on the jerseys (which are consumer-tested before league approval) and the temperature of the beer on sale to what fans are thinking and doing during breaks in the game action. According to modern thinking, the minds of the video generation require that something be happening every moment in order to prevent that dread disease, boredom.

If it's not the game riveting a ticket-buyer's attention, then there must be pizza giveaways for an entire row of seats, a mini-performance by the costumed team mascot, video replays on the Jumbotron (probably the week's most violent collisions), a chant breaking out, music in the air, or a free T-shirt in the air launched from a sponsor's shoulder-held giveaway gun. Put one way, even if the Flames lose 5–1, management wants fans to go home feeling they had a good time. Coach Page puts it another way: "Winning is not enough any more."

The league is marketing hockey – "Brand NHL" commissioner Gary Bettman calls it in his strategy sessions – not just as an everyday sport but as an exciting, hot, hip, edgy sport containing a collection of interesting, unpredictable personalities with amazing skills who mingle rapidly and sometimes violently. "These are attractive, articulate, friendly, highly skilled athletes," Bettman says. "If we want to stamp Brand NHL on the public consciousness, no one can do a better job than the athletes."

The goal is to raise professional hockey's exposure so that the letters N-H-L come consistently to mean the same to masses of consumers as the letters K-F-C do in chicken, T-I-M H-O-R-T-O-N do in donuts, L-A-U-R-A S-E-C-O-R-D in candies, and M-C-D-O-N-A-L-D'S in hamburgers. "We compete with other sports and other entertainment options for our fans," the commissioner says. "We have to make them feel good about spending their time and money with us. We have to make them want to do it again and again."

When Bettman arrived at NHL headquarters from the NBA in 1993, he felt instantly that hockey had to step out from behind its curtain. It was, for instance, the lone major professional sport without a national U.S. television contract. The league now has those contracts, which produce more coverage and more fans with every broadcast, and ultimately more income for teams to split. And the league has teamed with corporate sponsors such as Nike, Bud Ice, Fox TV, TSN, and CBC which now advertise the sport whenever they advertise their products or image. The league has teamed with corporate sponsors to drive the growth of in-line skating and hockey, which recruits new ice-hockey fans in the off-season and in the streets, and creates, in effect, a year-round sport, like basketball.

The league has moved its logo into new corporate-sponsorship areas. Companies now spend in excess of $150 million a year on joint promotions such as Play of the Year. The league has spread awareness of the sport into new social sectors by aiding and abetting the spread of in-line skating and roller hockey. And the league has moved teams into new geographic areas, which leads to new TV exposure, new sponsors, new merchandise sales, and new fans, all of which are called new revenue streams. If the Canadiens or Maple Leafs can become Canada's team in hockey, if the Dallas Cowboys can become America's team in football, and if the Chicago Bulls can have Europeans wearing their logo, why can't Disney's Ducks become America's Team or hustle clothing abroad? "What we are doing," says Rick Dudley, president of NHL Enterprises, the league's marketing arm, "is growing the pie. We want to make hockey as ubiquitous as possible."

And not just in North America; without making much effort to promote its non–North American players and personalities, fully 10 per cent of NHL merchandise sales already occur overseas. North America thinks of itself as owning the National Hockey League, but while fans there watch the Stanley Cup playoffs each spring, many others elsewhere can tune in, too – altogether the games arrive in 212 million homes in 170 countries and territories.

Such new thinking may bother some old-timers in Canada; they bemoan the Winnipeg Jets' move to Phoenix and the Quebec Nordiques' shift to Denver but somehow overlook or disparage the Senators' arrival in Ottawa along with the shift of two International Hockey League franchises from the American cities of Atlanta and Minneapolis into Quebec and Manitoba, not to mention the Flames' migration north.

But with billions of dollars at stake from TV networks, TV advertisers, and merchandisers in competition with professional football, basketball, baseball, NASCAR auto racing, and maybe someday soccer, the forces driving this change are financially powerful.

With ten times Canada's population and with hockey's popularity just blossoming across the lower half of North America, it is clear that the United States contains the greatest potential for growth. Even before the explosion of hockey's popularity there and the addition of four franchises (including an NHL return to Atlanta), Americans bought nearly 40 million hockey sticks in one year. That's 1.5 hockey sticks sold for every Canadian in Canada, or seventy-six hockey sticks sold every single minute every day all year. In 1990, according to USA Hockey, there were about 15,000 hockey teams in the United States. The number has now passed 30,000 and player members soared beyond the half-million mark even before the professional heroes of hockey played in the World Cup of 1996 and their first Olympics in 1998 – on global television.

When Canucks hats show up in Seattle and Flames jerseys appear in Montana, when thirty minor-league hockey teams compete across the American South, when Junior A games in some U.S. cities attract three thousand to five thousand spectators, and when one game pitting Wayne Gretzky against Teemu Selanne becomes the most-watched TV program in Finland's history, something is going on – and what's going on threatens to turn the old name, the *National* Hockey League, into a misnomer.

Even the CBC's venerated "Hockey Night in Canada," a Saturday-night institution in the homes, hearts, and collective memories of generations of Canadians and, incidentally, the longest-running television show in North American TV history, has caught the expansionist fever. Long dubbed by many Westerners "Hockey Night in Eastern Canada" for its proclivity to think the Maple Leafs game was by definition the week's most important, the program has now become a double-header, six full hours of nationwide hockey on Saturday nights which include a weekly Western game that spills well into the wee hours of Sunday in Eastern and Atlantic time zones.

In choosing the make-up of their own team, Flames officers now give careful consideration to the popular attraction of a player, as well as his hockey skills. Yes, a team always wants to win. But it must be seen to win in order to make money – seen by ticket-buyers who spend additional money on food, drinks, programs, and souvenirs, seen by TV viewers, "seen" by radio fans, and seen by fashion-conscious buyers of sports clothing. Fashion and identifying with fame and winning explain the sudden appearance across the American West in recent years of Colorado Avalanche shirts and hats adorning the bodies of humans who probably have no idea which end of a hockey stick goes on the ice. It also explains the ongoing popularity in southern Alberta of Flames shirts and hats carrying Fleury's name and number.

His fan-appeal was part of what made Theo Fleury attractive to the Flames on Entry Draft day back in 1987 when Ian McKenzie whispered the kid's name into the calculating ear of general manager Cliff Fletcher at that rickety table in Detroit's Joe Louis Arena. And the lack of popularity or a positive image – and the potential to develop a bad one – has been the reason for more than one Flames player's departure from the team.

"It may be from my PR-marketing background," says general manager Coates, "but a player's crowd-appeal certainly stands out in my mind. I try and put myself in a fan's place. What do I see and think when I see this fellow on the ice? There probably aren't more than ten or twelve superstars in the world, players that I personally would buy a ticket just to see, not their team, players like Michael Jordan and Wayne Gretzky. What brings people into the rink? What excites them? And what also helps the team win? It all has to go hand in hand. Our fan favourite right now is Theoren, clearly. I think Iginla will come on too with time."

When Ron Bremner was interviewed in 1996 to leave the presidency of BCTV and become president and chief executive officer of the Calgary Flames, the panel of owners had some questions for him. They asked Bremner why he wanted the job. "I don't know that I do," he replied honestly, "until I hear the answer to one question: What business is the Calgary Flames in?"

The owners replied, "The entertainment business."

"Good," said Ron, "then I am interested in this job." He explains his answer. "If they had said, 'the hockey business,' I'd have withdrawn. I want the Calgary Flames to be the Green Bay Packers of the National Hockey League, a pro sports team deeply rooted in the community, successful in athletics and successful in business, despite the smaller size of its market."

The fifty-year-old Bremner has an open, up-front, hands-on, self-deprecating style of speaking. "I tell people," he says, "that I was in the half of my graduating class that made the top half possible." Raised in the tough east end of Hamilton, Ontario, where General Sherman might have come from had he been Canadian, Bremner graduated from the University of Guelph and plunged immediately into a career in radio and TV sales and management. "I hate to lose," he admits. In fact, during father-son driveway hockey games, both Scott and Mark Bremner used to complain to their mother that their father shot the puck too hard. "I told them," Ron recalls, " 'Hey, this is life. You gotta learn to take it.' Well, being a small-city franchise is a tough life, too. And we're gonna learn to take it – and give it."

Taking over his office in August 1996, lining it with motivational books and mementoes, and installing a round meeting table to avoid impersonal across-the-desk encounters, Bremner immediately plunged into the Calgary community. Within ninety days he went through his first thousand business cards, the ones that list his direct line.

"I believe very much," he says, "that professional sports have become too detached from the people who pay the bills – our fans, our customers, our corporate supporters." One of the first things he did was record in his own voice the tape-recording that answers the Flames phone after hours. Soon after, he lectured Saddledome ushers about customer service. The Flames have about nine hundred part-time employees, always a tough group to train, manage, and maintain.

Bremner told them what he tells most audiences nowadays, that customer service and entertainment are paramount in the Flames organization now. He told them his working hours and private phone number and asked for their ideas.

"We need to keep returning value to our customers," he said. "Yes, it's important to make a profit. But it is also important to make a difference." He also told them about a goal: "Eventually, in a year or two," he said, "I would like each of our more than twelve thousand season-ticket-holders to be greeted by name by the usher in their section. Yes, it is a high goal. But that's the type of organization we want."

Next, Bremner spoke to Flames players. "Hockey players are a different breed," he said. "They are like police officers. Every shift they start could be their last. I told the players the reason they have the chance to make big money here for a while is because the fans – not management, but the fans – are willing to pay money to see them play. We need as players and as an organization to keep returning value. If we win 5–1 but the customers got a cold hot dog, a warm beer, and a half-baked effort on the ice, then to me that's a loss. I suggested every time they go out for a pregame warmup, each player look up in the stands and pick out a little boy or girl sitting there with their parents who maybe worked a little overtime to pay for this family outing. And I suggested that the players keep that customer in mind when they're deciding how hard they are going to play that day."

Bremner also set a goal for himself. "In a couple of years," he said, "I want the whole NHL turning to the Calgary Flames for advice on providing customer service to hockey fans and on providing the best possible product for your ticket money." This is a major cultural challenge in such a business organization; 90 per cent of Flames employees are low-wage part-timers, who work the Flames games or other Saddledome events and then go home to other jobs or school. Staff turnover – and, thus, training costs – is high, as is the risk to continuity in terms of customer-service attitudes.

There is also the ongoing 30 per cent or so currency differential between the Canadian and U.S. dollar, which means, in effect, that a Canadian franchise must sell $130 in tickets to acquire the same power to pay player salaries as an American team gets from $100 in sales. And Canada's elected officials have chosen not to award their country's businesses the same tax breaks American companies enjoy. For instance, hockey-ticket purchases in the United States can be deducted from income as business-entertainment expenses and the financial losses of American NHL franchises can be deducted from the income of associated non-hockey holdings. Thus, Wayne Huizenga's impressive financial successes with trash-hauling and used cars can help underwrite any losses of his Florida Panthers.

Five of Canada's six NHL franchises – Montreal, Toronto, Ottawa, Edmonton, and Calgary – rank in the bottom eleven teams for total payrolls. The sixth Canadian team – Vancouver – ranks eighth in payroll but has an American owner. And while player payroll on the books does not guarantee success on the ice – the New York Rangers and Pittsburgh Penguins have been number-one and -two spenders recently – it sure can help tilt the financial ice in favour of acquiring and keeping star players – Detroit, Philadelphia, and Colorado are in the payroll top seven, too. And Vancouver vaulted up the list with its multi-million dollar investment to acquire Mark Messier.

Bremner places the emphasis elsewhere. "In hockey," he says, "it's not how much you spend, but how you spend it. We intend to get more for our dollars spent." One way he invests money is on fifteen free breakfasts every Thursday morning. Each week the president of the Flames invites a dozen or so season-ticket-holders to join him for breakfast in a private dining room at the Saddledome.

On this Thursday morning at 7:30, these season-ticket-holders are ushered into the buffet and greeted by Bremner and several Flames staffers and introduced to a surprise celebrity guest, Zarley Zalapski, a player out for the year rehabilitating a knee injury. The buffet is bounteous – coffee, tea, juice, mountains of fresh fruit, and an immense variety of fresh-baked breakfast rolls.

Namecards mark everyone's place, as does a new Flames cap. These people have invested at least $4,000 per couple to guarantee themselves seats at every game. Those with tickets in the exclusive Chrysler club section closer to the ice have paid $6,644.70 plus a $300 membership fee for each season seat. Bremner's theory is that today such serious customers expect more for their money than a seat. They want to feel a part of the action and of the team family. "We want to develop more emotional equity with our fans," says Bremner. "Give them a genuine stake in us and we in them. Hopefully, it's harder to stop buying tickets from friends."

After selling every seat for every game every year for a long time and having a season-ticket waiting list, the number of Flames season-ticket-holders plunged a few years ago. It has now climbed back above twelve thousand. And as far as Ron Bremner is concerned, that makes more than twelve thousand opportunities to learn something.

"Please eat all the food this morning," the president says. "The leftovers just go to the accounting department.

"This morning we want to learn from you. But I thought I might take just a few minutes first to tell you some things we are doing here, where I am coming from. I love the look and the feel of this hockey club – the youngsters, the veterans, the coaches. Seven years ago we were the best in professional hockey. We had some internal business problems, became somewhat detached. But the owners stayed. No threats about leaving for more lucrative pastures. They invested some fifty million dollars in renovations.

"We need partnerships. We want to give you more value for your dollar spent with us. I want you to feel you have access to the Flames president. That starts this morning, but it doesn't stop this morning. So, tell me, what do you not like about the Calgary Flames? What do you want to see, besides cheaper beer? I hear that one all the time."

Doug Fraser is a longtime season-ticket-holder. "I like the direction of the team, what you and Al Coates are doing. I'm glad you got rid of that Reichel. We want a Canadian team for Canadian fans and I'd like to see some more seven p.m. games on weeknights and maybe keep the restaurants open after games."

Bremner seconds the praise of Al Coates's work, but omits mentioning that the Flames traded the disappointing scorer Robert Reichel, who is Czech, to the New York Islanders not for a Canadian but for an American, Marty McInnis. Ron notes the Flames might consider alternative restaurant times, like keeping one open after the game, but describes a previous experiment when they all were open before and after a game. "We doubled our staff costs," Ron says, shrugging, "but got no new business. After a game, especially a loss, it seems people just want to get out of here."

Bremner mentions that the room they are in and others like it, along with the kitchens and caterers down the hall, are always available for business and club rentals with or without games. He describes the newly varied menus at each Saddledome restaurant and then points out the additional variety achieved by renting out Saddledome concourse space to food franchises – Wendy's, Tim Hortons, Subway. "It's not traditional to go to a sports event and eat a caesar salad," he says. "But people are more health-conscious. We want to be open to serving our customers' very varied needs and wants. In Philadelphia, you know, the new arena has a working micro-brewery right inside. You can watch through the window and then buy the beer. Rumour has it they do twenty-five thousand dollars' business a night."

Another ticket-holder notes that the 1995 renovation eliminated rinkside access for kids seeking autographs. What about opening a lounge where fans could mingle with the players after a game? Zarley says after a game most players just want to be with their families. He doubts many would come without free food and an agreement they could leave after forty-five minutes.

"We forget," Ron says, "some players are basically shy. Many of them, of ours, are young, from small towns, and they are not used to such social interaction."

Ken Roulston suggests selling all unsold tickets at a discount in the last hour. "That's a possibility," Ron agrees. "But how'd you like to pay full price and end up in a seat next to a guy who paid only ten dollars?"

Ken responds, "I've never asked a stranger how much he paid for a ticket."

Someone says the Saddledome needs more ATMs. "We agree," Ron nods. "We're adding two more. And you guys probably haven't noticed but my wife did. We've added five women's washrooms this year."

Someone says section 106 is too hot. Ron nods to Bob White, who handles suite sales. "We'll look into that," Ron says. "Speaking of hot spots, I'm discussing a new sound system with the ownership. It'll cost six hundred thousand dollars, but eventually we will have sensors all over the arena constantly reading the sound reaching each section and adjusting it for that section automatically."

What's the deal, one customer asks, with all these interruptions during a game for pizza giveaways and all that?

"Good point," says Ron. "What we have here is a generational break. We have a generation – like yours and mine – that grew up with the original six hockey teams and we have a generation under thirty-five that never knew a tiny league and grew up with rock videos, pizza, and hey, while we're at it, we'll throw in a hockey game. They're all customers."

Frances Lane wants to make some points. "First," she says, "you should sign up Harvey the Hound for a hundred years. He is simply wonderful. He's great with kids and he lets adults be kids."

Ron agrees about the value of the team's performing mascot.

Frances also likes the Flames' new payment system for playoff tickets. Instead of requiring payment for all playoff tickets at once, the Flames will bill a season-ticket-holder's credit card for tickets game by game. "We thought this might be more convenient for our customers," says Ron. Everyone agrees. "Next year," he adds, "we'll be doing the same thing through the regular season for season-ticket-holders."

But Frances has a problem with her regular parking-lot attendant. "He's a human pylon," she says. "He just stands there and makes no effort to co-ordinate three lanes of postgame traffic trying to exit. All you want is the hope of getting out by morning."

"That's new to me," Ron says, "but that kind of thing annoys my wife, too." He gets Frances's seat location and orders a Flames staff member to meet her there after Saturday's game to ride out with her to experience the problem firsthand. Ron takes this opportunity to explain some difficulties the Saddledome has with Victoria Park, a struggling neighbourhood of aging private homes directly adjacent to the huge arena. Some Victoria Park residents appear to resent heavy event traffic. There are even suspicions that on game days angry neighbours leave their cars on the already snow-clogged streets on purpose.

"Hey," says Ron, thinking out loud, "what if we gave away some unsold tickets to neighbours every game, get them in here and having some fun, too?" Bob White makes more notes.

"I like the way the team is going," Greg Martin says. "They're a hardworking bunch of guys, not stale any more. There's a real sense of excitement about the team."

"Good," says Ron. "We're going to be building all the time now, not just every few years. You know, we're even getting into psychological testing of players. We want Flames representatives to be people with character, people with heart. They may not all be fifty-goal scorers, but we want people who want to be a part of this organization, who we can trust to represent the Flames in a group of a hundred kids at a shopping centre. We want the

Flames to have strong community involvement. We've got a grade-six literacy program going now, too. Kids who read a certain number of books get autographed bookmarks from Flames players."

Was there a chance of getting occasional video updates on the Jumbotron about the Baby Flames, the Saint John Flames? "Good idea. We'll look into that."

It would be nice to get the starting lineups posted in the lounge before the game. "It'll be done starting Saturday."

Mike Kehoe has been silent the whole time. Finally, he must speak. "I'm just a small businessman," he says. "I don't feel like I'm getting much value for my money. My wife, Aileen, won't come with me to the games any more since the players' strike. My boys come sometimes. But it's like I feel I have to use the tickets. It's no fun to come alone."

Zarley Zalapski interjects. "It was an owners' lockout, not a players' strike."

Some chuckles break out and Ron is smiling. But he is alert now. He suspects, accurately, an impending loss of at least two season-ticket-holders. "That's a very interesting point," Ron says. He is not eating and is leaning forward. "We want you to think of your season tickets as investments, not as spending. I'll bet we could identify the small-business owners among our season-ticket-holders and set up opportunities for them to network with each other more. They could buy insurance from you, Mike, and you could buy whatever from them. This is good."

But Ron was still worried about Aileen Kehoe's fading enthusiasm for hockey and the Flames. "Do you think Aileen would mind meeting with me?" Mike thinks that would be fine. "Good," says Ron. "You have my direct phone number. Check with her and let's set up an appointment for the three of us to talk about her concerns in the next week or two. I need to know what's on her mind."

Ron Kempe is an engineer who actually helped design the Saddledome. "Ron," says Ron Kempe, "I think you're doing a great job here. I like your openness."

The Flames president is appreciative. "You know, in business today," he says, surveying the entire room, "it's not good enough to sit in your office and wait for business to walk in. You have to reach out. This summer we're sending out a caravan of Flames players and coaches. We're going to claim Montana, Wyoming, and Idaho as Calgary Flames territory, and we're going to reclaim Saskatchewan and Manitoba. I want to see charters of fans flying into Flames games from Winnipeg. They don't have a team any more."

Hands are shaken all around. Both sides are very appreciative. The guests leave. Ron Bremner presides over a post-breakfast review. "Bobby," he says, "what have we learned this morning?"

"I like the idea of helping small-business owners network with each other through their season tickets," Bob White says.

"Me, too," says the president. "That's a half-million-dollar idea right there. And they can use Flames merchandise with their logo in their business."

Libby Raines, the Saddledome's assistant general manager, suggests a Flames breakfast club for such season-ticket-holders. The head coach and other Flames personalities could speak to them, she suggests.

"That's excellent!" says Ron. "Let's do it. Now, we need to work on increasing the accessibility of players. Having an autograph table in the lobby for injured players before every home game is great. But we need to do more. Will you give some thought to that, Libby? Good. Now, you know it's not good enough any more to say, about that parking problem, that we'll look into it. I want something actually done, okay? And then call Frances back and tell her what we've done, all right? Maybe we need to train these attendants more."

Libby is worried about the economics of opening restaurants before and after early games. "Well, who says we have to offer a full dinner at three?" Ron asks. "Where is that written in stone? So for early games we offer light snacks before and full dinners after.

"And, you know, about that staff turnover with the ushers and others? Maybe if we offered some more training, gave them more reason to stay. And the longer they work here the more discounts they get on tickets and merchandise? That might help. And the cheap seats, the nine-dollar ones way up at the top? What if we turned that whole section into a Kids' Zone? Let 'em make all the noise they want and maybe get everyone else fired up in here. That could be great. We want to set up more opportunities for magic moments."

This breakfast post-mortem appears concluded. Downstairs on the ice, the Olympias are finishing their first run of the day. The coaches and players are beginning to arrive for another day's practice, unaware of the fourteen season-ticket-holders returning to their offices feeling pretty good about the team and planning to mention to co-workers and family the breakfast meeting they just had with the president of the Calgary Flames.

The Saddledome ticket office is open. Brad Andrews, the manager, is pleased. For one thing, he is newly engaged to his girlfriend, Tonalee. For another, it appears that Saturday's one p.m. game will be another sellout. The Flames convinced the league to give them several midday weekend games. That is not popular for TV; one p.m. games are hardly prime time and one p.m. games are not the best for concession sales, since many fans eat lunch before arriving.

But Flames management is thinking about Saturday afternoons, and Tuesday and Thursday and Friday nights far into the future. One o'clock weekend games are great for Family Packs – eighty-eight dollars for four tickets, four pennants, four hot dogs, and four drinks. Family Packs, of course, attract families.

Families have children. Families with children at hockey games tend to have nice memories. Nice memories at hockey games have a way of creating future season-ticket-holders.

The Flames president stands up from the table. He already has put in a good morning's work. It's barely nine o'clock. "That was good," Ron says. He does not mean the breakfast; the Flames president hardly touched his food. Too busy listening.

Arriving at their desks down the hall, Flames office-workers see Ron Bremner stride towards his office. He seems unusually upbeat. They are unaware of the morning's events. Only those in accounting suspect something special was going on. They got some awfully nice leftovers.

It did not take long for Theoren Fleury to start feeling better after the operation. The recovery, if it happened, was going to take a long while. Knowing how energetic Theoren was and how confining a hospital and its rigid routines could be, Coach Fowler and his wife, Buella, planned a Wednesday visit to the Winnipeg hospital. After several long talks, they convinced Donna Fleury to ride along to see her son. No one knew how long the boy would be away from Russell.

Donna was very nervous, but the reunion in the hospital room went well. Theoren was enthusiastic and quite pleased to have visitors. He looked good. While they were all talking, the chief surgeon happened by. "Hello," he said to Theo's mother, "come to take your boy home, eh?"

Now, it was Donna's turn to look perplexed. She knew Theoren would be in hospital for weeks. "Oh," the surgeon said, delighted to be the bearer of good news for once. "This young man can go home today." Coach Fowler beamed. Theoren cheered out loud.

But Donna Fleury was not happy. In fact, she was nearly frantic at this unexpected turn of events. "I can't take him home," she complained. "I can't care for him like this."

The hospital room fell silent. "He can't come home like this," Donna said. "Who's going to take care of his arm?"

Doctors see families under stress react in a wide variety of ways. Sometimes, they come to know, it is better to be silent. There was an awkward pause in that room before Coach Fowler stepped in. He suggested many people would be available to help the Fleurys and, anyway, it wasn't like Theoren couldn't get around. The doctor emphasized the rigid rules necessary for recovery, not for the last time, because he knew different people heard different rules.

A week later Theoren was over at Len and Ede Peltz's motel. He would come to spend an increasing amount of time with them in the next two years. Ede suggested she might have a chance, finally, at winning a ping-pong game. "How long are you supposed to wear that sling?" she asked.

"A long time," Theo said. His father had described his own recovery from his broken leg and told Theo he could not use the arm for a long while. That did not seem right to Ede, who checked with Wally. Wally was adamant. Donna had told him what the doctor said. Ede suspected there were too many cooks in the kitchen. She called Dr. Robertson. "Oh, heavens," he said, "Theoren should have been starting to use the arm last week." In fact, the arm had started to stiffen and scar tissue to form.

Ede took charge. There were regular visits to a physical therapist, two or three times a week, plus required exercises at home. They had a mind-numbing routine to them. And it hurt to force severed and withered muscles back into shape. Worse yet, there was no sense of progress. So Theoren was not always diligent or punctual about the exercises or about keeping the appointments. So Ede drove him.

The recovery would, indeed, be demanding. There could be no contact sports – no hockey, for sure, no baseball. One more bad bump on that nerve ending and it would grow no more and this young man would never have any feeling in his right arm or hand. Golf would be good therapy in the summer and Theoren could skate come fall. But no hockey.

And then there were the hospital visits. Theoren found these to be ordeals, physically and emotionally. Once every month, in all kinds of weather, despite her own family's demanding schedule, Ede would drive Theoren all the way into Winnipeg to see Dr. Robertson. The doctor would prick the boy's arm all over with needles, trying to mark what progress, if any, the nerve growth was making down Theo's arm. When the needle hurt Theo's arm, that was good news. But it hurt nonetheless.

What hurt most was the emotional rollercoaster of the visits to the doctor. Few people over the years have had difficulty deciphering Theoren Fleury's feelings. He is remarkably forthright and open. His disappointments can explode as openly as his enthusiasms. He enjoyed his time with Ede – whom he always called Mrs. Peltz until just a few years ago – especially her acceptance and quiet reliability. But, frankly, he found the whole rehabilitation thing extremely confining. His arm was simply not healing as fast as he wanted.

Every month Theoren would get his hopes up. He would count the days to the visit, as if it were a release date from prison, or Christmas in someone else's house. Theo would tell Ede his arm was feeling pretty good, actually, and once the doctor heard that, he might just decide this time the recovery had gone so well that Theo could begin playing hockey again.

Ede was torn. She knew how important hope is to full recovery and to life. She admired Theoren's innate optimism. She never wanted to crush that. But as an adult she was dealing in the long term, the next couple of years. Theoren was dealing in the long term of a fourteen-year-old, the next week or two. Ede felt she had to be realistic. "We'll see what the doctor says," Ede would say. "Remember, he said this recovery was going to take a very long time." To Theo, it already had.

Theoren would be bubbly in the car en route to Winnipeg. He knew what would happen during the examination and tests. But he would block that out. His attention was focused on the results of the exam, which he was certain would show impressive progress. Ede found Theo to be remarkably stoic during the needle business. He winced only occasionally. At the end of every session, he would burst out, "Can I play hockey now?"

"No," was the inevitable reply. Dr. Robertson didn't even seem to think about it. "No, Theo, you cannot play hockey. It's important that we give this arm a long time to heal. We'll see you again next month."

Ede would see Theo's face harden. Once or twice, he tried to argue. But mostly Theo would say nothing until they were outside in the hospital parking lot. Then the anger and the tears would flow. Theo might lean on the car and sob. She remembers him thumping the car a time or two. He might sit in the car and cry and swear a bit, as well. The doctor was dumb, maybe even stupid. They all were at that hospital. Hadn't the doctor said himself that the nerve was growing? It was all the way down to here now. Had Ede seen that? So what's the difference from here to here? What did the doctor know about hockey anyway?

Ede let Theo get it all out. She knew him pretty well. Theo's anger was like a prairie thunderstorm, black and noisy, even scary, but also brief. In ten minutes, maybe fifteen, he would be his old self. Ede would try to plan some errand to do while in the city, like buy her husband a new putter for his birthday. Would Theoren help her pick out just the right one?

Ede came to realize how much Theoren enjoyed giving presents. Strangely, he did not seem too thrilled about getting them. He would be polite, pleased, but not as thrilled as most youngsters were. Getting gifts required patience and counting on others to remember or to choose well. Everything he had learned in the rented house on Augusta Street taught Theoren Fleury that relying on others was risky. And everything he had learned at his real home, at the rink, where he was inevitably cheered on home ice and booed on the road, led him to believe in doing things himself, without waiting. Waiting to be given something was dumb, especially when you aren't much over five feet tall. You can wait down there until hell freezes over and no one will ever notice you, let alone think to give you anything. So Theo Fleury learned early on that in the world he wanted to live in, taking was imperative. Take the puck. Then, take the shot, Theo. Take it now!

It was not until much later, when the clarity and accuracy of hindsight could focus her memory, that Ede realized what Theo was really angry about after those doctor visits. He was not angry because the recovery was not happening. It was happening; most visits the needles he could feel seemed to be farther down his arm.

Theo was angry because the recovery was taking so long by his own timetable. Theo had determined in his own mind that he was never going to be very tall or big. But he could compensate for that lack of physical presence by being a speedy presence, a scoring presence, and an annoying on-ice presence.

Teams might wait for an injured big guy to heal. But little folks who could not play due to injury are more easily discarded. They lose their place in line – and in the lineup. Theo was getting better at blocking out pain; he was getting a lot of practice with this arm business. But it was one thing to block out pain. It was quite another to overlook the fact that your right arm had blocked itself out of feeling anything.

While most people in his world were amazed that his limb seemed to be healing at all, Theo was growing impatient that this severed nerve refused to regenerate quickly enough to impress the doctor or to make itself susceptible to Theo's will. He felt that intense impatience experienced by people in a seemingly unmoving line at the bank or airport where their mounting personal anxiety seems to have no effect on anyone else.

Theo felt some days as if that arm, his arm, the one that had so reliably helped propel so many shots past so many helpless goalies, had somehow developed a stubborn mind of its own. Certainly, the doctor had. Internally, the arm had been reconnected. The muscle was healing. Theo could move it better now, though he had learned to sense where it was or actually look for it rather than fully feel it. But now, stubbornly, almost wilfully, this arm had the nerve to refuse to recover as rapidly as its owner desired. Theo may have been naive in his fierce hope for faster progress; he has always seemed fierce in his life and often seems naive, even today. But he was also right.

In fact, Theo probably was the only person who knew for sure that his arm would heal sufficiently for him to use it, and to use it in hockey. He didn't just *think* it would get better. He *knew* it would get better. No threats were necessary. It was going to get better. All of the adults in Theoren's life were more realistic – and wrong.

Coach Fowler was, of course, hopeful and included Theoren in team activities. That was kind. But Theo was not in his team's playing plans.

Wally Fleury knew the verdict, too. "I figured right then that was the end of his hockey-career days," Wally says. "I didn't know what the boy would do with himself."

Ede knew, too. Outside of Theo's presence, the surgeon spoke to her bluntly. "They didn't think Theoren would ever play hockey again," she says. "I mean, the boy couldn't even move his fingers at that time. And he's going to grab a hockey stick and launch one of his shots? I don't think anyone told him what was not possible. I did tell him, 'Theo, you're going to need your arm to earn a living as an adult, whatever you end up doing. So you've got to give it time to heal as much as it can and not hurt yourself.'"

Throughout Theoren Fleury's life, summer has been the toughest season to endure. Without hockey, through childhood and adulthood, summers can seem absolutely endless. Waiting may be necessary. But it is also a waste of time. One day, years later, there would be serious physical conditioning to do with his personal trainer. That would provide a sense of progress towards the first faceoff of fall.

But that first summer after The Injury, Theo began his long, passionate love affair with golf, which appealed to him precisely because it was not a team sport. His grandfather gave him his old clubs and Theo played almost every day at the Russell Golf and Country Club: Len and Ede paid his dues and Ede usually ended up driving him there each morning and fetching him come evening. Golf was great therapy for Theo's arm and for his mind, and it played to his superb eye-hand co-ordination and to his competitiveness. And there were no goalies.

In addition, the Peltzes and two or three other Russell families chipped in to pay Theo's tuition at the Andy Murray Hockey School in Brandon, Manitoba, that summer of 1982. On his first morning at that camp Theoren burst onto the ice with a display of speed and hustle that caught the eye of at least one instructor, Graham James. When that same instructor blew the whistle for the campers to assemble, the first student to skate up obediently and eagerly was Theoren. He introduced himself. James recognized the name as a developing legend in Manitoba youth hockey. But he had not realized how small the boy was. As hockey scouts do, James filed the Fleury name away in his memory.

He knew the youngster was not allowed to play contact hockey at the camp. The family, or someone, had written that loud and clear on the application form. And the boy had announced his temporary limitations just as eagerly as he performed every hockey drill all week.

Wally and Donna Fleury did not mind others sending their son to camp or involving him in athletic activities. In many cases, they didn't know about it. Donna felt sufficiently overwhelmed by housework, overseeing her two younger boys, and the threats of daily life that, as far as she was concerned, the absence of Theo was just fine. Often, in the evening she would ask him about his day and Theo would reply as fully as he felt the need to.

It took quite a while, adults being adults and as stubbornly realistic as they are, for the fourteen-year-old to convince the grownups in his life that he was going to get well enough to play hockey again.

"I remember," Wally says, "we were watching television together real quiet like one evening right on this couch. His arm was hurting him a lot. There were a lot of days like that. He was just sitting there holding his right arm close to himself with the other one. He never complained, but you knew it hurt a lot. And he looks over at me and he says, 'Dad, I think when this arm gets good, I'm going for it.'

"Of course, I knew what he meant. I kind of swallowed, you know, 'cause I didn't think at that point the NHL was going to be for him. And I said, 'Okay, but one day at a time, boy. You're going to miss one whole year of hockey.'

"And he says to me, 'I know. But I'm going to skate every day. And the doctor says golf is good for it. So I'm going to play golf every day. And I don't think I'll be far out.'

"And I looked over at him. He was even smaller after The Injury than he was before. He was looking up at me, holding that arm real tight, and looking up at his old man. No way could I say I'd been a doubter. And I said, 'Well, son, you've got the skills. You're a super skater and a super shooter. You've got great hands and good eyes. You've got the speed and the love of it. If you have a dream, you have to follow it.'

"And, you know, I think my boy taught me something that day."

Of course, progress was not constant throughout the year. Theoren had to test the rules at times, do some things he shouldn't, if only because someone said he shouldn't. One summer evening Theoren did not show up at the motel as usual. Ede became suspicious, like a parent suddenly noticing the absence of noise from a child's busy bedroom in mid-afternoon. She drove over to the ball park just to check. Sure enough, there was Theoren playing second base for Russell. He saw her coming. Ede walked right onto the field. The game stopped. She said nothing, but held her forefinger up and beckoned Theoren towards her. "C'mon," she said, "let's go."

No one protested to that woman that night, not even Theoren. They could see her face. Theo followed Ede off the field and into her car where he sounded angry but acted obedient. They went for an ice cream together.

Later, the coach called to complain. Theoren was an important team member, he said, and Theo wasn't complaining about his arm. "I see," said Ede, "and when he gets hit on that arm and can't use it for the rest of his life, are you going to stop by his house every day and say, 'Them's the breaks, boy, but it was great having you on the team'?"

One time at a party Theo tried to show off his handicap. Might as well get some use out of it. He stuck his finger in the flame of a candle and held it there to impress everyone with his stamina. Actually, he could not feel a thing. The flesh got burned and then infected. "Exactly what were you thinking?" Ede asked. Theo shrugged. He'll still show anyone the scar.

When hockey started in the fall, Theo went to all of the practices and skated. He never missed a team game, made all the trips, and always shouted encouragement. He even offered teammates advice on moves that might work against certain opponents. "I knew," Coach Fowler says, "how much it hurt for Theo not to play. But he'd cheer his mates on and lead songs in the car coming home. Those times showed me he was definitely a real team player."

"Hurt?" recalls Theo. "I was dying inside because I couldn't play. But I could hang around with the guys and I could still skate, do the skating drills and stuff. That had to be enough for me for then, I guess." Also, for a few dollars Theo would referee other hockey games, even adult games, anything to get on the ice. These games included some involving his father. But that didn't affect Theo's penalty calls. "Oh," says Wally, laughing, "he called 'em straight, real straight. He'd call me as quick as anyone. One time he saw me trip someone and, boy, his arm went right up and he looked at me and said, 'Yes, you did.' I skated over to argue. He sticks his finger right in my face, like this, and says, 'Don't!'

"So I didn't."

Sometimes Theo would suggest to Ede that he could play hockey because, after all, it had been many months since the operation. "You do," Ede said, "and when you come out for warmups, you're going to find two women, your mom and me, sitting at centre ice knitting." Theo seemed to enjoy that response and sought it many times.

There was some grumbling in the café about Len and Ede's rigidity in holding out Russell's best youth athlete from important competitions. But that did not affect her resolve. When Ede heard a rumour that Theoren was secretly scheduled to play in a hockey tournament in Carberry one weekend, she and Len drove the 130 or so miles to be there. Just before every Russell game that weekend, the two of them appeared near the Russell bench in case anyone had any crazy ideas. Number 9 did not play. And Theoren didn't know about those parental patrols until many years later.

Ede dates the turning point in Theo's recovery to a conversation in her car on the return journey from yet another discouraging visit with the doctor in Winnipeg. Theoren said he still thought he would play in the NHL some day. Ede knew what the doctors thought. But there's something about Theoren's fierce determination and careless optimism that eventually convinces others of the impossible. Ede said, "Well, if you are seriously interested and really want to try and play hockey and go into Junior and improve yourself, I will promise you one thing: I promise that as long as your drive and your energy are what they are, I will support you in any way I can. You give me your commitment and desire and dedication – and, boy, did he ever teach me the meaning of commitment – and I will give you my time. But when your desire stops, then mine will, too."

Theo simply said, "Deal."

To this day, whenever she is at Theo's games, Ede usually wears the number-14 Calgary Flames jersey he gave her and perhaps the number-14 earrings he gave her. And across the distance from the stands to the rink, they exchange a secret signal.

"It wasn't long after the conversation in the car," Ede says, "that it became clear Theo was going to be able to return to hockey and move up to the next level."

"Ede and I would go into the specialist in Winnipeg every month," Theo recalls. "We'd talk on the way. I'd get my hopes up, big time – bigger and bigger every month – that this time he was going to let me play. And absolutely every time I went in there I just got totally crushed. Totally. He'd say, 'There's no way you can play. You just can't play yet.' But I knew I was going to play again. So I'd tell him that. I'd say, 'You know, I am going to play hockey again.' And he'd say, 'Well, not yet.' But I knew what I was going to do."

Almost an entire year passed. March came again. To some people, the uninformed and uninvolved, March might mean that in a few weeks the ground would no longer be as hard as iron. To others on the prairies and across Canada, those families with hockey schedules stuck on their refrigerators, March means tournament time. Life on the ice is sudden-death. The doctor had won a reprieve from Theoren's silent anger by finally issuing his medical clearance. Russell was facing Roblin at home in front of the hometown crowd. It was Theoren Fleury's first shift in his first game since The Injury. Could the kid make a comeback, at age fourteen?

Theo took the opening faceoff. He skated towards the goal. He shot that puck. He scored.

"It was totally weird." Theo says. "Weird but good, like I'd never been away. But it was wonderful. I knew I could do it then."

About two weeks later a small package arrived at Winnipeg Children's Hospital. It was addressed to Dr. Robertson. Inside was a hockey puck. On it was a small plaque. It carried the simple date: March 4, 1983. It also carried an even simpler message: Thank you.

❖

One of the best birthday gifts Matthew Naylor ever got was his Theo Fleury hockey jersey. It's a home jersey, white with lots of red, some gold, and Fleury's name on the back with a huge number 14. It wasn't cheap. But Dave and Sheila Naylor made the investment for their seven-year-old son because Matthew likes Theo, and Matthew's parents like the idea of their boy admiring a public figure, like Fleury, associated with excellence.

Many parents even use that juvenile admiration at times to instil desirable patterns of behaviour or useful lessons for life, speculating out loud, for instance, that Theo would likely be going to bed in good time the night before a game. Fleury, of course, knows nothing of the important formative role he is playing in such families, though he might suspect something were he to look simultaneously into the eyes of such youngsters and their parents when they happen to see him.

Matthew even got his shirt signed by Theo Fleury at a hallway encounter once, one of many the hero willingly signed that day, which means Sheila has to be extra careful to preserve the signature when that shirt shows up in the laundry. Matthew may remind her to be careful, just in case.

There is a Theo Fleury poster in Matthew's room, too. It was one of the first things that went up after the Naylors moved into their new house. Matthew can see the blown-up photo of Theo in action from his bed. Theo Fleury in action is the last thing Matthew sees when he goes to sleep at night and Theo Fleury is the first person Matthew sees when he wakes up. Theo is always there. In fact, the image of Theo Fleury lives in many homes like an extra family member. When anyone talks about "Theo," everyone knows exactly who they mean.

Before Matthew goes to bed on Flames game nights, he and his father watch the sports news on TV to make sure they know what happened that day, because normal slumber would be impossible without that knowledge. At breakfast before leaving for school every morning after a game night, Matthew and his dad read the sports pages together. They check the Flames' box score to see how Theo and the Flames did and exchange thoughts on what that means and what the team could have done differently.

"There's a lot of guy talk at breakfast about momentum and the playoffs," Sheila says. Though she's a fading Leafs fan and still an Oilers fan, Sheila rather likes to see that shared father-son passion. It makes her feel good somehow, as if life is proceeding normally, at least her family's life. So she also cheers for the Flames if only to promote peace at home.

"When the Flames win," she says, "they're both so happy, especially when Theo scores. And they're both down and sad when they don't. But it doesn't really matter to Matthew. He loves Theo anyway, no matter what."

So, what is it about this man who passed Matthew in a hallway once that causes the little boy among many to hang the player's picture by the bed, wear a shirt just like the player's, and check the newspaper most mornings to see how the player's day went at work? "I like Theo best," he says, "because he's small – like me. And feisty – like me."

Four or five times a year father and son plan a hockey outing together. They pick an opponent they haven't seen yet or lately. Dave gets two tickets, usually for a Saturday or Sunday game. The afternoon games are best. Sheila plans a matching outing somewhere with their five-year-old daughter, Nicole, who does not like hockey or her brother most days.

Like hundreds of young people and some not-so-young at every home game, Matthew naturally wears his Fleury shirt and perhaps a Flames hat for good measure. You can see them all over the stands. Sometimes they get their picture on the Jumbotron. Even some dads wear Fleury shirts. Ritually on game days, the Naylor males head out early for the Saddledome because it is very important for team luck and momentum for the pair to be in their seats and game-ready to witness the warmups in their entirety. The pair also hits the men's room on the way in, so there need not be any interruption during actual play.

"There he is!" Matthew announces. And Matthew's father knows who "he" is. They might discuss how "he" looks during the warmups, how focused "he" seems, how "he" doesn't always wear his helmet to warm up, how "he" even helps pass out the pucks for shooting practice, how "he" can move the puck so delicately and precisely, and exactly when "he" leaves the ice for the team's final pregame meeting in the locker room somewhere mysterious down that dark ramp under the far stands where no doubt magical things happen.

Magic is a crucial ingredient to merchandising professional sports, as Mark Mason knows. He is director of retailing and merchandising for the Flames, a job he designed and won in 1988 despite his lifelong allegiance to the Chicago Blackhawks. Hockey had been an integral part of his Calgary childhood since he tried to get his Grandpa Mason's attention in the living room and was shooed away. "Don't bother me, son," the old man said. "There's a Leafs game on."

"Grandpa had never put on a skate," Mark said, "but he was mesmerized by the game. You pick up on that kind of thinking." So Mark played hockey every day for the rest of his childhood, into Junior, and, now well into his thirties, three nights a week in senior play. When Mark grew tired of selling furniture, selling hockey stuff seemed a natural thing to do. He joined the Flames about the same time Fleury was finishing in Junior.

In one sense merchandising hockey is easy in Canada and, increasingly, in the States. "When sports merchandising exploded in the 1980s," Mark said, "people obviously wanted to be associated with winners. It's the bandwagon effect. That explains all of the Bulls, 49ers, Cowboys, and, more recently, Avalanche paraphernalia you saw on people's heads and backs. But now, we seem to be getting back more to local and regional team allegiances."

The NHL has merchandising agreements with about three hundred companies to use league and team logos on everything from trading cards, credit cards, and video games to clothing, lamps, towels, and street-hockey gear. It's about a billion-dollar-a-year business at the retail level. Royalties are split evenly among all teams. Clothing and other items featuring individual players are licensed separately by the National Hockey League Players' Association, which keeps the royalties.

"Our goal," said Rick Dudley of NHL Enterprises, the league's marketing arm, "is to have hockey everywhere. We draw the line, however, at hockey toilet seats." Indeed, every hockey shirt or hat is not only an individual sale, it transforms that head or body into a walking advertisement for the sport. Licensing sales have grown 600 per cent in five years, Dudley says. Part of that has been continued expansion of products such as additional third jerseys, which is, in a business sense, just like Campbell's adding a new soup or Dairy Queen a new flavour. Third jerseys, which every team will get eventually, are carefully designed, tested for consumer appeal, and must be approved by the league.

Expansion can also come by adding teams, which not only brings $80 million each in initiation fees split among existing owners, but also expands the television markets for home teams and the audiences exposed to the sport in general. An Albertan hockey fan is quite likely to watch, say, a Toronto–Detroit game on TV. Until Florida sports fans had their own teams, they were unlikely to watch any hockey, or so American thinking goes. For now, American television viewership, and therefore the money, is largest where the game is played. So the league intends to locate in the largest TV markets and let the spaces in between fill in over time with fans newly exposed to the game through TV.

Merchandise tastes vary by region, according to Dudley. Merchandise for the NHL's original six teams – Boston, Chicago, Detroit, Montreal, New York's Rangers, and Toronto – tends to sell better than others, reflecting the enduring appeal of nostalgia or heritage symbols, especially if they win the Stanley Cup. The newer teams are freer to innovate. League-wide, sales of Flames merchandise rank in the second tier of teams, Dudley says, behind the original six, Colorado, and the Mighty Ducks.

But in Calgary, of course, Flames merchandise far outsells that of any other team. And anything with Fleury's name on it far outsells anyone else's. "As soon as Theo arrived here," Mark Mason says, "he became the most popular player for merchandise. If it's got Fleury's name on it, it'll sell. He sticks out, giving

110 per cent every night. People want to be associated with that kind of talent, skill, and success." Each season Flames players go through two sets of home and away jerseys. Fleury's four used jerseys will bring a thousand dollars each in one of the Flames' three retail stores.

Part of Mark's job is to keep Flames merchandise up-to-date. He knows from his marketing experience that Canadian consumers, including Calgarians, are historically uninterested in running out to buy the newest anything, the way Americans are. But still, each year Mark will approve some new design on the hats, a new patch on the jerseys, or a new-style T-shirt, just to keep the Flames' image fresh and hip, though he must anticipate what will be fashionable months in advance. Mark must ship those designs and orders off to manufacturers in Asia by December to be ready to sell them the following autumn.

To Mark, though, merchandising Flames gear has two major points. First, of course, it provides income for the club. "We have only forty-one days a year to sell our home games," says Mark, who wears a Flames hat in his office. "But with our stores and catalogue we can sell merchandise 365 days a year."

Second, Mark sees merchandise as a teaching tool to promote a more daily, routine kind of loyalty among fans rather than an episodic one tied only to the team's games. "We need to re-educate the fans today to support their team through thick and thin," says the man who is still waiting for his Blackhawks to win their first Cup since 1961. "Too many people now are into instant gratification and if the team loses a few games, they fade as fans. What kind of fan is that? Being a fan should not be based on last night's box score. Being a fan should be a lifelong continuum, like it is for kids."

In fact, sometimes a day or two after attending a Flames game in his Fleury jersey with his dad, Matthew Naylor can be hard-pressed to recall the exact score. It's not the score that really seems to matter. It's the whole day's experience and excitement that he cherishes, talking about various aspects of the athletic spectacle for days afterwards with his dad and buddies at school.

And for Matthew and everyone else in the Saddledome that spectacle starts with the pregame festivities. That's when the huge arena suddenly falls into total darkness and the Calgary fans grow even more silent and the big Jumbotron screen shows the colourful video with the flaming comet hurtling noisily out of space towards earth in general and Alberta in particular and Calgary specifically. It plummets so rapidly at that familiar skyline, streaking faster and faster straight for the Saddledome with a wraparound roar that says something very big is on its way, something very big is about to happen. And just when that flaming body from space is about to hit the very building where the fans are sitting, without warning fireworks explode from the scoreboard. The lights flash on. And there are the Flames, his Flames and his Fleury, leaping onto the glaring ice with those bright uniforms and confident strides so full of hope and energy and promise for this new game.

And Matthew and his dad are right there in person, together, not only to witness but to own the entire experience. "Yes!" Matthew will exclaim.

Neither father nor son need say out loud how great that moment is; Dave Naylor patting his son's knee says it all. Matthew smiles at the touch. Absolutely nothing has happened on the ice and yet these two are already having the greatest time. Together, they will moan and groan and cheer throughout the action. With everyone else, they will object vocally if the referee misses a flagrant foul on Theo. Their emotions will rise and fall with the fortunes of their gladiators on the ice. The father and son actually will feel the same momentum they know is felt on the ice.

It all seems so much more exciting in person. Their allegiance to the Flames is compounded exponentially by sharing it with so many other partisans in the same room. When the other team scores, many slump in their seats in silent disappointment. When the Flames score, though, Matthew and his father will be so excited together and so busy high-fiving that they will forget to look up at the ceiling. They only feel the blast of heat on their foreheads from the twin yellow propane flames that explode briefly above them. But it'll be exhilarating nonetheless.

And if it's number 14 who shot that puck, then life very suddenly is very good. Matthew will start yelling before that announcer with the familiar voice even gets Theo's first name out.

With the clarity of youthful vision, Matthew notes how busy the Flames games are. Every moment there is something going on somewhere. If it's between periods, some lucky fans are shooting pucks or basketballs down on the ice for a chance to win a Chrysler Canada product just like the one now being driven onto the ice with its blinking lights pleading, "Look at me, look at me." Two youth teams put on a mini-scrimmage for a sponsor while the pro players rest in the locker room.

During each period, Matthew is unaware that there are at least four seventy-second pauses in play. These have nothing to do with player rest periods; they are for TV and radio commercials, the extra price that ticket-buyers must pay in time waiting so that thousands of people in their Alberta homes or back in Toronto, Ottawa, Chicago, and Philadelphia can see and hear the same game for free.

According to the modern rules of mass entertainment, those times and other shorter pauses in play can never be left void in the arena. Something must be happening somewhere at every moment. And if that certain something also brings in money, so much the better. So these times are filled with a variety of commercial promotions. The Jumbotron video screen shows a compilation of this week's hardest, on-ice player collisions from around the league, called "Crunch Time." As soon as it is done,

Flames employees distribute Nestlé Crunch candy bars free in some lucky section of seats. A moving company sponsors "the move" of two fans from seats high in the Saddledome down closer to the ice. Lucky numbers are hidden in every Flames program, giving the holder a chance to win Flames merchandise. Canadian Airlines may run a promotion for a free flight for two to somewhere outside Canada that is warmer than Calgary.

One section of seats may get free Tim Hortons donuts or Little Caesar's pizzas, if they yell loudly enough. One fan gets on the Jumbotron screen to sing for his or her supper, a free dinner at a local restaurant. Another gets a chance to answer a hockey trivia question while eighteen thousand kibitzers yell their own answers. There is the SportChek Loot Launcher, a bazooka-like air gun that can fire wadded T-shirts from the rink into the highest reaches of the Saddledome, if that section yells loudly enough.

And then there is Harvey the Hound, the Flames' mascot. "Harvey is a big, playful puppy who wants to meet everyone and try everything but is not always successful," says Grant Kelba, who is thirty-seven years old. Although he never owned a real dog as a child and still doesn't, Grant ought to know. He is Harvey during Flames games. Or maybe Harvey is Grant between games.

It's so hard to tell, and the identity of Harvey's human is supposed to be a secret. What is not a secret is the almost universal appeal of this mute dog. According to some Flames employees, Harvey is a great mascot, and Grant is a little weird, the way goalies can be weird. This might be explained by Grant's having spent almost half of a lifetime inside a dog, intentionally. "Harvey and I," says Grant, the pair's spokesman, "just try to create little magic moments for people here and there wherever we go together."

The pressures of being a team mascot today can be great. And with the explosive global growth of team mascots, the

Flames hardly being the only pro sports outfit that wants pleasing entertainment between plays, Harvey (or Grant) is very busy advising and consulting teams all over the world on how to be publicly lovable without speaking. Harvey the Hound, Consulting Mascot. The last four digits of Harvey's phone number, by the way, are RUFF.

First of all, you need to know that Grant (or Harvey) is a performer, not a cheerleader. There's a big difference. Harvey might act like a cheerleader at times, when he's banging a drum, for instance. Actually, that's a signal to Willy the organist way upstairs in the sound booth. Cheerleaders, especially professional ones, are sideline sycophants who would likely be ignored by spectators were it not for their obvious and strategic lack of clothing.

So Grant is a performer who rehearses, psyches himself up for big games, fusses over Harvey's costume, does physical training, gets butterflies before going on, and appreciates applause, though he can hear little of it inside all that ersatz fur. Grant (or Harvey) is also a rare creature, a native of Calgary. So much of that mushrooming city's population – now approaching one million – is like Fleury, virtually all of his teammates, at times his coaches, general manager, and president: they come from somewhere else to an emerging metropolis large enough to provide urban diversity yet sufficiently small to let individuals feel they can still make a difference.

When Grant first began to realize he was destined to live a dog's life, Fleury was scoring a hundred goals a year in a Manitoba kids' league of under-twelves and telling everyone who would listen that some day he would play in the NHL. Everyone also thought Grant couldn't do it. A few even said so. Think about it: Someone just emerging from his teens announces to family and friends he has this idea to build his career around a mascot that a team would hire to entertain spectators by doing goofy and endearing things whenever nothing was happening in the game.

You're going to make a living as a grown man pretending to be a dog? Well, good luck to you, Grant. We'll be sure to watch for you.

But Grant didn't listen to the non-believers. "Speaking for both of us," says Grant, "we are Theo Fleury fans, big time, very big time. Against all odds he has succeeded. Forget the odds, everyone said he couldn't do it. And he didn't just make it. He succeeded at it. Wouldn't we, each one of us, like to be able to say that about ourselves? I know Harvey would."

Grant was determined, very determined, to become Harvey or something like him. And nothing was going to stop him. He practised and practised and practised. He watched animals. He watched people. He watched cartoons. He watched people watching animals in cartoons.

Grant instinctively understands the engaging appeal of anthropomorphism. That's the big non-cuddly word for the powerful, relentless, and never-ending Western, especially North American, cultural and emotional drive to attribute human feelings and characteristics to most mammals. North Americans even name these animals, be they cartoon bears (Yogi), tigers (Tony), horses (Black Beauty), elephants (Dumbo), dolphins (Willy), mice (Mickey, Minnie, and Fievel), rabbits (Bugs, Thumper, and Easter), reindeer (Dasher, Dancer, and six friends), kitty cats (Sylvester), deer (Bambi), chipmunks (Chip and Dale), pigs (Porky), coyotes (Wile E.), or ducks (Donald, Daisy, and Scrooge). We endow these characters with all kinds of human qualities – love, anger, jealousy, fear, mischievousness, hunger, stupidity, revenge, longing – every human drive save perhaps sex.

In Asia, families eat dogs while talking at dinner. In North America, families eat dinner while talking to dogs. They may even hand-feed their dogs from the table, if the animals sit and beg politely. Truly, North Americans love their dogs – Lassie and Pluto and Benji and, well, Old Yeller. Fleury and his wife

Veronica live with two dogs – Hat Trick and Ditto. When Theoren leaves home for a game at the Saddledome, he turns on the TV to keep the dogs company; he even selects a channel showing hockey. And when Veronica taped the recorded message on the telephone answering machine at their lakeside home with the hockey rink cleared off the ice out back, she naturally included the dogs' names among those unable to come to the phone right now.

So what better character for Grant to become than a dog? Grant has long admired dogs' basic friendliness, loyalty, faithfulness, and, above all, their unconditional and ever-forgiving love. He modelled Harvey on the Siberian Husky, a sled-dog breed famous on Canada's frontier for its work ethic, loyalty, endurance. Endurance is a big deal in the Canadian psyche. "How's it going, eh?" Canadians ask each other. "Not too bad," is the inevitable reply, as if that's the best one can hope for.

Grant's first incarnation as a canine was named Ralph. Grant and Ralph performed along the sidelines at the football games of the Calgary Stampeders. Not as exciting as a live horse galloping about, but Ralph was very popular. And then in 1983, Grant got his big break.

The Calgary Flames were still new in town, trying to establish a team identity. They were looking for a mascot. But which one? If the Calgary Flames were in Europe, they'd likely be named for a natural-gas company which would dress someone up as a flame and call him Sparky. He would become, in effect, a walking corporate logo.

In North America, however, the Calgary Sparkies just wouldn't catch fire. Teams often are named after large animals, though birds are okay if they are tough like bluejays or cardinals. Team names are supposed to connote something strong and powerful (unless the team is owned by Disney, which can be cute). The mascot should be something fans can identify with, something possibly catchy, but surely something distinctive with appealing, test-marketed colours that the fans will want to spend lots of money on and wear all over their bodies.

Lions and Tigers are good, Panthers, too. Sabres, Bruins, Hurricanes, Kings, Jets, Devils, Lightning, Senators, Sharks are strong. An Avalanche can kill people, but the name might do if we put a cartoon Big Foot on the shoulder. Or Stars. Maybe something patriotic or chauvinistic – Canadiens or Canucks. Something professional or regional – Oilers, Capitols, Blackhawks, Islanders. But, for instance, you'd never want to name a team after parts of an animal's anatomy, like the wings, or after some goofy animal that waddles on the ice like a penguin. Or how about naming a pro sports team after a leaf? There's an exciting name.

So the challenge for the then public-relations director of the Calgary hockey club in 1983 was to find a mascot that fit the Flames. Al Coates had on his desk a four-inch pile of detailed mascot proposals. On the phone he asked Grant Kelba how this dog character of his would be any different. Shortly after, an immense, friendly Harvey the Hound sauntered into the Flames' public-relations office with an amazing amount of unwarranted confidence, silently shook Coates's hand, and then licked it.

Grant (or Harvey) became a Flames entertainment subcontractor. Harvey appears without fail at every single Flames home game – forty-one regular-season appearances, plus exhibition and playoffs. On his own, Harvey accepts another two hundred or so public appearances from private parties to shopping-centre openings, and probably turns down another two hundred invitations. He has become so popular locally that a hockey team of real tykes chose to name itself after the pro team's pretend mascot: Harvey's Hounds.

It all makes for additional free exposure for the Flames and additional income for both Harvey and Grant. "The harder Harvey works," says Grant, who drives him pretty hard, "the more additional opportunities I create." Currently, there are Harvey dolls, Harvey pins, Harvey T-shirts, Harvey keychains, Harvey pucks, Harvey posters, and, best of all, Harvey trading cards.

Grant chose the name Harvey because it is appealingly alliterative, Harvey the Hound. And it sounds better than, say, Desmond the Dog. "And how," Grant wonders out loud, "can someone named Harvey not be your friend?"

Harvey is actually quite large. He is basically grey with a white face, belly, and left arm. He has no tail. "If Harvey had a tail," says Grant, "you might as well post a sign: 'Pull me.'" Harvey's eyes are very blue and perpetually open, as is his friendly, possibly panting mouth with the long tongue hanging out. With his little hat perched on his huge head and his ears perpetually perked up, Harvey stands about seven feet tall on two legs and acts just like an irrepressible puppy.

He usually wears red shorts to go with his red cowboy hat. On New Year's Eve, of course, Harvey dresses up with the Calgary crowd and dons a tuxedo. He also has appeared as a canine Batman, a dog-eared Elvis, and a large-nosed Phantom of the Opera. During the recent Dalmatian craze the hound showed up for work wearing 102 black spots.

Harvey is everybody's friend, even drunks. When some spectator, who has perhaps had ample beer, starts acting up and trying to steal Harvey's spotlight, the dog will watch this little spectacle quietly for a few moments, his head tilted quizzically. Then, the dog will shrug. He will remove his red collar labelled Harvey. He will place it around the drunk's neck. And Harvey will take the drunk's seat to watch the game.

"This is without a doubt the best job in the entire world," Grant says. "You can be a friend to every single person you meet and no one looks like they think you're crazy." Grant says he and Harvey especially watch for bored youngsters. "We come up to everyone with our tail wagging, figuratively speaking," he explains. "How could they not like us, right? It's me, Harvey." Men tend to be a little more reserved towards Harvey, Grant says, especially if they're wearing a necktie but not if they've been drinking. Children can be intimidated by the animal's size. So Harvey lets them approach him. The back of the paws on each four-thousand-dollar costume are intentionally very soft. "As soon as they feel softness," Grant observes, "the kids are Harvey's pals."

Grant was surprised that women are the most forward with Harvey. "Maybe a mascot makes it safer to be flirtatious," he says, "but every woman greets Harvey warmly and with a smile." In an instant, women will dance with Harvey or high-five or hug. One time a woman in the stands ripped open her blouse to bare her chest to Harvey. Harvey stood there, tilted his head this way and then that. Then, the dog turned around to thousands of onlookers. And he shrugged.

But Harvey's work is hard because he is a very physical hound. Grant must be in fine shape. It helps that he's around fitness buffs; he sells physical-fitness vacations and health spas on the side. And he works out year-round, there being no off-season for Harvey. The biggest crowd responses come to Harvey when he appears to risk life and limb in one of his stunts. There are the times he somersaults off a mini-trampoline – in skates. The crowd seems to love someone, even a mascot, who just keeps trying hard. And what team would not want its members or mascot to be known for trying hard?

But pleasing the crowd has a physical price; Harvey never gets hurt but Grant has separated both shoulders, hyperextended both knees, twisted his back. "Harvey likes to push the envelope physically," Grant says, shaking his head over the dog's eagerness to please the crowd. "He'll try anything several times." He will even walk along the top of the glass surrounding the rink, exhorting the crowd.

Suddenly, Harvey will seem to fall straight down with the glass between his legs. That brings an audible groan from many onlookers. Harvey's body stiffens. He tumbles off the glass completely and lands on the ground, arms and legs sticking straight up. He bounces back up. Clearly, the dog meant to do that – or means for us to think so. He's fine. Everyone cheers. He'll surely try again later.

If the score of one of those between-periods youth-hockey scrimmages becomes lopsided, Harvey is likely to hassle the goalie of the leading team, move the net to catch a wide shot, or perhaps start a snowball fight with players. If the game ends in a tie, Harvey is very happy.

But when the real hockey game is on, Harvey is usually off. "The fans don't want to miss one second of the game," Grant says, "so we usually sit down, or else we're hustling through the concourse to get in position for the next break." An unobtrusive assistant usually hovers nearby, warning Harvey of unseen obstacles and the clock. He will say, "Giveaway at the thirteen-minute mark in section 103." Harvey will dispense just enough hugs and shake just enough hands in section 230 so that he is at the top of the steps in 103 with 13:05 left in the period when, from on high, the voice of Allan Beesley says, "And now in section 103 Harvey has a gift for a special someone."

The spotlight and Jumbotron camera instantly find Harvey – a seven-foot dog not being that hard to spot even in the Saddledome. Suddenly, Harvey is on for his thirty-second mini-play without dialogue. "Essentially," Grant says, "Harvey is a mime. So everything, every gesture or motion of his, needs to be exaggerated. Harvey is relating to one fan, but he is also playing to eighteen thousand others plus the TV camera. So he's got to know where he is at all times, even inside that suffocating outfit. He just tries to create warm memories wherever he goes."

The game resumes. Harvey finds an attractive woman near an aisle. He invites her male escort to stand and shake the dog's hand. Then Harvey takes the escort's seat. Later, he'll make his way to the next spot, or take time to wander down by the opposition team's bench to gesture defiantly, safely behind the glass.

There are, of course, some things Harvey will never do. "Harvey never wants to come on too strong," Grant observes. "He will never shine the heads of bald men. Harvey will lick the ladies' hands, but not their faces." Also, Harvey does not lift his leg on anyone.

Grant is typically nervous before a game. So two hours before game time, about the same time Theo Fleury is driving into the Saddledome parking lot in his new pickup truck, Grant too arrives. Grant and Harvey have a pregame meal together. As soon as that Harvey head goes on and the strap on the football helmet inside is snapped, there is no Grant Kelba. "When I'm Harvey," says Grant, "I'm Harvey – for three people or twenty thousand." At those times there is only the creature who answers to Harvey. He will mingle with the arriving crowd, pose for pictures, issue hugs, and turn thumbs down at anyone wearing the other team's shirts or hats.

"The purpose of a mascot," Grant says, "is for an identifiable character to provide additional entertainment and stimulation to paying customers at an event. The team can't control what happens on the ice so it needs to ensure entertainment off the ice. Fans want to come for the overall experience and not just for a win. We're treating them less like fans now and more like guests. What a wonderful change!"

"Actually," Grant confides, "this is a very lonely job. Very satisfying but very lonely. You can't talk. You can hardly hear, just some cheers if they're loud for a goal or something. Hockey is the most difficult sport for a mascot. There is no sideline. The sport moves so fast. Everything is tight quarters. Steps are everywhere. I end up inside talking to myself a whole lot, saying out loud to myself what I want the people to see Harvey saying outside through his motions."

Several times during the game Harvey will disappear into a locker room to replenish some of the ten pounds in fluids Grant will lose during the five hours of Harvey's life from arrival until the game's end. If he sweats too much, he may even have to change costumes. Only then do Harvey and Grant discover the score of the game they are at. So Grant often tapes the game at home to watch later.

"These games could be a ballet for all I know in there," Grant says. "Fleury and the guys have the ice to play on. I have the entire stands."

So does Karla Piper. But no one sees her.

Karla Piper is what happens when the daughter of a minor-league defenceman from Saskatchewan gives up figure skating for marketing. She sits unobtrusively in the handicapped seats, speaking quietly into a headset and directing the entire entertainment extravaganza that these hockey games have become and that all the people around her, including Matthew Naylor and his dad, have come to expect but don't know is being controlled from the next section.

"We'll do the shootout at the second," Karla says into her mouthpiece in her own showbiz shorthand. "As soon as the Yahoo goes we'll go right to the S.O.J." More than a dozen people are on Karla's communications network around the Saddledome: cameramen like Neil Scott, Mark Fuller, and Ron Ratke; Rocky Anderson on the sound board; trumpeters like Ken Shoults; Dave Glowaski, the fiddler; plus Harvey's assistant, Kevin Hogg; Willy Joosen on the keyboard; Beesley on the loudspeaker; Mark Neustaedter, an announcer who roams the stands, and Brian Funfer, who runs the Jumbotron from a windowless cubicle in the basement.

The actual hockey game may be spontaneous and unpredictable. But for the last several days Karla has been writing a thirty-two-page script that will control everything the crowd hears and sees whenever play stops. She knows when the pizzas will arrive, when the Loot Launcher will launch, what time in the game the Telus Trivia Question should come on, when she wants to show the *Calgary Herald*'s Face of the Game, when the

Santa Fe restaurant's Sing for Your Supper promo will happen, when Crunch Time will be shown, at what point the league's Saves of the Week video will run, and precisely what time the CBC needs Tony Rino to start singing "O Canada."

It's a tricky business directing a show within a game. So right about the time Fleury is shucking his street clothes in the locker room, Karla gathers her team in the grandstands for a run-through. It is particularly tricky to have a Chrysler Neon driven onto the ice for three contestants to shoot baskets and pucks for and get everyone off safely in nine minutes so that Mike Duben and Keith Thomson can have their four minutes and fifty seconds to prepare the ice so the thin layer of warm water will have time to freeze just before the CBC's Canadian Tire ad ends and the network switches back to the Saddledome for a brief narrative introduction to the next period's play.

Down below the grandstands in an unmarked room sits a key player in Karla's entertainment arsenal. For many recent games it has been Brian Funfer, a nervous thirty-seven-year-old natty dresser who can chew gum, tap a pencil, and run a twenty-two-ton scoreboard at the same time. From this room, which is soundproof until Calgary scores, Brian and his seven-person crew can control the scoreboard, the recorded music, and the game pictures shown on the TV monitors by the concourse food stands. Flames management determined that fear of missing some exciting plays was keeping too many people in their seats and away from buying food and drinks.

Brian has vivid memories of childhood hockey games on cold Saturday afternoons followed by hot chocolate in the living room while he watched Bugs Bunny cartoons until dozing off on the couch. He would awaken to the smells of dinner cooking and the sounds of "Hockey Night in Canada," featuring the Maple Leafs or Canadiens.

To Theoren Fleury, who is by now taping his sticks just down the hall, and to Brian's mother, who once again will be yelling at the refs and the Flames' opposition on her TV or radio, the athletic encounter on these nights is a game. To Brian, the entire game is a show.

By the mid-afternoon before an evening game Brian is feeling the butterflies. He will eat a hearty pregame meal, maybe a steak. Although no one but his jeans-clad crew will see him, Brian has donned a dark pinstripe suit with a red tie and his tasselled loafers. He'll come into his windowless world and go over Karla's script, pick some of the rock music he wants ready on the computerized sound system, check the electronic gear with his crew, and remind everyone of past mistakes to avoid.

"I don't like the butterflies," he admits. "But I do like the adrenaline rush just before the first faceoff when you know you are as ready as you can be. You've practised. You've prepared. You don't know exactly what's going to happen, but you know you'll be challenged and you know everybody will be watching and you hope to be as prepared as possible. This is the Big Time right here. I try to remember what it was like to be sitting in my seat at the game and wondering what was going on. When that whistle blows to stop play, I want every set of eyes looking up at my Jumbotron." In fact, close scrutiny of both players' benches reveals that many of them watch the game on the Jumbotron as well.

Brian will remind his cameramen what to look for at various times. Part of Brian's job is to balance what gets shown on the giant screen, roughly equal numbers of beautiful women and handsome men and lots of cute children in families. "We'll come out of replay," he says into his microphone, moving the gum more rapidly now, "and go to a kid."

Mark Fuller is on camera one, the one in the stands that can swivel like a turret gun. He swings his camera around to find what he knows Brian wants, a kid. And that kid better be wearing some kind of Flames gear, preferably a jersey and hat. Brian will keep the kid's picture on the screen until the youngster suddenly sees himself eight feet tall and eleven feet wide. The youngster begins to jump up and down and wave. Brian cannot hear the chuckles sweeping the crowd, but he knows they are there. He will have handed out fifteen seconds of lifetime fame to one more person and filled one more entertainment void with a warm moment.

Later will come a sleeping baby, several people with faces painted in Flames colours, and perhaps a young woman and her boyfriend who plans to propose as soon as Brian flashes their images for all to see. The woman is shocked, sees herself, covers her face, and hugs her new fiancé. The crowd applauds. Ten minutes later Brian will order the camera back on the couple. As soon as everyone can see them, Brian orders two words added to the screen: "SHE ACCEPTED." Now, the crowd cheers.

In fact, Brian can seem to direct the crowd's reactions like some absentee orchestra conductor. He orders up a tight shot of Fleury's intense face on the bench. Theo is usually chewing one lip. Thousands of cheers erupt, many from children, if the higher pitch is to be believed.

Brian talks to Neil Scott on camera two. His camera cable keeps Neil closely tethered to the Olympia entrance. "Everyone gets their fifteen minutes of fame," says Neil. "My job is helping people do that."

Neil is not a big-time hockey fan, but he is a serious Fleury fan. "That guy is a heckuva digger," says Neil, another working man. "He makes up for small size with big drive and big heart." Neil knows he has to look for the unusual for TV. Nothing normal should pass through his lens. "You're always looking for someone who sticks out visually," he admits. Neil sees much of the stands through one eye, but little of the game. He is situated maybe twenty-five feet from the goal, but can't tell when one is scored until he hears a roar, or groan.

On the headset Brian tells Neil to find someone in the visiting team's jersey. Neil looks, finds, and focuses. Brian puts the

Boston fan on the Calgary scoreboard for everyone to see. Boos break out. The boos spread. "Hold it. Hold it," says Brian. The director is watching and waiting. And waiting. The Boston fan senses something. He looks up. He sees himself, points to the Boston emblem and holds up one forefinger.

"Gotcha!" says Brian. "Hit it!" Suddenly, a bright red circle with a line through it falls over the visiting fan's face. The laughter is thunderous.

But back to action on the ice. A fight breaks out. Currently, the league allows in-house cameras to show a fight on the scoreboard but not a replay. "We're not trying to incite anyone here," says Brian. "I know some purists don't like fights. But some people do. They're part of the game. So we show them in proportion." While officials sort out the penalties, Brian plays the theme from the film *Rocky*.

Brian's crew immodestly claims partial credit for one win over Pittsburgh. The Penguins were killing the Flames, 4–1 or something. Brian decided to hassle Jaromir Jagr, Pittsburgh's prolific scorer and hair-grower, who was about to take a faceoff. Brian ordered a tight shot of the Czech's head with its bounteous black hair flowing down the back. Then Brian ordered up some special music, George Thorogood's "Get a Job, Get a Haircut."

The control-room crew thought it was hilariously clever. The faceoff was delayed. Jagr heard the crowd laughing. He looked up and saw himself. He skated around and around, but the camera followed and followed. Eventually, Jagr lost the faceoff and the Flames surged back to win, 7–5. "I think we got him flustered," Brian says. "Anything we can do to help our boys."

Brian Funfer has long wanted to be a record producer, but as long as it has lasted, putting on at least forty-one shows a year on a scoreboard larger than some cottages is a pretty good job. Sometimes as he depressurizes immediately after a game, Brian walks the Saddledome's concourse level and mingles with the departing crowds, his audience, listening hopefully for comments about the game's production. "We all want people here to have fun," Brian says. "When the whistle blows, we need to dazzle everyone for seventy seconds. That's our show time. Regardless of the score, we want them to get their money's worth."

Up in the sound booth at the northern end of the press box that seems to hang precariously over the arena, Gary Sweitzer and Jeff Phelps manipulate their computer to produce the moving graphics on the scoreboard, the clapping hands, for example, the stats, and player photos. After six years in the booth Gary and Jeff do not get the same rush they once did, tapping their keyboards and seeing the message flash on the Jumbotron much larger than life. But it's still fun seeing and hearing the crowd react. "We try to help keep the energy level up in this place," says Gary, "to keep the fans in the game."

From nearly ninety feet above the ice Theo looks even smaller than usual. "You gotta love that guy," says Willy Joosen. Willy is from the Netherlands, which isn't big either. He doesn't know Russell, Manitoba, from Moon River. But maybe if you hum a few bars, he can pick it up. Willy is the electronic keyboard player. "I've been playing this Flames gig since just before they won the Cup in '89," he says as his fingers fly over the keyboard, sending another tune showering down on the inattentive crowd below. "It's fun, man. And I get to see the games. I don't get nervous. I get excited. Nothing beats live hockey for excitement."

You'd get excited, too, if your job was to match live music with the action on the ice without any sheet music, or time to look at it even if it were there. Willy does what he can to share his excitement and feed the fans' fervour. But Willy says he's played fiftieth-wedding-anniversary gigs that were wilder than many Flames crowds. "They're ponderous here, man," he says. "They're afraid of getting rowdy because it would be too American."

To liven things up, Willy can be a very sly organist. The Flames have warned him about that. For instance, after a bad call by the ref there is to be no more playing "Three Blind Mice." So, instead, Willy has played the theme from "Mr. Magoo." "Probably nobody but me gets it," he says, "but, hey, you gotta have fun, right, man?"

If there is a sizable fight, Willy will play "It's a Wonderful World." When an opponent enters the penalty box, he might concoct the sound of a dungeon door closing.

But perhaps one of the best jobs in the whole Saddledome belongs to Dean Campbell. It is not a difficult job. But it is an urgent job, an important job, a dramatic job. He must always have his hand at the ready. Dean is the propane man, director of pyrotechnics, exploder extraordinaire. The moment any Calgary player knocks the puck across the opponent's goal line, Dean flips the safety switches and in one motion punches two buttons high on the wall.

Instantly, two huge red and yellow flames explode near the ceiling over both ends of the ice. WHOMPF! WHOMPF! More startling and dramatic than a standard siren or foghorn, of course, and very emblematic of an energy-rich province to burn off a gallon of propane to celebrate a team's goals. But it's startling nonetheless.

Some eighteen thousand heads jerk up, perhaps thinking that pregame comet has finally landed above them. The blast of heat is powerful. It seems the ceiling should melt. But immediately there is Beesley's familiar voice intoning, "CALGARY GOAL SCORED BY . . ."

And when Allan says the scorer's name, Dean hits those buttons again. WHOMPF! WHOMPF!

◆

There were no propane flames when Theoren scored his first goal on the Russell rink after his year-long medical sabbatical.

That goal came at about the same time as the Saddledome was nearing completion and Harvey the Hound was striding into the Flames offices for his audition.

It had become clear quite quickly in Russell that, after a seemingly endless recovery period, Theoren Fleury had overcome the odds once again. He had had to learn how to use his arm all over again, and that was tricky since he could not always fully feel where it was. Theo never would regain complete feeling in that arm; to this day he can barely pick up coins with his right hand and cannot feel which coins they are.

Some people thought Theoren's shot was not as hard or fast as before The Injury. But these typically were not people who saw Theo's shots coming right at them.

According to the experts who study young hockey players the way horse-buyers study thoroughbreds, many youth hockey stars peak at twelve and never get better. Other players catch up to them in skill and size. Perhaps the youthful stars' egos get wounded, as the long, brutal Darwinian principle of survival of the fittest – and meanest – takes effect, reducing the ranks of young men progressing through the sport's many levels. The teams at the top, awaiting each year's crop of eager newcomers, count on that winnowing.

Theoren would invest valuable time teaching his Russell teammates certain moves or tricks that he had perfected during his own endless private practices. He always seemed to have time for that. Ted Petz remembers several lessons from Theo about out-waiting a goalie on breakaways. Theo had made a science out of collecting, trying, refining, and relentlessly practising various little feints or dekes that would cause an eager young goalie to make a physical commitment before the shooter. "It's a game of chicken," Theo had said, shrugging as if being patient under pressure in front of noisy crowds at age fourteen was simple. "That's all it is."

It had become clear to most of the adults around Theoren that even at that ripe old age he was going to have to leave Russell if he was going to develop his hockey skills and escape his troubled home environment. One or two teachers suggested he pursue sports through the university and possibly obtain an athletic scholarship at an American college known for hockey. There were several right next door in Minnesota. Len and Ede, however, believed Theoren would apply himself to hockey around the clock but studying books was something else. "Theo was not much of a reader then," Ede says.

Growing up in Manitoba, of course, Theo knew the route to the NHL was through Junior, typically the rugged Western Hockey League, which is to the NHL what boot camp is for the military. Except that relatively few WHL players graduate to The Show, as the NHL is called. Manitobans had long cheered for their main WHL representative, the Brandon Wheat Kings. Theo and his teammates had occasionally seen the Wheat Kings play. They were so impressive, even glorious, and seemed somehow larger than life in their black and gold uniforms. There was also a whole host of other teams, Tier II, for instance, for young players to dream about and work towards. The skilled players aiming for U.S. colleges went into Tier II because getting money from Major Junior teams like the Wheat Kings would destroy their amateur status for collegiate play in the States.

Theoren was known to scouts all across Manitoba. He was known as speedy and an incredible scorer, which is always important. But after age twelve or thirteen, size starts playing a more sizable role. By then, the bigger boys are starting to fill out. Some are getting into weights, so their arms, legs, and necks are growing thicker. Size is the first thing people see. For some scouts, it may be the only thing. Even though he could not play in Junior for two years, Theoren Fleury had been drafted that year by the new Winnipeg Warriors, whose scout, Graham James, had spotted him at that Brandon camp. The Warriors were a hopeless new team attracting few fans and fewer victories, but still they were in the WHL.

Rather than see Theo mark time in hockey by spending another year in Russell, Len and Ede made inquiries about Theoren joining a Midget team in Winnipeg. They contacted James, who was building his reputation as a youth coach. It is not easy for a new player simply to move onto an established local team at that Tier I Midget level, positions having been allocated for those already resident in that playing area. But James helped place Theo onto a suburban team, the St. James Minor Midget Canadians.

No one needed to convince Wally Fleury that his boy had outgrown the Russell hockey program. Theo begged Ede to lobby his mother hard to permit the move. This proved unnecessary. Donna did not object. And so a year before he could legally drive a car, Theoren Fleury left home to pursue his hockey career.

He was very excited. He was going to the big city to play hockey. Of course, to the people of Russell, even Brandon looks like the big city. It was exciting to be on the way to Winnipeg and possibly beyond.

It was something else when the familiar car with the Manitoba plates from Russell pulled away from his new city billet without Theo. The reality of being a country boy away from home for the first time, living in a single room in a house belonging to strangers, an elderly couple who didn't think much of hockey or what they had heard about hockey players, and attending a brand-new high school totally devoid of friends was daunting, even for Theo.

The first day he walked into Silver Heights High School for grade ten, Theo was wearing his best golf shirt and his only rugby pants. He was overcome by the intimidating novelty of new slang, new fashions, music, and sounds. The teachers, halls, books, rooms, and routines were all unfamiliar. Even the class bell had a different ring. The youngster saw teenagers with orange and green hair. And the music sure wasn't Charley Pride. Theo's first thought: "I think I'm a little out of my league here."

That first day or week may have been the low point. "I was a lonely kid doing my own thing," Theo remembers. There were times when Russell, or at least the familiarity and memory of Russell, seemed awfully good. And there were nights when the country boy alone in the city cried himself to sleep.

Whenever Theoren Fleury has felt out of his league in life, he has, after a brief pregnant pause to think, bellied right up to the challenge. He has looked it straight in the eye. Well, actually, given his height, Theo has looked the challenge right in the chest. In Winnipeg, he looked right at loneliness and isolation and focused even more intently on hockey. Fortunately, training camp started soon after school opened. And by Christmas he was happily in his element with skates on his feet, a hockey stick in his hand, and teammates all around.

In effect, Theoren practised with two teams, St. James and the Warriors, while playing games for only one, St. James. This double commitment would test his skills as a centre and his physical conditioning without exposing him in games to players possibly five years older. "The other guys were huge," Theo recalls. "You'd have guys six-foot-something, 200 pounds. And I was five-foot-nothing and 135 pounds soaking wet with rocks in my pocket – and rocks in my head, too.

"I guess people talked a lot about that. I never thought of them then as bigger than me. I blocked it out. I still do. What's *their* size got to do with *me*?"

The Warriors were an awful team. "I think they were probably the worst team ever in the WHL," Theo says. "They'd lose like 19–1. I think they won nine games that year out of seventy-two." Worse, from a financial standpoint, the team drew fewer than a thousand spectators per game – for one game only 837 tickets were sold – when sales of three thousand were necessary just to break even. But Theoren practised and learned with the Warriors. He made friends. And he did the same on the St. James Midget team.

One of his Midget teammates – linemate, in fact – was Mike Rolling, who had learned to skate on the Russell rink while his father, a Mountie, was stationed there briefly. When Mike was ten, his father stayed over in Thompson one day to have Mike watch this Fleury phenomenon play in a tournament. Mike's dad once played on the Russell Senior team with Theo's dad, though their sons were not friends then.

Playing with Theo in Winnipeg sticks vividly in Mike's mind. "He was quite simply the best hockey player I ever played with," Mike says. "He was always the smallest guy on the ice and always the highest scorer. I'd be skating up ice thinking I was moving pretty quickly. Theo would flash by me with two or three guys chasing him. He'd take them outside. All of a sudden, there's the puck right in front of me. He knew I'd be open and he knew exactly where I'd be open. He'd have the goalie way out of position. I'd get another goal. And Theo was as happy as I was."

The boys became good friends, even close, but never quite as close as Mike hoped. "With Theo," he says, "there's always something you're never sure of." The pair enjoyed teenage adventures together, like the time they boarded the wrong Winnipeg bus, talking hockey constantly, and spent an hour riding in the wrong direction out into the countryside completely, obliviously ignorant. On the ride back they still talked and argued hockey. Mike was a Winnipeg Jets fan. Fleury was in love with the New York Islanders, especially Mike Bossy and Clark Gillies.

Theo and Mike hung out together, sneaking into any hockey game they could find, including Jets games. With his brazenness, Theo even got both of them into the Jets' press box for a game. They watched from on high amid luxury and free food.

There was no time for girls then. The boys played hockey and practised hockey. Theo would don his gear efficiently and quickly. Then he would take many long minutes preparing his sticks, getting the tape just right and the length exactly where he likes it – two inches below his chin. But once on the ice, it was all business and all hockey for Theo. "There was one guy on our team that everybody, even Theo, hated," Mike says. "One game the other team took a run at this guy. Theo came flying in there like a demon, the smallest but the first one to protect his teammate."

It was also difficult to get Theo off the ice. Sometimes he would wave a teammate over to the bench, as if the coach had ordered a line change, and then Theo would leap on the ice for an extra shift.

"We always had to drag Theo off the ice," Mike recalls. "He never wanted to leave. When our ice-time was up, the guys would be in the locker room talking about girls or what movie they were going to see. And all of a sudden we'd realize Theo is still out on the ice, deking this way and that, shooting here and there. He'd usually try to stay with the next team just to get in more skating and practice. He would practise and practise and practise, building up his collection of moves. Eventually, everything about hockey became second nature to him. He hardly had to think.

"People see Theo do phenomenal things in a game. But people don't see the endless hours he has always invested on the ice practising everything that we see him do today.

"If we got kicked off the ice, we'd go out and freeze our asses off waiting for a bus to another rink. Theo would do the talking. He'd talk real nice and polite to these guys, even lots bigger guys, and ask if we could, you know, maybe play a little on their ice with them. And they'd say, 'Yeah, sure, kids. Why not?' And ten minutes later Theo is talking back at them and faking them out of their skates and scoring every time he gets the puck. And they're asking, 'Who is this little shit and why can't I take him?' They might try to run him, but they never could catch him. I look back and say, 'We were crazy!' I mean, who goes out at fifteen looking to take on large adults in hockey?"

If they couldn't play indoors, then Theo and Mike would put on most of their gear and go looking for an outdoors opportunity. "We'd wander around town until we found a pickup game on some pond," says Mike. "I see Theo playing for the Flames on TV now and I see him doing lots of things I saw him practising back on those Winnipeg ponds when we were fifteen."

Theo was very competitive. If a teammate bobbled the puck, Theo would simply snatch it and score. That was not exactly endearing behaviour, but winning smooths such edges. Even years later when Mike and Theo played on the same team in a charity golf tournament, Theo said, "Just like old times, eh, Mike?" They had much fun that day. But when too many of Mike's drives went awry, Theo got on his old linemate for not playing well enough, just like old times again. The next winter came another familiar gesture. Mike was coaching a team of ten-year-olds. Theoren knew this. Right about tournament time a batch of autographed Theoren Fleury photos arrived at Mike's house, one for each of his players. Mike was a big hero at the subsequent team dinner.

Mike also remembers Theo always being very vocal. "Back in Winnipeg," Mike said, "he'd say anything to get the other side off their game. Theo was always yap-yapping at someone, complimenting them on their missed shot or thanking them for letting him score another goal. After a while Theo can get to you. They'd start yapping back or take a penalty. And the crowd would get into it, even mothers yelling at him, 'You smart-ass, who do you think you are?' And Theo would just smile. Nothing got him off his game. He'd score and then he'd skate along the glass and wave at those mothers."

After a while Theo could get fans upset even before taking the ice. "We'd be warming up in our end," Mike remembers. "You'd hear a buzz go through the crowd. Without looking, we knew Theo was coming. Sure enough, he'd get somebody yelling at him as he was coming up the ramp. I think he did it on purpose. It got his juices going. Or he'd take a penalty right after the first faceoff. I'd say, 'Theo, what are you doing?' And he'd say, 'It gets me in the game.' And then, as soon as he'd get out of the box, he'd score."

Often, it seemed, Theo would end the day by following Mike to his home where the two boys would play some vigorous basement hockey games with tape balls, Theo vs. Mike and his little brother. Or Mike and Theo would watch hockey on television. They would turn down the sound on "Hockey Night in Canada" and take turns providing their own play-by-play. Both remember being quite good at it and slipping each other's names into the running accounts. "There was never any doubt in my mind," Mike says, "that I really would see him in the NHL someday."

When it got late, Mike's mom would invite Theo to spend the night on their couch. Theo gratefully accepted. Come morning, Mike would wake up to the scrumptious smell of bacon and pancakes cooking. He would shuffle sleepily down to the kitchen and there would be Theo talking up a storm with Mike's mother as she cooked up pile after pile of pancakes and served them, steaming hot, to a grateful Theo.

"Oh, good morning, Mike," Mike's mother would say. "Theo was hungry." Theo is always hungry, Mike would think.

Theo was extremely complimentary about Mrs. Rolling's cooking. "These really are delicious," Theo would say, washing down another stack of pancakes with another glass of milk.

This mother-with-someone-else's-son breakfast scene occurred on so many Saturdays and Sundays that Mike lost track. By the time Mike had raced to the bathroom, washed and dressed, and returned to the kitchen for the few surviving pancakes, Theo was fully fuelled for a day of physical activity. He had his hockey gear by the door, prepared to head out in search of a game. He'd look at a hungry Mike. "Ready?" Theo would say.

Mike has another memory. The hockey season was ending. Theo, the league's leading scorer, was returning to Russell to complete the school year. The Winnipeg Warriors had been sold and the next fall would become the Moose Jaw Warriors with Graham James as the new head coach briefly. Theo would follow the team there and, afterward, who knew? Theo stayed one last night in the Rolling home. But when the family woke up the next morning, they found their regular house-guest had already departed.

On the kitchen counter, however, right at Theo's regular place, Mrs. Rolling found something addressed to her: a paper bag. Inside were several new glasses, just like the ones Mike's mother poured milk in for Theo on those many mornings of family breakfasts.

◈

If a player arrives in Canada's Western Hockey League with any innocence or unwrinkled clothing left in his gear bag, he will soon lose both in the demanding, rugged, and much-coveted life of a WHL player. There are eighteen teams in the league scattered across four provinces and two states, a world within a world for everyone involved.

That means that in addition to playing some six dozen or more hockey games against other young men also fighting to capture a life in pro sports, throughout the long bitter months of Western winters the tired players spend hundreds of hours travelling thousands of miles across the vast West in fume-filled buses with seats that do not quite recline.

Fleury never took an airplane to play a North American hockey game until he reached the pros. He remembers endless bus trips, some thirty-six hours long, with take-out food and no chance to shower, that ended with tired players stiffly walking off the bus, playing a complete hockey game and reboarding for four more hours to the next day's game site. Whenever they are at "home," in the rented billets with families, the players must also attend school. For this, they receive five or six dollars a day.

But these young men also receive the adulation of local fans, youth players, and some attractive young women who gather by the locker room or rink doors to shower on them the kind of attention, and perhaps affection, that the players think they would love to endure in the NHL. More importantly, the players receive the regular opportunity to hone their skills and try their luck impressing the pro scouts who make the rounds of Junior towns like military spies infiltrating the same aging rinks where stale popcorn, oily coffee, and leather-skinned hot dogs are the common provisions. Sitting silently in the press boxes or even the stands of such unlikely places, these veteran hockey eyes try, without tipping off their competitors making the same predictable rounds, to find that one player who possesses that certain spark that the other scouts have overlooked.

In recent times, Canada's three Major Junior leagues have provided more than half of the players drafted by the NHL. And the WHL, widely regarded as the most demanding because of its longer travelling distances and more physical style of play, often provides the most players of the three leagues. WHL alumni who made the big time include Bobby Clarke, Mike Vernon, Grant Fuhr, the Sutter brothers, Mike Modano, Cam Neeley, Esa Tikkanen, Bill Ranford, Trevor Linden, and Mark Messier.

"I never saw Fleury before he got here," said Bearcat Murray, the Flames' longtime trainer who once drove a travel bus in Junior. "But I knew if he could make it through four years in the WHL, he was one tough s.o.b., regardless of size."

Even in 1984, WHL teams were recruiting male mountains. Few now are much under six feet or two hundred pounds. A bespectacled Fleury appeared poised and confident, yet still shy, about making the team when it arrived in its new home in 1984.

A reporter for the *Moose Jaw Times-Herald* asked, once more, about his size. "I think I have a good chance of earning a place on the team," Theo said then, "because I'm a good skater and I have good puck-handling skills. My lack of size might be a minor drawback, but I think I'll be able to overcome it because of my speed."

The same reporter noted how many players from Fleury's Bantam draft were already out of hockey. Fleury smiled for the photographer. The headline read: "SMALL, BUT A TENACIOUS WARRIOR."

They play physically in the WHL, as if the puck belongs to them, and they play hungry, as if someone is watching them. This is why several thousand fans pay ten dollars or more to watch boys with pimples play Junior hockey, and why the same teams eagerly admit the familiar band of older men who bring with them something far better than a ticket – a notebook with the logo of an NHL team.

"Theoren Fleury was too small," Art Schoenroth, president of the Moose Jaw Warriors, recalled at Fleury's WHL "retirement celebration" in 1988. "That nonsense was repeated again in 1985, again in 1986, and there were still sceptics in 1987. You heard that in the stands, you heard that in the streets, in the press, and it was accepted knowledge in the highest of NHL offices. How wrong can self-proclaimed experts really be?"

"If you didn't know Fleury well," remembers Greg Kvisle, who did not know Fleury well when he became Theo's coach after the first year in Moose Jaw, "you'd look at that little guy with the neatly combed hair and the glasses on that boyish little face. And you'd say, 'Where's his briefcase? The guy's a wimp.' But nobody thought that as soon as Theo took the ice. I don't think he's got a low gear. When he's playing hockey, he's all adrenaline. He wasn't a locker-room leader. He was a leader by example. Two minutes left or fifty-eight, up by nine or down by two, the guy was giving 110 per cent. That's contagious on a hockey team. And that is precisely why he is a pro today.

"Except sometimes his teammates would stop playing and watch him. Me, too. He was a blur. You'd say, 'How the hell did he do that? And what the hell did he do?' I swear Theo was faster with the puck than without."

When Theoren Fleury arrived in Moose Jaw, he was in yet another new billet, at another new high school, in a new city 250 miles from home, on a new team in a new life. He made an important decision, not for the last time. He decided he was going to do anything – including some things he had yet to think of – to get noticed.

Although Theoren didn't know it at first, back home in Russell both of his parents, inspired in part by their oldest son's determination, made important decisions for themselves, also not for the last time. They each decided to seek help for their addiction problems.

"I got so sick of feeling sick," said Wally, who would stumble on occasion but has stayed largely sober since. He's had time to think now. "You know," he says in continued amazement and appreciation, "I never had money for their hockey. But they never, not once, ever came to me and said, 'How come you got money to drink, but you don't have money for us?' They could have said that. I feel real bad, for sure. But I'm there for them now. When I saw Theoren out there in Moose Jaw or in the NHL, I feel great. It's like a part of me is out there playing like an all-star."

When Donna watched Theoren leave for Moose Jaw, it was as if her perpetual daze began to clear. She announced to Ede it was time to get better. She entered a residency program. And as part of the therapy, she drew a map for Ede of everywhere in her home on Augusta she had stashed pills so she would always have some within reach. Ede Peltz and Ted Fleury then collected every pill bottle they could find. When they finished, they had filled two grocery bags and part of a third. Donna has struggled through several treatments.

One time, Ede took Donna and Wally to see Theoren in a tournament in Regina. After the game, Wally disappeared. To spend some time with his mother, Theoren opted out of a pizza celebration with his Warrior teammates. But after five minutes together, Donna announced to her son that she was too tired to talk and went to bed. Theoren went home alone early.

Later treatments proved more successful for both parents, however. Donna still requires non-addictive maintenance medication for anxiety. But the delusions and dazes are gone. And she has even gone downtown alone to volunteer at the Russell ice rink. "I regret my problems from before," she says. "Theoren and I are closer now."

Theoren's renewed decision to go all out in his play for Moose Jaw was actually not a new decision. "I had decided I would do anything to get to the NHL," he recalls. But Moose Jaw was a bigger stage than Midget with bigger crowds and stakes. And despite his size, he had a higher profile in news coverage.

Coach Kvisle nods when he hears about that decision. "The ones that make it to the NHL," he said, "have decided they will make it to the NHL."

His first year in the WHL Theoren scored 29 goals and had 46 assists in 71 games. He also acquired 82 penalty minutes. His second year, 1985–86, everything went up: 43 goals, 65 assists, 124 penalty minutes in 72 games. In effect, he spent two entire games in the penalty box. His third year Theoren scored 61 goals and 68 assists in 66 games. He also cut his time in the penalty box to under two hours – 110 minutes. That third year was the one that went down in the notebook of a man named Ian McKenzie, a former law-enforcement officer who knows how to read evidence.

His fourth year in the WHL, 1987–88, Theoren Fleury scored 68 goals and 92 assists in 65 games to accumulate 160 points, over half the Warriors' team total, and to share the league's scoring championship with a Swift Current player named Joe Sakic.

Fleury points out that the Moose Jaw team produced a number of NHL players: Lyle Odelein, Kelly Buchberger, and Mike Keane. Keane, a tough winger from Winnipeg nicknamed Zeke, ended up being Fleury's bodyguard. Theo would trip someone, spear someone, fire a puck at the goalie right after a whistle, or crash into the goalie so he'd think more about Fleury coming in next time. And the goalie's teammates would jump on him. So Keane would have to jump in to protect his linemate. Pretty soon, Fleury would squirt out the side and skate away. Penalties would be assessed. And Theo would have more room out there to skate and shoot. One time against Medicine Hat a fight erupted during pregame warmups. Kvisle just knew Fleury was involved.

As a rookie, Fleury had to sit in the middle of the team bus. As his four years passed, he worked his way up to the widest back seat where he could read or lie down and sleep. As the team bus rolled through the long prairie nights and everyone else slept, the coach would spot one seat light on in the back. There would be Fleury, glasses on, intently reading for his high-school homework. "He was very proud of being the first person in his family to graduate from high school," the coach says. "I know he had a tough childhood. But you see that family together and there's a lot of love there somehow."

Not much love for Fleury on the ice though. If Moose Jaw's opponents tried to line Fleury up against the boards, like as not they'd find he had darted in, gotten the puck, and departed before the defenceman slammed into the suddenly Fleury-less corner. And Theo's intensity was just as hard in practice.

Coaches recall his running right over teammates if he didn't think they were working hard enough. They said Theo had two gears: high and overdrive. They called him Fleur and, when he got them angry, some other things.

That last year Fleury racked up 235 penalty minutes. "You don't really try to coach Fleury," says coach Kvisle, still shaking his head. "You try to control him a little bit. You remind yourself, these kids are only seventeen, eighteen, or nineteen. They're immature. I don't know how many talks I had with him. I said, 'Theo, you ain't gonna score from the box, boy. Use your head sometimes.' I made him work on his defence. He wasn't good in his own end because he always wanted to be in the other end. He was all energy. I'd call him over to the bench to settle him down sometimes. We'd be up by five goals and I didn't want him getting his leg broken. I didn't tell him, but he was the team. And he'd cuss at me 'cause I was keeping him from playing. Nothing slowed him down.

"I don't think you can like people like that. But you can respect the hell out of them."

Again or still, Fleury would do the unexpected. In one game against the Pats in Regina, the Warriors were ahead 8–2 with maybe three minutes left in the third period. Theo got a break-away. He was going in at full Fleury speed. Maybe ten feet from the goal he poked his stick between his own legs and, while straddling it, shot the puck into the top right corner of the net. Score: Moose Jaw 9, Regina 2. To complete the act, Theo skated past the Pats' bench riding his stick like a witch's broom. He also waved. When the ensuing brawl ended, Fleury was found watching from his own bench.

"You wanted to kill him sometimes," coach Kvisle says, "strangle every living ounce of life from that little body. But then he'd win another game himself or inspire the team with his example or he'd be over with some handicapped kids in wheelchairs talking and signing autographs as long as they wanted.

"The other teams and their fans loved to hate him. One time in Portland they held up the game a half-hour to get everyone in because Fleury's Warriors were playing. In Swift Current, they played that Weasel song whenever Theo skated on. Theo could really be irritating. And they'd be chasing him all over and we'd score. He looked like a wild man at times. But when you'd look into those bright eyes of his, you'd say, 'I'll be damned. He knows what he's doing every single second.'"

Theoren Fleury has an unusually broad and precise vision of the ice; all of his coaches have said that. He can see so many possibilities to play a puck before most players even see the puck, let alone anticipate where that seven-ounce piece of frozen rubber is going.

And Theoren Fleury has had a similar developing knack for understanding the visual and show-business aspects of the game. His hockey eye also informs him when kicking an opponent's skate out from under him would be least noticed and when allowing his own natural exuberance to bubble over would be most effective on the crowd and his team. Being liked was not important. Being noticed was.

When you don't get noticed much by your parents in childhood for who you are, for just being there, and for being their child, when you must earn most attention by doing something good or bad, you quickly learn what to do to get noticed, good or bad. In that mode of thinking and at that height, being penalized is better than being ignored. And if being noticed in such ways gets your hockey opponents distracted and off their game, even if for only a moment, then that helps make up for a lack of size.

Theoren Fleury got very good at getting noticed. And no notice was more important than one that he was totally unaware of at the time. That's the way scouts like it. The man who noticed him was Ian McKenzie. A former hockey player himself until he joined the Mounties at age eighteen out of his home town of

Calgary, McKenzie actually never left the game. Wherever he was stationed – all over Alberta and B.C. and in Ontario – McKenzie kept his hand, head, and heart in hockey. He was always deeply involved, in the community, in hockey, and in his own players. He coached youth teams, usually Bantams or Midgets; they're more focused at that age, or at least as focused as boys can be, yet still malleable.

Ian had a pretty good eye for players, so when the soon-to-be legendary coach Scotty Bowman wanted someone to scout some Western prospects for the St. Louis Blues, he hired Ian part-time in the late sixties. The assistant general manager of the Blues then was a man named Cliff Fletcher. Soon after, Cliff Fletcher became the first general manager of the Atlanta Flames. He remembered Ian and he remembered Scotty's admiration for Ian's eye for talent. So Ian became an employee of the Flames organization a year before there was a Flames team. He is now the longest-running Flames employee.

He has abandoned Calgary and its winters for a home on the warmer West Coast, but Ian McKenzie is still racking up thousands of frequent-flyer miles for the Flames, packing his battered suitcase and notebooks around the world as a talent scout.

Good scouting is a knack built on experience and eyes as acute as the best shooter's. Scouting is an important business. It is invisible to the world of the fan, who gets only inklings on Entry Draft day when some young player gets chosen or a known player gets picked much higher than he is ranked. Some scout somewhere has seen something the team wants.

Scouting is essential to the future of a team. You need not be a Mountie to get your man in hockey, but having their determination and savvy sure helps because finding good hockey talent is not a science. Its satisfactions are silent. Scouting is not easy. Nor is it gentle. Those who object to bust measurements in beauty contests as sexist might become physically ill watching scouts break down the physical attributes and skills of hockey players.

In the weeks before the Entry Draft the top players are flown around to receive more physical exams collectively from NHL teams than some people get in a lifetime. With so much money at stake, in salaries and potential gate and merchandise receipts, pro hockey teams are even getting into the uncharted Arctic waters of psychological testing, trying to gauge the internal mechanisms that win games but show up on no stat sheet – yet.

Hockey scouts have eyes as cold as the rinks they inhabit. They're supposed to. Their job is to travel alone all over the world like grizzled prospectors seeking to uncover the perfect personnel for their teams. That takes the tricky ability to track a player's development, actually many players' development, over a period of time. You saw them last year, last fall, last winter, this past spring, and now again tonight. Are there patterns to their play and behaviour? Has there been growth in skill? In savvy? In size? In speed? Will those advances continue? Now, extending the lines of growth, do they cross somewhere the possible needs of the team back home? And how do you measure the intangibles?

"You're looking for heart," says Ian, "and leadership and size and skill and savvy and skating and strength. There are no perfect hockey players. Wayne Gretzky has faults. He's not a great skater and he's not physically strong. But everyone knows what he has done. Could anyone have predicted what he has done? What I look for are the best players available when we're going to be drafting. Frankly, a lot of the time in this business you're not looking for the perfect player. You're looking for the player with the least wrongs."

Leadership is a tricky trait to track down, especially in young players. Scoring, blocking shots, those things you can measure. But leading? You can't measure leadership. Teams need it and want it. They won't win championships without leadership. Some scorers have it, some don't. As Ian puts it, "How many Stanley Cups has Gretzky won without Messier?"

Some selections are easier than others. Ian recommended Brett Hull, for instance. "Hull was overlooked in Tier II," Ian says. "The knock on Brett was he was too heavy. I kept watching him. I liked him. We took him in a later round and he developed well in college. *Sports Illustrated* asked me if I liked Brett Hull because his father's name was Bobby Hull. I said I liked Brett Hull because he scored 105 goals in one season at Penticton. You don't do that by accident."

Ian McKenzie cannot remember how many miles he has travelled and games he has seen since Scotty Bowman phoned Red Deer and launched him on his never-ending journey from Penticton to Sweden to Brandon to the Czech Republic to Lethbridge and Seattle and then to Russia via Boston and Denver. But Ian can remember the first time he saw Theoren Fleury play hockey. Ian was in Moose Jaw on a regular visit. It was the fall of 1984. Ian had his list of players to watch and to ask about in a casual but businesslike fashion for development and attitude. Fleury was not on that list. Fleury was way too small.

What did Ian think of Fleury that first time? Ian shakes his head as only a wise veteran scout can. "I didn't give him a hope in hell of making it into the NHL."

Shannon Griffin can remember the first time she saw Theoren, too. She was more impressed than Ian. "He was kind of cute," she says. "Not movie-star cute, but cute. He was little and skinny and he had all his teeth then."

She first saw him at a barbecue welcoming the Warriors to Moose Jaw. Like most Junior players, the young heroes were away from their home towns for the first time, living in the homes of others, playing hockey and travelling at all hours, attending school when possible. Their peers back home are still hanging around the lockers in the high-school hallways, checking out the girls checking them out. These hockey boys try to look tough in their new uncertain world. They need to be tough.

They can be traded or cut today. Or their knee could be blown out tonight, and it's "Thank you very much, son. Good luck with the rest of your life." But their hollow swaggers carry over off the ice. They may try to grow beards or goatees and talk louder in public than might be acceptable back home.

Still, despite all of their potential on-ice savvy and obvious toughness, there is about these young men the air of lost dogs. Even in public, they hang together in packs. And they clearly have not been wearing – or selecting or tying – neckties for very long.

Sensing this vulnerability, the teams' home towns, encouraged by the teams seeking to expand their followings, tend to adopt these hockey players rather like sons-at-large. There might be a booster club that sells souvenirs and tickets to dinners to raise money for things like bus trips and even cakes to be delivered to individual players on their birthdays. Each player will be invited to share a family's holidays to ease the absence from his own.

The players will be interviewed by the local newspaper and radio, maybe even TV, and quoted before and after games. The team's front office will love each story as a spur to ticket sales. Talking about hockey makes the players more comfortable. In interviews they can practise dispensing opinions about surprising topics like their favourite colour (Fleury's is green). Possibly, some smart players will learn what they can modestly admit to about themselves and what they can say honestly about their team and the upcoming game that is not inciteful to the opposition. The players will also practise complaining to teammates about being misquoted.

Some players are invited out into the world to speak to wide-eyed grade-schoolers about the importance of reading or school. That impresses the youngsters and doesn't hurt the team's reputation. Other players will visit children in the hospital and deliver a team pennant. They may show up from one to three p.m. at a local store to pose for pictures and sign T-shirts, and the team captain may just happen to show up at the radio station to chat, on the air, about both of this weekend's home games.

A few players may also learn that if they get into, say, some under-age drinking problems, the team and local authorities will work it out for them in a spirit of quiet co-operation because, after all, what good could come from a talent like this being publicly embarrassed and missing some games? And no doubt the boy has learned his lesson. Or a lesson.

Outside the rink before and after practice there will almost always be at least a small gaggle of fans seeking to see the local players, maybe even to talk briefly. The scene is as familiar and predictable as the seasons. The little boys will have pens and pieces of paper. The teenage girls will have come in twos and threes. They probably will have neglected to mention to their parents that they were going to hang around outside a room where naked teen boys were showering. Later, the girls could claim it was a spur-of-the-moment thing, which might sell until their father sniffs an unusual amount of perfume for a Thursday afternoon.

The boys will emerge in groups, too, their hair still soaking wet. They, too, could claim not to care about the gathering of young women were it not for all of the after-shave lotion that seems to have spilled on their faces. Most of the girls will appear incapable of much communication beyond giggles or sideways glances. Good luck in the game tomorrow. Hey, thanks. In the aisle of the grocery store, where players might stop for snacks on the way home, total strangers will now smile and nod familiarly at them, and the players may hear their name whispered excitedly after passing someone.

This is where the real aura of celebrity begins.

Of course, some of the players were recognized back home in youth hockey. They won the MVP trophies at the team's annual dinner, heard their name on the loudspeaker, and saw their parents snapping pictures while other parents applauded. The newspaper published an article, which probably was written by the coach. A teacher in school might have mentioned something good about a game. But that was more of a neighbourhood reputation. Back home, people, especially girls, did not wait outside to see you. They didn't create phony encounters – and bring their cameras.

Junior hockey is the same game as always, only bigger time, bigger players, bigger goals, bigger hits, bigger crowds, bigger stakes. The same goes for its fame. In fact, this fame stuff tastes pretty good. And what could possibly be wrong with something that tastes good and makes you feel better?

Shannon was at the Warriors' welcoming team picnic with her friend Dawn, whose mom worked part-time at the team's ticket window. Shannon never would have considered attending alone. But it was a welcome party and one with a fair number of athletic young men. Dawn and Shannon discovered while talking with Theo that this cute little guy was from Manitoba and, well, Dawn had relatives in Russell, Manitoba. Had he ever heard of Russell?

Shannon attended the Catholic school, Vanier High. All of the players that first year in Moose Jaw went to Peacock High School. So Shannon could not stage an encounter with any players or that player in her school hall between classes. And because they were new in town, none of the players was in the phone book. So, soon after the barbecue, when she needed a date for her baseball-team picnic, Shannon sent word through a friend who was dating a player who knew the little guy that she was the one with the girl who had relatives in Russell and she was wondering if the little guy would like to go with her to her baseball-team picnic. Would he call? She waited for his call. And waited. And waited.

He never called. He never showed.

Shannon couldn't really ask anyone else, just in case. She waited and waited. Then, she went to the picnic alone. But she went late to give him a little more time to get there. The picnic was not the same as she imagined it could have been in the company of that player.

Had that guy gone with her to the picnic, Shannon might not have liked him after all. He might not have liked her or baseball or her friends. Maybe he had a girlfriend, though Shannon's girlfriend had told her she had not seen him with any Moose Jaw girl. Indeed, Shannon knew very little about him.

There are a lot of things to think about in the mid-teens – new feelings and old fears and future hopes and so many present uncertainties. In fact, one of the few comforting certainties of life at that age is that, later, as an adult there certainly won't be as many uncertainties. Shannon thought about the player's non-appearance a lot. She did not talk about the non-incident much at home. Shannon has four older half-siblings who lived far away and she would not know them well until years later. There was one older sibling with her own mom. This was the second family for Shannon's father, who was a travelling salesman and away a lot.

Shannon's parents were casual hockey fans. They went to some Warrior games and Shannon went along. Or Shannon might attend with friends. The Moose Jaw team was still new and supporting it bore the flavour of civic duty. She saw that player there. He was pretty good. He looked larger on the ice, but the bottom of his number 9 still got tucked into his pants in the back.

Shannon decided that he might not have received her date proposal. In fact, she decided that was exactly what had probably occurred. That would explain everything and erase any possibility of rejection. Some weeks later Shannon was at the mall with a friend. The mall is not far from the arena. As long as they were in the area, Shannon suggested seemingly on the spur of the moment, why didn't the two girls stop by the arena? Maybe they'd see "some" Warriors.

The girls were early for practice. But, then, so was Theo Fleury. Always. Shannon struck up a conversation. He seemed to remember her. He seemed nervous. He had to go on the ice soon. He forgot to ask for her phone number. So Shannon offered to give it to him. "So, uh," she said, "do you want my phone number?"

What was a young man, even a hockey player, supposed to say? No, I don't like the looks of you? He took the number. Some days later he used the number. They agreed on the movies, *All of Me* with Steve Martin. Shannon had a car. Theo wouldn't for two more years. When she arrived to pick him up, Theoren was in jeans and shirtless. Despite conscientious digging, he was having trouble finding his shirt, the pink golf one. Shannon surveyed the scene. Obviously, a tornado had recently passed through the hockey player's room. She imagined nothing could ever be found in that mess.

The movie was funny, though Theoren remained so nervous he absentmindedly kept kicking the chair in the next row. After some time its angry occupant stood up and leaned back towards Fleury. "Don't you kick my seat one more time!" he said. The couple laughed later. They walked in the park. They got along pretty well, in fact, very well. "He has a certain spark," Shannon says. "He seemed vulnerable and needed someone. I was vulnerable too, I guess. I needed to be needed. It felt really good to be needed."

The two of them were together almost ten years. Shannon was the organized one. Fleury's Moose Jaw landlord did not like messy tenants. Shannon organized Theo's room as a reclamation project. When Theo transferred to Shannon's high school, she would pick him up each morning. Theo was very determined about graduating from high school. Even when the team returned from a distant game at four a.m., he was ready for school when she arrived at eight-thirty. Shannon admired that determination. She was near the top of her class and could help with some subjects. She could introduce him around town. She enjoyed being with the team's developing star. "There is a powerful loneliness about Theo," Shannon says now, "even in a crowd. I thought I could help fill that need. But I always knew that women with hockey players always take second or third place to hockey. Women who can't handle that are toast, burnt toast."

There was always a deep unknown sector about Theoren, which intrigued Shannon until near the end. His silences seemed full of meaning, even mystery. Then, because he had no money, he would hand-draw her a birthday card.

Shannon enjoyed being useful and she was chronically organized, as organized as Theo was determined. Years later, feeling protective of his interests and future, it was Shannon who would return the countless phone calls from reporters and others that Theo would ignore. She would dial the number and hand him the phone. He sounded very nice on the phone. It was Shannon too who organized his mounting fan mail, arranged what needed autographing, and had it mailed back. "Those fans poured themselves out to him," she says. "We just couldn't ignore them."

At first, that was a definite relief for Theoren, who couldn't finish mowing Len Peltz's large lawn, and felt the same about other non-hockey activities. With Shannon on the case, he didn't have to keep track of many things, from fan mail to phone calls, daily non-hockey schedules, and even laundry. Later, this organizing would become confining like a schedule or shirt that was too tight. Then, Shannon's organization became nagging. But by then, there was a child involved.

Shannon remembers in Moose Jaw Theoren writing her letters on long road trips. They usually had to do with the events in and scores of games, how he had played in those games, and pro scouts he thought he might have seen. It had not been a hard job, but Theoren had convinced Shannon he was going to make it to the NHL. "The NHL was a given," Shannon still says.

The Warriors never were a good team during Fleury's tenure. They had five coaches in six years. Kvisle remembers thinking

Fleury might make the NHL as a third-line centre for five, maybe six years max. "You'd watch Theo for ten minutes," the coach recalls, "and you'd probably hate him. He was always stirring everything up. I'd call him over and say, 'Don't do that any more.' And he'd say, 'Okay, Coach.' And he'd go and do something else. And most of the time it worked. He had such great self-confidence on the ice."

But not in the eyes of scouts. Scouts don't talk with each other about players they are really interested in. So there was a fair amount of talk about Fleury. And head-shaking, too. Yeah, the guy racked up points, all right, so far anyway. But he also racked up the penalty minutes. Fleury seemed durable enough – he missed games rarely and shifts never. One scout heard he assigned himself extra shifts. But Fleury was so small, dinky, actually. The guy would surely get killed in the NHL.

Ian McKenzie came across Fleury now and then at games where he was scouting someone else. Ian would watch a few of Fleury's shifts. How could you avoid it? The guy was everywhere. Pretty good speed, too. But Ian agreed with his peers. The guy was way too small for the big time.

Coach Fowler remembers Theo returning home to Russell on holidays. His mother had been in and out of various drug treatments. And Theo would ask to practise with his old youth team. "He could have been the big shot," Coach Fowler recalls, "the hot-shot WHL player coming home. But he wasn't. He never showed off, just did all the drills like everyone else. I was surprised, pleasantly."

Shannon recalls being at a cousin's wedding in June 1986. Suddenly, Theo disappeared for more than an hour. She found him in the parking lot, too quiet. It was Entry Draft day, that all-important day when NHL teams select their future players. That's the day these young men discover what it's like to be a teenage girl waiting at home for that special someone to phone – and he doesn't. The Junior players don't talk about Entry Draft day much; they don't need to. Theo had called home, collect, to see if he'd been invited to The Show.

The answer was no.

"Maybe next year," Shannon said, full of hope. She did not know how this draft business worked. But she knew Theo would make it to the NHL; he had told her so.

Theo did not reply. She was quickly learning what a Theo silence meant.

Theo was a very determined hockey player his third year in Moose Jaw. He reduced his penalty minutes. He increased his scoring, racking up about one assist and one goal every single game. He was invited to try out for the Canadian World Junior Team. No one gave him much of a chance. He phoned Ede from the tryout camp the night before the final selections. "I don't know, Mrs. Peltz," he said. "I'm afraid I won't make it this time."

"Well, Theo," Ede would say, "all you can do is your best. And your best always has been pretty good."

But, of course, Theo did make the Canadian World Junior Team and gained Canadian and international exposure that enabled even more people to say he was obviously too small to go to the next level. That was the year of the riot and the Canadians' disqualification with the Russians. So some people thought Theo had not been able to show what he could do.

By the end of his third year in Junior in the spring of 1987, Fleury had filled out to maybe 145 pounds. Entry Draft day was a quiet prairie summer day in Russell, Manitoba. Theo and Shannon had gone there to visit his parents. Shannon was four months' pregnant then and easily tired. She went into the bedroom for a mid-afternoon nap.

When the NHL's top brass gathered in Detroit's Joe Louis Arena that morning, there was a quiet plot afoot among the Flames' leadership assembled around the team's table. A lot of people, including Theoren Fleury, contributed to Theoren Fleury's growth as a person and as a hockey player over the years. But Theoren Fleury is a pro today because of a minor corporate conspiracy on that draft day. And Ian McKenzie was chief plotter.

It had finally dawned on Ian at a game either in Lethbridge or Swift Current, it doesn't really matter where. Once again, Ian was making his WHL rounds. With the draft barely four months away, he had gone there to scout a dwindling list of prospects. Fleury was not on the list, of course. But Ian found himself scouting Fleury anyway. "I'd seen him all the time in Major Junior," Ian said. "Maybe forty times. And every time I would say to myself, 'What a great player. Too bad he's too small.'"

Ian had seen the riot at the Junior Worlds. Fleury was on the ice at the time. Ian thought Theo might even have been the instigator of the melee. That was no minus in Ian's mind – or in his notebook. He sees the Russians play all the time and some full-sized North Americans don't have the will to stand up to them or their skating skills.

Now, back on the prairies, Ian would remind himself every shift to watch those other guys and every shift he'd find himself waiting to see what the little guy would do. This was becoming a routine for Ian. Here is the pro scout, who knows better, and all he can do is watch the little guy, who is incredibly consistent and, according to what Ian heard from all over town, the most determined individual anyone had ever seen. About the second period that night in the late winter of 1987 Ian McKenzie added Fleury to his list.

"I said to myself," he says, " 'What's it going to take, Ian, for you to get the message that Theo Fleury is a player? Every time you go to his games, you end up watching him. And he ends up doing something spectacular. And everyone talks about him like he's six-two. Screw his size. The kid's a big-league player.'"

But Ian was in a very small minority. In fact, he *was* the minority. Ian was the only Fleury fan on the Flames. Theo's name was not on the team's list of top 125 prospects. The NHL's

Central Scouting Bureau had listed Fleury – in spot 197 out of 200 draft prospects. Ian had been working on general manager Cliff Fletcher for months, stressing Fleury's speed, scoring, and obvious fan appeal. "If the kid never plays one day in the NHL," McKenzie told his boss, seeking any edge, "he'll fill the arena for our farm team in Salt Lake." Fletcher was noncommittal.

So the draft got under way. Calgary's first pick was a left winger named Bryan Deasley. Everyone was big on him. Next came Stephane Matteau, another winger, followed by another second-round pick, Kevin Grant. Then the Flames picked Scott Mahoney, Tim Harris, Tim Corkery, and Joe Aloi.

Ian whispered in Cliff's ear, "Now's the time for the Fleury pick." But, no, the committee went for Peter Ciavaglia instead.

Drafting Fleury for the Flames had become a personal matter for Ian. He knew in his head and his guts and his bones that the kid would make it. The Flames' eighth-round turn came. "Now, Cliff, now," Ian whispered.

"Gentlemen," the general manager said, "this next pick is mine and Ian's. Ian?" Flames people looked at each other. This was unusual.

McKenzie made the announcement. "The Calgary Flames select Theoren Fleury of the Moose Jaw Warriors."

Some laughter erupted nearby. Ian's eyes fell on a fellow scout at the Philadelphia Flyers' adjacent table. "I wanted to punch him," Ian said. "I leaned across in front of Bobby Clarke and I said, 'What the hell are you laughing about, a little short-assed s.o.b. like you?'"

At least one of Ian's Flames colleagues threw his pen on the floor in disgust over this wasted pick. When he realized it was his favourite Cross pen, he scrambled after it.

The phone rang on Augusta Street moments later. It was Ian McKenzie. "Theo," he said, "the Flames have picked you eighth, 166th overall. Congratulations."

In the bedroom Shannon heard the phone. She heard Theo answer. She heard him say, "Really? Eighth? 166th?"

When she got to the living room, Wally and Theo were hugging each other. The phone rang again. It was someone named Peter Maher from CFR Radio in Calgary. Maher knew Fleury was drafted merely to become an IHL fan favourite in Salt Lake City. "Well, sir," Theo said in his first interview as a Flames property, "I'm very happy to be a member of the Calgary Flames."

On the other end of the phone line the radio voice of the Calgary Flames was silent. The kid doesn't know, Peter thought.

A number of people smiled in similar ignorance that day as the news flashed through town and out across the prairies. Doug Fowler smiled. Greg Kvisle smiled. Mike Rolling. Ted Petz. Ann and Jim Petz smiled. Ede and Len Peltz smiled. So, of course, did Shannon Griffin. She had already learned how uneasy summer makes Theo. "He is totally lost without hockey," she says. The Entry Draft day's events would get them through at least this summer, she thought. She was grinning broadly herself. But Shannon had never seen Theo with such a big smile.

And it did not go away until training camp.

❖

By the time training camp starts late each summer, Brenda Koyich has already had a very busy year. In fact, her off-season is much busier than most people's on-season. By training camp, Brenda pretty much has organized the team's entire year of travel from October well into April. No one may yet know who will be on the team, but Brenda can tell you exactly where they will be at any given time on any given travel day – unless one thing goes wrong. Usually, more than one thing goes wrong.

Brenda is secretary to general manager Al Coates. From her desk in the corner of the Saddledome, all Brenda has to do for the Calgary Flames is reserve airplane tickets and airplane seats for hundreds of thousands of miles of travel between the United States and Canada; pre-arrange scores of bus rides to hotels, to arenas, to alternative practice arenas, back to hotels and out to airports in twenty-five cities in two countries with differing rush hours and holidays; set aside for late arrival an adequate number of single and double nonsmoking rooms with extra-large beds and, for the coaches, VCRs in hotels that are good luck for the Flames and have not booked a convention at the same time; prevent lobby waiting by arranging pre-registration with roommates prescribed by the coaches; pre-plan three meals for every day on the road, taking into consideration the remarkable appetites of professional athletes and their differing nutritional needs and desires on game days and non-game days; and set up one labelled envelope for each travelling Flames employee containing sixty-five dollars in cash for each road day, taking into account sixty-five dollars in Canadian funds for each travel day in Canada and sixty-five dollars U.S. for each travel day in the States.

The only complicating factors are the diverse tastes, sizes, temperaments, ages, skills, and superstitions of forty different men from a half-dozen different countries on three continents; the unpredictability of aircraft machinery and buses, highway construction, and accidents along normal travel routes; sudden changes in winter weather from hurricanes in Florida to ice storms in New England; the shifting value of Canadian and American currencies; and the certainty that injuries, trades, call-ups, and send-downs will change the cast of team members substantially and unpredictably.

Other than that, Brenda Koyich's job is fairly simple.

"I love it," says Brenda, who always seems calm even when her boys arrive at the Newark airport intent on getting to Boston

Fleury measures up to teammate Todd Simpson, practice 1997.

1997, versus the Avalanche.

Theoren Fleury, meet Rob Blake.

MIKE VARTY

Right: Harvey the Hound walking the Saddledome glass. Below: Fleury convinces a Boston player to play on his knees and help Calgary.

KEVIN UDAHL

Practice, practice, practice.

The front teeth go missing – again.

NHL scars.

Right: Fleury, son Beaux, wife Veronica. Below: Fleury with son Josh.

where a fogbank has just rolled in and closed the field. In her spare time Brenda also handles the paperwork for players' contracts and the logistical arrangements for trades and call-ups.

Brenda is actually from Edmonton, where she did similar work for the Eskimos of the Canadian Football League. She and her husband, Mike, a travelling chemical and plastics salesman, moved to Calgary in the early 1980s. She was going to apply to the Stampeders. Then someone said they thought Calgary had a hockey team. She looked in the phone book under "Flames, Calgary." The next day Cliff Fletcher called back. He hired her on the spot. She's been with the hockey club ever since.

She loves the excitement of professional sports, but has seen some changes recently. "It's all the money in sports now," she says sadly. "Money changes the way people think, act, play, and treat each other. You suddenly take youngsters away from small-town homes and working families, give them lots of money, and treat them like royalty. And most of them are going to change. Some handle it better than others. But either way they are different for it."

Brenda associates Theo Fleury's arrival on the Flames with the birth of her daughter Jessica. Now, after a hard day at the office, Brenda rushes home, throws together a quick family meal, and everyone returns to the Saddledome where they have become serious hockey and Fleury fans. "You see all of the people coming into their seats," says Brenda, "and you think about all you've done to help make this game possible. Sometimes, of course, you see players and their families and you know they are going to be traded right after the game. And none of them know it yet."

Her desk and Al Coates's office are busy places leading up to the Entry Draft each summer. What she could tell people about the different interests and human demands of each player! She won't tell anyone, of course. But she could.

But chief travel planner is her major title come July, when the team gets from league headquarters its preliminary computer-written schedule of eight-two games. Arriving at that schedule is no simple process either. Every NHL team, for instance, must play every other NHL team at least twice, once in each city. But teams must play conference opponents more often.

Overlay these requirements with the often conflicting schedules of the arenas, which book ice shows, rock concerts, curling competitions, collegiate and high-school athletic events, circuses, basketball games, monster truck races, and tractor-pulls, among other activities. Now add the differing traditions and holidays of two diverse countries; both have Thanksgiving, but on different days in different months, and Americans stay home to watch pro football on TV on that Thursday. New Year's Eve games are a big Calgary tradition, so the Flames want an original-six team that night, if possible. Only the United States marks Martin Luther King, Jr.'s birthday with a civic holiday that might cause fans to go out, but only Canada has Boxing Day, which keeps most people at home. Adjust the hockey schedule for other sports events: the NBA schedule largely mirrors the NHL's, and you might not want an NHL game to go up against a World Series. And now the Winter Olympics require a two-week break.

Now, mix in the demands and programming needs of television networks and stations that are paying big bucks to show the games and charging even bigger bucks for beer, auto, and Canadian Tire advertisements that will be watched by millions of viewers, who in the Atlantic time zone will be heading for bed by the time the Canadiens face off against the Kings in Los Angeles for a seven p.m. game in the Pacific time zone. So how about a Sunday afternoon game, except that mid-afternoon and early evening games cause fans to eat at home first and positively kill important concession sales at the game site?

Now, toss into the scheduling brew the specific requests of individual teams. The Flames, for instance, are trying to change the demographics in the team's fan mix to create a new generation of family ticket-buyers; the Flames want several Saturday and Sunday matinee games at 1:30. That's 3:30 p.m. in the Eastern time zone, which might do little for the CBC or Philadelphia's Sportschannel. But that's 12:30 on the West Coast and might draw well if the opponent is the Sharks or Canucks.

But Brenda's concern is logistics, smoothly but cost-effectively moving twenty-four players, four coaches, four trainers and equipment managers, four or six media representatives, and possibly a general manager, an owner or two plus their spouses, and a couple of contest-winners. "You want to make things go as smoothly as possible," says Brenda, "so the guys can concentrate on their game. But as hard as you might try, you can't plan or anticipate everything."

When George Greenwood told Brenda the Saddledome had been booked more than a year in advance for a two-week curling championship one future March, Brenda knew that was good for Saddledome income but potential trouble for her: a two-week Flames road trip two years hence.

In July, Brenda also saw trouble with a road trip following immediately after a recent January All-Star break. Typically, players not in the All-Star Game scatter across the continent for a few days in the sun, if they are single, or a few days with family, if married. The coaches, management, and usually Fleury will be at the All-Star Game. Now, how best to resume the regular schedule by getting the others from Calgary to Pittsburgh as efficiently – and cheaply – as possible in time for their only practice together in nearly six days before a crucial game?

When the league's draft schedule reaches her in late July, Brenda sits down with general manager Al Coates, the head coach, and Mike Burke, director of hockey administration, and walks through every trip. From their long experience they have certain scheduling preferences. Brenda knows most coaches' strong desire for practice time on the road, which is more difficult to arrange than a practice at home. She knows on that

Pittsburgh trip, for instance, the coach will want the team to meet him there in time for a Monday practice, which means the team must leave Calgary sometime on Sunday. As it turns out, Pittsburgh's Civic Arena is unavailable on Monday. So Brenda must find and reserve ice-time at an adequate suburban rink. That means another bus reservation and more calls.

The Flames can get a game-day skate in the Civic Arena before Tuesday night's game. And don't forget to arrange for the forty late check-outs that day. Now that game will no doubt end too late to make any commercial flight to Toronto for the Wednesday-night game. That means she will need a charter flight from Pittsburgh to Toronto late Tuesday. Late at night after a game means the players will need food and plenty of it. But can the charter get to Toronto before the one a.m. airport curfew on landings? Or should she plan to land in Hamilton? Either way, the team will need a bus in Canada after midnight and again in the late morning from the hotel to Maple Leaf Gardens for the game-day skate.

This time the Flames will try a different hotel in Toronto. The new one is quieter and, some hope, may help to break the string of losses to the Maple Leafs that some on the team believe may be tied to their usual hotel.

That road trip's next game is Friday night in Ottawa. Is it better to practise in Toronto at the Gardens on Thursday morning before going to the airport? Or should the Flames fly to Ottawa first and practise there, which will mean a longer bus ride out to the Corel Centre?

And while solving these problems, Brenda also needs to remember that all of these people she is phoning are in a work day two hours ahead of Calgary's Mountain time zone. So Brenda's mid-morning is Ontario's lunchtime, and she better have all of her eastern calls done by two-thirty in Alberta. That's when she turns her attention to the West Coast trips.

Of course, Brenda cannot know in July about the ice storm headed for Toronto on the same night as that Pittsburgh game. Or the possible airline strike in February. Or the trades that will change the roster before the March trading deadline.

Now, the last time the Flames were at that New Jersey hotel several players sent word that the salads were wilted and the pastas too spicy. So Brenda must correct that with the chef.

She also must bargain for the best deals everywhere. Whenever possible, the Flames stay in Canada to avoid costly currency transactions. Likewise, whenever possible the Flames fly on Canadian Airlines, their Saddledome sponsor and discount travel partner. But Canadian Airlines does not fly everywhere. So where can the Flames get the best airfare deal without staying over a Saturday?

And so it goes over an entire season.

It's exhausting just to hear Brenda recount an August work day. So how do the Koyiches – Brenda, the travelling secretary, and her husband, the travelling salesman – relax together?

They plan their own trips every March and July.

Only someone who did not know Theo Fleury would be surprised by what he did at his first Flames training camp.

"Gecz," says Terry Crisp, Calgary's head coach when Fleury arrived, "I saw that little pecker get out of the cab at training camp. He was challenging everyone in sight, everyone, especially the goalies. He thought he had to make his statement right off. I said, 'If this kid doesn't get killed in his first forty-eight hours, he could be great.'"

Fleury's reputation preceded him. When Bearcat Murray realized Theo Fleury was Wally's son, he knew the kid was tough enough to make it. "You don't survive the WHL without being a tough character," says Bearcat.

Lanny McDonald did not remember the ragged youngster pushing forward to get his autograph after that Winnipeg game, but he took one look at the kid's WHL stats and he knew something was there, beyond the little body. "Great numbers in Junior," Lanny recalls, "usually mean you were on a helluva team or you're real good. Theo was not on a helluva team. In fact, it was a helluvan-awful team. So we knew he had something."

As usual, the scouts had briefed the coaches on the new players. Ian told them, 'Don't panic over the kid's size. Give yourself some time with this little guy and let him convince you, as he did me.' This first pro training camp would be a time of first impressions and assessment for all of the Flames' new players, only two of whom would stay in the league for long. With one year of junior eligibility remaining, the assumption was that Fleury would return to Moose Jaw for a final year of seasoning, if not growth. He came into camp at 155 pounds.

It did not take long for those 155 pounds to make an impression on the coaches, who liked him, on the veterans, who disliked him, on the goalies, who hated him, on the media, who loved him, and on the fans, who were intrigued.

The way newcomers are supposed to come into town in the close-knit hockey fraternity is to be quiet and modest, take time to feel their way around, learn the ropes and routines, downplay any individual importance they might have and play up the importance of the team. Theo Fleury was the smallest newcomer. But as Len Peltz still says about him, "Theo is short. But Theo is not small."

Nor did Theo come on small. "He walked into that locker room," Lanny remembers with a fond smile beneath that immense red moustache, "and he said, in effect, 'Here I am, larger than life, literally. I'm here to save all of you.' Theo sometimes has a way of saying things, and they may be true, but they don't come out quite right. So, some people take offence. Actually, Theo royally pissed off an awful lot of veterans.

"I used to think Theo could say some things a little softer, you know, not get everybody so riled up. But getting everybody riled up is probably why he's been so successful over the years. He doesn't believe what people said, about how someone that small is not going to survive in the NHL, let alone succeed."

Coach Crisp was amazed. "I thought Flower had some kind of Charles Bronson Death Wish," he says. "In practice, without fail, he would automatically take on the biggest guy. Did you hear the goalie story?"

Everyone on the Flames remembers the goalie story. Players at Flames training camps – sixty or seventy in all – are divided into four teams for purposes of drilling and scrimmaging. In one drill, a defenceman lies down on the ice. The puck is dropped near a forward. The defenceman must get up and stop the forward's rush towards and shot at the goalie.

Players in those training camps watch each other quite closely, maybe as closely as the coaches watch. They are not yet teammates. They are all auditioning for the same jobs, sometimes viciously. Very quickly in that camp, Fleury gained a reputation for quickness. So worried was the defenceman about Theo's speed that he started to get up before the puck was dropped. A coach blew his whistle for a restart. But Fleury ignored the whistle. He skated past the defenceman, who was initially startled and then embarrassed that he had become an on-ice spectator, and Fleury shot the puck at the goalie. Gasps were not audible. But they could have been, for this was a severe violation of macho hockey protocol: a nineteen-year-old rookie firing a warning shot at a veteran. The goalie retrieved the puck and fired it at Fleury, who retrieved the puck and shot it back at the goalie. Whistles blew all over. But everyone got the wordless message loud and clear: this little guy was different, intentionally and defiantly. And what were you going to do about it?

"Theo is always driving it at you," says Mike Burke. "He's always trying to bite your ankles. He figures if he makes everyone feel confused and hassled, then they can't find him, let alone get him."

Drafting Fleury was perhaps more a sign of the general manager's faith in Ian McKenzie's scouting skills than in Fleury's NHL future. But Cliff Fletcher quickly became a Fleury fan. "If we were so smart," says Fletcher, "we should never have waited until the eighth round to take Fleury. In all candour, when we drafted him, from my perspective the bottom line was he'd be a real entertaining player for our farm club in Salt Lake City. Anything more would be great. But that competitive fire of his was unbelievable. And his instincts. He was simply going to defy the odds and prove everybody wrong."

Burke adds: "Theo loves it when it's him against the world. He's always at his best in the biggest-pressure situations. And he is never intimidated. Never."

Coach Crisp loves players like this. "There just is no quit in Theoren Fleury," says the man who affectionately called Theo Fleury everything but Theo Fleury.

"Crispy never called me by my name," Theo says now with a smile. "He called me Flower, peckerhead, and some other things, but never Theo. He knew I play my best when I'm pissed off."

Fleury struck many as cocky. Not Crisp. "No, he wasn't cocky. Cocky can be hollow. Theo was just very, very confident. And sometimes that bothers people who haven't worked as hard as he has to get where they are. But Fleury knew he had practised endless hours. He knew what his considerable skills were. He'd take the puck and come flying down the ice and make some kind of incredible spinnerama move with the puck between his legs and shoot and score. Now, maybe many rookies can make that move. But few of them would be likely to try it for fear they might fail. Fleury was not afraid of failing. He knew he had to make an impression.

"And he succeeded."

Glen Sather, who still presides over the archrival Edmonton Oilers after many successful years with Messier, Gretzky, and crew, remembers the first time he saw Fleury. In fact, he can remember precisely when Fleury was drafted.

"I think it was the eighth round," says Sather. "We had talked about taking Fleury. But our scouts were reluctant because of his size. I had not seen him play in Junior. I said to our people, 'How the hell can this little guy get so many penalty minutes and so many points?' I think we played the Flames in an exhibition game during training camp. We hadn't taken him in the draft, obviously. That was the first time I saw him play. Right away, I turned to our staff and said, 'I think we've made a terrible mistake.' He's a great competitor."

That competitiveness and spunk, not to mention those points, made Fleury a Calgary fan favourite from his second shift. The big city's newspapers were full of stories on the "little man" with the baby face. It's all part of the hero-making – and, eventually, hero-unmaking – machine; what did that new little guy do yesterday? "Our world loves overachievers," Burke observes. "The kids especially are drawn to Fleury. They identify with him – 'Theo Fleury could be me.' In fact, sometimes Theo still seems like a kid in many ways."

At the end of training camp that kid was headed back to Moose Jaw, as expected, for a final year of preparation in Junior, after having made his desired impact. In pro sports the youngsters are supposed to push the veterans from below. And the veterans are supposed to see this as a stimulating professional challenge instead of a threat to their million-dollar salary. Ian told Theo to work hard and stay focused. Theo told Ian he was going to win the WHL scoring championship.

And he did just that. He scored 160 points in 65 games that year, tying Joe Sakic for the league lead, and all that while accumulating 235 of Moose Jaw's 3,472 penalty minutes. Fleury also would have his captaincy suspended for a half-dozen games for, as Theo puts it, "beaking off in the papers." Always a prime target for reporters, Theo had supplied them and their readers and listeners with frank quotes about the team's troubled season, frank quotes which, frankly, the coaches did not like.

Fleury did not call a news conference to announce his views on losing so consistently. He issued no news release, sought to plant no rumours by going off the record, and did not steer the reporters to others who would back him up.

Fleury's stubborn openness and sometimes troublemaking candour have always made him easy pickings for story-hungry writers. All they have had to do is get him alone and talk like friends. The reporters in Moose Jaw asked the developing star, quite sincerely, what Theo thought about the team losing so much. The answers to such sports questions are eminently predictable. They are asked by reporters who have already decided on the gist of tomorrow's story or column. It's safe to say the player is not going to respond: "No, I really don't mind losing a lot. We've done so much of it here in recent years and we are getting even better at handling defeat as this season goes on. In fact, I believe we still have a very good chance of missing the playoffs once again."

Predictably, Theo Fleury told the inquiring minds what he thought about losing so much: He didn't like it. Who would? The team had not succeeded for a lot of years. Fleury also thought somebody ought to do something about it. What's it going to take? The team's record spoke for itself. So did Fleury's mounting scoring numbers. No one could question his effort.

Of course, when the stories came out, Fleury's thoughts sounded less like the solicited views of a short athlete answering a provocative question from a friend while towelling himself off and looking for his socks. They sounded more like the provocative, premeditated demands of an uppity nineteen-year-old team captain who refused to accept his place in life, especially to the ears of a possibly insecure coaching staff that knew the team's record only too well and was secretly and justifiably worried about its own future. If Fleury has something to say to team management, the coaches wondered, why doesn't he come in to them and say it? Why talk to outsiders?

The truth is the reporters asked Fleury. Management didn't. And being famous, or on the way there, raises the volume of everything you say. If a regular (i.e., non-famous) person says he'd like to come back and visit his school, no one cares. If a visiting celebrity utters the same words, the crowd applauds. Same words, bigger deal. Another truth is that some of Fleury's teammates also resented his apparent fingerpointing, though they had shared his sentiments before the interview. But their views were not as eagerly sought as the captain's. Being eagerly sought makes someone important nowadays.

That year Fleury would go on to become the tenth leading goal-scorer in WHL history, the twelfth in assists, and tenth in points. Fleury again made the Canadian World Junior Team and gained additional exposure. There, he played with Sakic, Adam Graves, and Trevor Linden and was chosen captain of the Canadian team, which brought tears to Ede's eyes when she saw the "C" on Theo's shirt on TV. The Canadians went on to beat the Russians for the gold medal in Moscow. How sweet that was! And by the time Theoren returned to Moose Jaw, the Warriors' coach had been fired. And Theo was reinstated as captain.

If anyone had asked him then about the change of events, Fleury would probably have shrugged – and maybe smiled. But he kept on working.

On November 18, 1987, Theoren Fleury and Shannon Griffin became the parents of Josh, an eight-pound-two-ounce future forward. Theo and Shannon discussed giving him up for adoption but dismissed it as soon as they shared the sight of the infant. Josh would be the embodiment of their commitment to each other. Marriage, however, would have to wait; the Moose

Jaw church would not permit the vows within its walls. Theo, however, could not wait to proclaim his joy at being a father. During a nationwide TV interview from Moscow, Theo said he wanted to say hello to his son back in Moose Jaw. His son was likely not watching; he had yet to turn two months old. But others were and they thought it strange that Theo would say hello via satellite TV to Josh but not to Josh's mother.

About that same time Theo learned a painful lesson about fame. He had become a celebrity around Moose Jaw, which is not Calgary but is a whole lot larger than Russell. The media are always delighted to have a celebrity, perhaps even to help create one; having someone the public wants to know about does help sell the product that's going to give them details of the celebrity's career and life.

The Warriors were delighted to boost Theo as their celebrity. The team had received the required payment from Calgary when the Flames drafted Fleury and another cheque would be forthcoming if Fleury actually played in the NHL. Having a possible future NHL star as captain and leading scorer helped sell tickets, even during what would be a dismal 18–52–2 season. Fleury, in fact, was responsible for 160 of the Warriors' 308 total points.

Fleury was prepared to spend unlimited time doing team promotions, sometimes patiently signing autographs for two hours or more at the shopping mall, which was considerably longer than he ever applied himself to, say, mowing grass. The kids especially liked Fleury. And the Warriors knew the effects of children's desires on the spending of a family's entertainment dollar.

Theo was recognized all over town. It was about this time that Fleury first sensed that fame, which starts out as being warm and inclusive, can become a cage, nicely furnished but confining nonetheless. He heard the whispers after passing a couple of people in a store aisle. One would say: "Hey, that's him, the hockey player." Or, "Hey, look! That's Fleury." Players soon get good at ignoring these surreptitious honours, until the fans take the next step. That's the not-always-shy request for an autograph on anything handy, a T-shirt, cap, the back of the grocery list, or even their skin. They must have something to prove to others, and perhaps to themselves later, that the encounter really took place. For a moment they were in the presence of fame.

Over time, the repetition of such encounters, each individually intended innocently enough, can also create a continuous sense of confinement, even imprisonment, as if the celebrity's every action, even the most routine in a convenience store, is being monitored and, quite likely, judged.

Fleury met people everywhere in town, on the street, and at the golf course where he played regularly and worked in summers. Many people want to meet sports stars, even teenage sports stars. It may be normal for nineteen-year-old hockey standouts to find people, some two or three times their age and others much younger, lining up just to shake their hand and wish them good luck in Friday night's game. But that is more fame than most nineteen-year-olds ever confront. It's a heady experience and proves addictive for some.

Star or not, Theo had failed his driver's exam on the first try, parallel parking and routinely checking over his shoulder proving to be his temporary downfall. But with some coaching and test runs with Ede, Theo finally passed. Now, as a newly drafted pro player, the boy wanted his own car. At the suggestion of one of those many people who seek to encircle celebrities, a man whom Fleury considered a good friend, Theo invested 10 per cent of his $35,000 Flames signing bonus to buy his first car, a used Chevette. Six months later Theo traded the Chevette in for a newer Toyota Supra. Only then did he discover he had paid twice the proper price to his "friend." It was a lesson even an exhausted Theo could recall late one night ten years later with the clarity that accompanied recollection of another major wound, The Injury.

But all that was forgotten on March 12, 1988, which was proclaimed Theoren Fleury Night in Moose Jaw. It was to be his last home game for the Warriors. Fleury had long been widely admired as an overachiever, a successful underdog, but he cemented his place in civic affection – if not team management's – by refusing a late-season trade to another WHL team in playoff contention. Moose Jaw might have received several good, younger players for the future. But Theo said the Warriors had given him his start in Junior when others had shied away because of his size. So, he said, he wanted to finish his Junior career as a Warrior. In fact, he had even had a huge Warrior chief's head tattooed on his arm. Team loyalty is a big deal to Fleury. Plus he wanted to get on with his pro life as soon as possible.

Sports speed up life. In the pros, they talk about the decline of players who have barely become thirty, which is about the time those in many non-athletic professions are just finishing apprenticeship. Cricket aside, everything happens so much faster on – or off – the rink or field, which is part of sports' appeal. No waiting for verdicts, beyond a couple of minutes occasionally during games for video reviews. The fans can be intimately, vocally, and emotionally involved in the action occurring before them while also being safely removed from it. Talk is cheap for fans, even in the expensive seats.

There are no grey areas in sports as there are in real life. There are fewer ties and compromises. Mayhem is cheered, not feared. Impatience is a virtue in sports. Greed, too. And sports are very tidy. There are good guys (ours) and bad guys (theirs); no need to worry about the bad in the good guys or the good in the bad guys. Without feeling any qualms, fans can turn real-life players into living caricatures. The beginnings and endings of everything are more decisive and clear-cut in sports than in real life, which has no precise periods and loud horns announcing their conclusion. Scores are easier to keep on ice than in life. And there are stats to mark the progress of every player and every team.

Given this haste with life, this compaction of a life chapter into one three-hour game inside a chilly building, and the distorting glare of fame and celebrity, no one involved in Theoren Fleury Night saw anything strange in all the talk about the "last game," "career end," or "retiring" the number of someone still three months short of his twentieth birthday. It all seemed a perfectly normal, even touching, gesture of programmed appreciation by a team organization and community for the focused physical action Fleury had allowed them to share with him for four hockey seasons.

So Moose Jaw went all out. The Warriors announced they would bestow on Theoren the ultimate team accolade: permanent retirement of his jersey number 9. It was the only time Moose Jaw had done that. The Chamber of Commerce Information Centre put up a sign: CONGRATULATIONS THEOREN FLEURY ALL OF MOOSE JAW IS PROUD. Warriors' president Art Schoenroth told Theoren, "You have carried the name of Moose Jaw Warriors throughout the world and have made us proud. When your father Wally told our executive that his son Theoren would build our franchise, he wasn't playing an idle fiddle tune. Our city, which is now your city, owes you a debt that we want to honour."

Coach Kvisle said, "The memories, fond in the hearts of Moose Jaw hockey people, and perhaps not so fond around the WHL, will always be there to cherish." Previous Warrior captains sent admiring messages. Mayor Scoop Lewry sent a congratulatory letter, as did Moose Jaw's members of Parliament. Shannon and Josh were there, as was a quiet Donna Fleury, a beaming, ebullient Wally Fleury, and a proud pair of Peltzes. Loyal fans offered tributes to Theo: "I like him," said Danny Sahl, who was eight at the time. "He's cool. I like when he gets mad."

Before the game, there were presentations at centre ice from local businesses, the team, the team's board, the team's booster club. Theoren responded. He was cheered. He was moved. He thanked many people; they never forgot the feeling of being mentioned so publicly by a celebrity. Those that Theoren left out never forgot the feeling of not being mentioned by the famous person. "Theoren Fleury has had to be so self-contained in his life," one of them noted, "that he has a difficult time saying 'Thank you' – or 'I'm sorry.'"

But no remarks that night were more moving than those delivered in person by Michael Smedley, a five-year-old Ontario boy who would never play hockey due to muscular dystrophy but had adopted Theoren Fleury as his idol. Clorox of Canada paid for Michael's trip to Moose Jaw and Theo gave him the game's official puck. Flashbulbs flashed all over the arena.

With his Junior career officially complete, the *Hockey News* named its Junior Player of the Year: Theoren Fleury. He travelled immediately to Salt Lake City to begin his pro career in the IHL, just in time to help the team win the Turner Cup. In two games he racked up seven points – three goals and four assists – and an equal number of penalty minutes.

The summer of 1988 seemed to take forever to end. When training camp finally opened, it was a disaster for Fleury. After all those years of going his own way, Theo had listened to everyone who offered him advice. He could not make himself any taller, but he could get larger. Theo had put on some weight, actually a lot of weight. In 1987, Theo came to the Flames camp at 155 pounds. In 1988, he arrived weighing 175 pounds. Now, in addition to taking a lot of penalties, he was slow.

"When you're small," says Cliff Fletcher, "you can't lose even a half-step. The game becomes so much harder that way."

Ian McKenzie remembers his disappointment at that second camp. "People told Theo," Ian says, "that he looked like a drowned rat at 150 pounds. So what? He was a very quick drowned rat. So he added weight. But the truth was, he couldn't carry it. The first year, he intimidated defencemen with his speed. The second year, he didn't. He couldn't. So we sent him down to Salt Lake before the season started. I told him to get in shape and lose the weight."

"LITTLE MAN GONE," said the Calgary headline. Fleury thought that might be the end of his NHL career, before it even began. He was crushed. After a few desultory games, coach Paul Baxter, famous within the Flames organization for his tutoring of young players, laid out the choice bluntly for Theo: You can either play your way into the NHL or sulk your way out of it.

Theo chose to play. In forty IHL games that year, he scored 37 goals, had 37 assists, and earned 74 penalty minutes.

In the early weeks, Theo lived with Brian Patafie, now the Flames' trainer. "The team felt Theo was a little young to be living in a hotel," Brian recalls. "He was making $27,500 in Salt Lake, eating fast food, living for each day's hockey game or practice, and almost every night calling his dad. Theo was a regular guy then. And he's still a regular guy, despite all of the money and fame. You gotta love someone who doesn't let money change them."

The Flames had a very good team in that 1988–89 NHL season. But as the fall progressed, Coach Crisp became increasingly worried. The Flames were not as good as they could be. Something was missing. The team needed a spark. Speaking of sparks, how was Fleury doing? His name was always popping up in the conversation of Flames coaches, as it had in Ian's mind before then.

"For some reason," Coach Crisp recalls, "our team had reached a flat spot. The Fleury kid was lighting up the IHL. I thought, hey, let's try the youngster, bring in some excitement, some of *his* excitement. If it didn't work, we'd send him back down."

Shannon Griffin had just returned on December 28 to Salt Lake City from a Christmas visit to Saskatchewan. The day after she got back, her birthday, Theo had proposed. Now, it was

New Year's Eve. She was all dressed up for the team party after the game against the Denver Rangers and waiting for Theo outside the locker room. And waiting. And waiting. Suddenly, one of the players ran out and yelled, "Theo's going up."

In Russell, two phones rang at New Year's – at the Fleurys' and the Peltzes'. It was Theo. "I'm going to The Show," he said.

Instead of the team party that night, Theo packed in their apartment while Shannon did the laundry until near dawn. On January 3, 1989, Theoren Fleury played in his first NHL game.

He had been right all along.

❖

One of the first people to know about any roster move is the equipment manager. In the Flames' case he is Bobby Stewart, a conscientious, chunky Montreal native who remembers the day when he became a stickboy for the Canadiens; on that day Bobby thought that life could get no better. He quit playing hockey himself at sixteen, but became the trainer for a Montreal Junior team, which was where the new Flames hired him in 1973. Oh, the miles he has put on since! "I've been at this for twenty-four years," says Bobby. "I'm going to do this until I get it right."

Bobby's job is to ensure that every player has everything he needs to compete – pads, uniform, stick, tape, sharp skates. He's got an old sewing machine for ripped jerseys, boxes of rivets, piles of laces, different-shaped face shields (and the screws to fit them), a skate-sharpener, various sizes of jockstraps and plastic cups, hacksaws, garter belts, socks of various weights, and hundreds of wood, aluminum, and graphite hockey sticks of varying dimensions, weights, and stiffness.

Like Brenda Koyich arranging the travel schedule, Bobby's goal is to minimize hassles, to cater to the players' every possible need, so that they can concentrate on the game. He gets help from the representatives of equipment manufacturers whose job it is to recruit new players and to see to it that they and the veterans are seen using the company's sticks or gloves or helmets. Custom-made sticks, for instance, are provided free in unlimited quantities. All Bobby has to do is tell the Jofa representative he is running low on Theoren's favourite style, and a fresh bundle with Fleury's name stamped on the side is shipped immediately, even to meet the Flames in a distant city.

It's one thing to ensure the ready availability of all of this at home in the Saddledome. It's something else to do it on the road, far from the familiar drawers and boxes. Bobby also has to remember which heavy-duty rubberized bag of five dozen contains the CCM plastic blade holders and which one holds the spare jerseys with the proper name and number for the new player being called up from Saint John tonight or, even more challenging, for the traded player arriving from another organization come morning. Bobby better have brought along sufficient spare letters to spell out any Russian name.

Bobby doesn't spend much time sitting at his little desk in the Saddledome; there is always some crisis or chore to handle. "Exactly what happened," he asks out loud of no one in particular, "to all the Russian players who never wanted their skates sharpened?" But on his desk sits his favourite inspirational sign: YOU NEVER FAIL UNTIL YOU STOP TRYING.

Bobby has collected a Stanley Cup ring for the championship the Flames won in Fleury's first year. From a quarter-century of working in and loitering around pro hockey rooms, Bobby has also collected some skill at reading the behaviour and demeanour of thoroughbred athletes: "One night they're quiet and they go out and play great. And the next night they're noisy and go out and play great. And vice versa. You figure that out."

Many staff members pitch in to help Bobby and he does the same for them. Brian Patafie, the trainer, will round up gear. So will Terry Kane, the physical therapist, and Tony Oumerow, a Russian masseur whose nimble fingers work out pains before, during, and after games and practices.

As they waddle off the ice between periods, several players will toss their gloves to Tony, who attaches them to an intriguing array of Rube Goldberg devices. They are actually a series of hair dryers adapted with PVC piping that blasts the hot air into the damp gloves. "Drying gloves to keep players' hands comfy is something that's changed since I started in this business," offers Bobby. So many dryers have been plugged in on the hallway floors of some arenas that the fuses blow.

Something else that has changed in recent years is the team's attitude towards the community. There always has been some sense of connection, but now the Flames work hard at it. Much of the responsibility for the new emphasis rested on Rick Skaggs, another Manitoba boy who went west to join the Flames. Previously, Rick was Winnipeg sales manager for Molson's sports promotions, a logical link to public-relations director of the Calgary Flames.

Smoothly assisted by Bernie Doenz, Rick and Kathy Gieck, his assistant, facilitate the media's links with the team, mainly the players. For some games there can be as many as forty-five media personnel requiring credentials and attention. "That means we feed them," Rick says, laughing. Whenever a player sees Rick approaching in the locker room, he knows someone wants to talk with him. It could be a TV broadcast between periods, a visiting network reporter, a radio station. He is not always a welcome sight. "My job is easy when we're winning," says Rick, "and not so easy when we're losing."

The team does some player training in public relations. "Many of our players are young and inexperienced," says Rick, who is neither. "We want them to feel comfortable dealing with the public and the media. It's an important aspect of their job." There have been some public-relations hurdles in recent years:

the lockout, the Flames' regular disappearance in early playoff rounds, the Saddledome's renovation, which displaced many season-ticket-holders. "We need to scramble now," says Rick, "and build and keep a higher community profile."

The team has its autographed-bookmark program to encourage children's literacy. Recently, the players chipped in to lease a seventy-thousand-dollar luxury box for the season, dubbed it the Junior Flames Locker Room, and made it available to youth programs every game. In 1997, the Flames also bought the Calgary Hitmen Major Junior team from a consortium of owners, which included Fleury and Joe Sakic, and laid plans to make that WHL franchise and Saddledome tenant more of a joint draw and perhaps even a fan feeder system with the Flames. "We look at this," said Ron Bremner, Flames president, "as a great opportunity to expand our presence, expand our market, and have some new marketing opportunities in a new and exciting demographic. The fans who are fourteen years old today in ten years are going to be good potential season-ticket-buyers for NHL tickets."

There is an amazing number of requests for something from the club: player appearances at stores or car dealerships, autographed pennants for children in hospital, pucks, Flames gear for charity auctions. Bobby Stewart keeps a special garbage can near the locker room for discarded sticks, even stick fragments, to fulfil such requests. "It's more important these days," Rick adds, "to create a team image and to give something back to the community."

Rick and Kathy help find help for the players to handle the growing volume of fan mail. "Our guys can get overwhelmed with this stuff," says Rick. "Their mind is supposed to be on hockey, but you can't ignore some kid in Saskatchewan who sends in his hockey card for an autograph. And you'll never guess which Flames player gets the most mail."

Less visible but of some importance to the team's success and attraction is the quiet back-room work of Gary Taylor, the

Flames' longtime video man. From a little cubicle in the corner of the Flames' Saddledome workout room, Gary runs twelve VCRs off of five satellite systems, videotaping games of future opponents as well as some Junior games to scout prospects. His first taping involved a Flames game in 1980 in the old Corral, using a handheld videocamera.

In fact, Gary lives his whole working life on tape; although he has gone on an occasional Flames road trip, Gary has never seen a Flames home game in the Saddledome. "I'm standing here just eighty feet from the ice," Gary says, "and I can't get out there."

Gary's twelve-to-fourteen-hour daily schedules are not the smoothest or most predictable. He may come in at five-thirty and work all morning, editing tapes of the last three games of the next opponent into segments for the head coach and his assistants to study either at home, in their office, or in their hotel room on the road. There will be tapes of the opposition teams' power plays, their penalty-kills, their special teams, forechecking, and defensive-zone coverage. Gary can expertly turn an entertaining three-hour game into an incisive twelve-minute, commercial-free action tape that will alert coaches that Vancouver has just changed its defensive strategy. Then he'll take the afternoon off and return in the evening to aim his five huge antennas out back at unseen satellites floating in outer space broadcasting that night's games of upcoming opponents.

Gary might be taping simultaneously five games elsewhere and the Flames game across the hall when a special request comes down from Kevin Constantine on the Flames bench. By the next intermission, Gary, please make up a tape of power plays from the current game so the assistant coach and resting players can analyse a new pattern and make adjustments.

Gary also keeps running video scrapbooks for players of goals and hits, even favourite Flames fights. The fight tape of Sandy McCarthy, a combative winger sometimes protecting Fleury, is getting quite long. For entertainment and a little learning, Gary makes tapes titled: "Good Aggression," "Defence to Offence," "Breakouts," "Power Play Goals," "Cycling," "In Your Face," "Regrouping," and Gary's personal favourite, "Oh No's."

"I love this game and this job," says Gary, "trying to capture and then find and use just the right visual moment to trigger our guys. It's my job to have these tapes ready for the coaches, no excuses. And I've never missed one game I was supposed to have."

Gary particularly admires Theo Fleury. Gary has his son helping Theo handle the stream of fan mail that flows into the Flames offices. "Don't ever tell Theo he can't do something," Gary says with a confident smile. "I'll bet he'd take on those NBA players if you challenged him."

Given his longstanding expertise with videotapes, satellites, and tape players, is Gary Taylor available to help others program their VCR to catch tonight's game? "Actually," says Gary, "no, I'm not. I don't really know how. I do everything manually. I can't trust technology to do it for me."

◈

Fleury had instant NHL success. He earned his first assist against the Los Angeles Kings in his second NHL game on January 5, 1989, and his first goal two days later in his third game, which was against Grant Fuhr and the Edmonton Oilers.

Even though they spend most of the first twenty years of their lives trying to get into the NHL, players still have some major adjustments to make once they get there. Players in the NHL seem bigger. Everything, including the skating, seems to go faster in the NHL. The lights are brighter. The headlines seem bolder. The crowds are bigger. The money is bigger, too, of course, but so are the consequences – of stellar play and dumb mistakes.

Some players' heads get bigger, as well. "For a brief time when he first came up," says Al Strachan, a nationally noted hockey writer, "Theo was a real, uh, dip. He thought he mattered quite a bit and he lacked some social skills. But that didn't last long. You know, we forget how young these guys are, how narrow their interests have been, and the money and material things that most of them did not have growing up.

"But there was never any doubt about his skill, his heart, his guts. Theo is the consummate Canadian hockey player, especially Western Canadian – rugged, tough, never intimidated. He knows as long as someone is screaming at you, you don't have to fight them. Theo thinks like the Sutter brothers think: 'You got a problem? Well, get over it. It's only pain.' In the States I think the athletes are coddled more with athletic scholarships and simply more people to tell them they're wonderful. In Canada, even the biggest star in Junior rides the bus through the night like everyone else."

Like many fans, Al has a favourite Fleury story. "I remember the '91 Calgary–Edmonton playoffs. The first game. An absolutely perfect back-and-forth classic game. I think it was 2–2 in overtime. Fleury steals a Messier pass at centre ice, races in, and drills it past Fuhr. Flames win. Fleury was so excited that even up in the press box, it was infectious."

John Davidson is a Calgary boy, a goalie, who went on to fame and fortune playing for and broadcasting about the New York Rangers. "Hey," he says, "any time I hear Mark Messier speak in glowing terms about someone, their ability, emotion, heart, will, and the way they handle adversity, like he speaks about Fleury, I take note. When you think about the small players like the Richards, you can't think of anyone who has played the game better than Fleury. And he's done it consistently from youth hockey in Manitoba to the NHL and World Cup."

Davidson says as a goalie he always hated playing against small players like Fleury. "The little guys are just that much quicker than the large ones – their dekes, their stick-work, their windup, their release. It's only a millisecond. But it fools your eyes.

"The trick for stars in the NHL these days," he adds, "is not getting too comfortable though. Few of them have had much in their lives. Suddenly, there's a lot of money and a lot of fame and the temptation to coast at times can be pretty strong. Plus, those little bodies put on a lot of miles out there running around with – and into – the big boys. Calgary's been rebuilding in recent years with a lot of rookies, and a veteran like Fleury probably feels like he's the Lone Ranger at times."

Fleury reminded coach Crisp of those Indian-rubber balls. "You know, the harder you throw them against the wall, the harder they come right back at you," he says. "I played with Bobby Clarke and those guys and we never worried about a player's size like they do today. So I don't always pay attention to size. I think that bus that brought him up from Salt Lake could still be waiting to take Flower back to the minors for all I know.

"But I know too that I was never sending him back down. I used him to kill penalties right from the start. That's a sign of great confidence. You want guys killing penalties who always – always – work hard and won't make dumb mistakes. He knows the game. He's always thinking the game. He has great anticipation. He's like the Russians, always gets himself open. He doesn't stay in traffic standing around like a post with his mind in neutral. I tell you, every team would like to have a Fleury. But there aren't enough Fleurys to go around.

"I give a lot of speeches nowadays," the coach adds. "Motivational kinds of speeches. People want to hear how coaches do it. I say coaches don't do it. Players do it. And I always cite two players I had in Calgary – Dougie Gilmour and Theoren Fleury. In my mind Theo is like Henri Richard, similar kind of player. If there's a dull game, those kinds of guys don't mind going in and shaking things up. Theo would take a run at the largest player out there. Then, he'd take a run at the second- largest player and so on."

Lanny McDonald recalls one game against Montreal. "Larry Robinson was a foot taller than Theo at least," Lanny says, smiling. "Robinson had the puck. So little Theo takes a run at him. No one ever expected that. Theo got our guys pumped up. 'Geez, if Theo's doing it, I better, too.' Theo turned the game around. As a team, you build on little things like that and they become big things. Yeah, Theo rubs some people the wrong way. He always has. I suspect he always will. But he answers all the questions out on the ice. The code of athletics, whether you are Michael Jordan, Dennis Rodman, Albert Belle, or Theoren Fleury, is if you get the job done in the game, bottom line, it's all okay in the end."

"Well," Theo says in response, "hockey is a physical game. There's nothing in the rules that says I can't hit people out there just because they're bigger. I like to go into the corner, dig the puck out, and create some opportunities. I wish I had a dollar for every time someone has said I'm too small to play. See, that's the difference in our society. A small player has to prove he *can* play. Big guys have to prove they *can't*. Big guys get the benefit of the doubt. That's all right. Maybe we've opened some doors for smaller players."

When Kevin Constantine was head coach of the San Jose Sharks, he knew Fleury only as an irritating opponent who became the most successful scorer against the Sharks in team history. "Fleury is so good in this emotional game," says Constantine, "because he is so emotional. Sometimes that helps him score. Sometimes that gets him in trouble." Kevin keeps game notes in a little laptop computer where he types in observations and comments on most players he sees. He had a lot of comments in there about Fleury.

Suddenly a few years ago Constantine was fired by the Sharks. He was in his mid-thirties and it seemed he would never again chew another piece of bubble gum behind an NHL hockey bench. "For two weeks after the firing," he said, "I sat around at home feeling angry." Then, he began organizing a hockey camp and playing with computer programs that addressed the needs of hockey teams and coaches. Just as suddenly as he was fired, the Constantine phone rang. It was Pierre Page, an old friend from Minnesota hockey days. Calgary's assistant coach, Don Hay, had just been chosen the first head coach of the Phoenix Coyotes. Would Kevin come to Calgary as assistant?

One of Constantine's biggest surprises in Calgary was Fleury. "I have discovered," said Kevin, "that Theo is much more intelligent than I anticipated. He's not just rambunctious. He's incredibly savvy. I've seen countless situations where you'll watch and no play is possible and then he'll score. He sees things that others can't. And he has no fear, absolutely no fear at all. He'll go to the net and get hit more than some bigger boys. Look, anyone who walks around with two missing teeth and a huge gap in the front of his mouth at age twenty-eight is sending a message of some kind. As a coach, I like that message."

Fans love that message. Fleury is the only player left on the Flames from the 1989 Stanley Cup champions. He remains a most recognizable local celebrity. People wave to him everywhere. "Hi, Theo," complete strangers say. "Hi, how ya doin'?" the Flames captain replies.

"He's an attractive, distinctive subject," says Dave Elston, who needs distinctive subjects in his business. Elston is the well-known sports cartoonist in the *Calgary Sun* and the *Hockey News*. Cartoonists need characters or caricatures to make a living, which is why Dave Elston loves players like Esa Tikkanen, Marty McSorley, and Theo Fleury. "We don't seem to have the same kinds of characters in hockey today," says Elston. "They're more like athletic businessmen."

Elston did several famous cartoons featuring Fleury. There was one showing a penalty box. Only the top of a helmet marked

Fleury was visible. Another showed a Flames line change with several players leaping over the boards and a pair of hockey gloves coming up a little ladder by Fleury's spot.

The word was that Fleury was not all that delighted with those cartoons – until he met the cartoonist. Elston is ten years older and three inches shorter than Fleury. "I'm one of the few people," Elston says proudly, "that Theo can call 'Shorty.'"

Calgary fans have noticed a gradual change in Fleury in recent years. Other coaches and general managers have discovered over time that to neutralize Fleury as a scorer, and skilled distraction, they need to distract him. "The best way to play Theo," says Cliff Fletcher, "is to agitate him, get him off his game."

Coach Crisp is one of Fleury's favourite coaches. "The coaches I've played the best for," Theo says, "are the toughest on me, but in a nice way. Crispy knew how to push my button almost till I hated him."

"I didn't ride Flower much," Crisp says now. "You don't need to get him fired up. You need to calm him down some. He's a real treat to work with." But now Fleury is coach Crisp's opposition twice a year. He tells his Tampa Bay Lightning players simply, "Hassle Fleury early but don't, whatever you do, piss him off. That's when he gets great, when he's mad."

Simply put, Fleury has matured. "He's a much smarter player now," says Fletcher. "He knows when to expend physical energy and when to save it. He's become one of the better forwards in the NHL and one of the best players Canada has. The tougher the games are, the bigger they are, the harder he plays. You can't teach that competitive fire. And he's so durable, too. Potentially, he's got a lot of years ahead of him. He just can't afford to lose his speed."

"Theo has definitely matured," adds McDonald, who played 1,111 NHL games himself and had his number-9 jersey retired by the Flames, which explains Fleury's switch to number 14 for the NHL. "As a professional, you put incredible pressure on yourself. You know thousands, perhaps millions, of people are watching you all the time. Whether you play one year, five years, or sixteen years, sometimes you expect more of yourself than yourself can produce. [NHL coach] Roger Neilson once told me, you play 50 per cent of your games ordinarily and you play 25 per cent of your games absolutely outstanding and you play 25 per cent of your games as hard as you possibly can and nothing matters, you stink. Now, that means you are a dog in twenty games every year. It takes maturity to always try to be great but to learn to accept those times you are not. Maturity takes time."

"Playing hockey for me now," says Theoren, "it's like I'm two different people. I'm really kind of laid-back off the ice. But on the ice I'm aggressive. I look angry all the time. I'm emotional. People have told me it's like Superman going into the phone booth and completely changing personality. I look at tapes from before and I kind of cringe. I don't believe I did some of that stuff. My emotions got the best of me."

Is he aware when he is getting under an opponent's skin? "Oh, for sure," he says with a very small smile. "I draw on their hate. It gives me an advantage. Hopefully, they discover I'm under their skin when we light up the scoreboard. But I can't get so wrapped up in that any more that it gets me off *my* game. I need to pick my spots. I'm working on that."

Anybody else would be delighted with five consecutive thirty-goal seasons, four All-Star appearances, more than 170 multiple-point games, an average of more than one point per game for each of his more than seven hundred NHL games, one 51-goal, 104-point season (1990–91), and two other 40-plus-goal seasons (1993–94 and 1995–96). They would be pleased with a second 100-point season (1992–93), almost certainly with becoming the Flames' all-time leading goal-scorer (Joe Nieuwendyk held the record at 214), finishing among the Flames' top three scorers for at least seven consecutive years, missing less than 1 per cent of his games due to injury, going three-for-three on career penalty shots, and setting an NHL record with a plus-nine rating on February 10, 1993, against San Jose.

By anybody's standards, a 29-goal, 38-assist season in 1996–97 might at least be adequate. But Theoren Fleury was not satisfied and neither was coach Page, who oversaw the team's disappointing 32–41–9 record. It was only the second time in seventeen years the Flames missed the playoffs. Page saw the year as an investment in the Flames' youthful players. There was Fleury's closely chronicled scoring slump. The coach publicly questioned his star's work ethic and physical conditioning. At one point, he benched Fleury, though he carefully refrained from using that word. Fleury was angry at the time but agreed with the coach after the game, saying his play had been "awful" and he was not getting his face dirty enough scrapping for the puck. "I have to look at myself in the mirror," Theo said, "and be better."

There was also the off-ice distraction of the Graham James case. A native of Prince Edward Island, James had built an impressive reputation as a Manitoba youth hockey scout and coach, briefly with the Warriors in Winnipeg and Moose Jaw and then with the Swift Current Broncos from 1986–94. With Swift Current he won two WHL championships and one Memorial Cup. In 1994, he was hired to run the Calgary Hitmen but resigned in 1996. James was subsequently convicted of hundreds of instances of sexually assaulting two of his Swift Current players, including one player later to play in the NHL. Sheldon Kennedy of the Boston Bruins identified himself as that player. In January 1997, James was sentenced to three and a half years in prison.

Because of the heinous nature of the crimes and how they underlined the vulnerability to their coaches of young men seeking professional hockey careers, the case ignited a firestorm of debate, discussion, news coverage, and worry across Canada and in the hockey world beyond. Because the case involved one well-known player, who as part of his personal therapy went on nationwide sports TV to tearfully recount his experience, and then launched a campaign against sexual abuse, the matter might – who knows? – involve other famous people, who had chosen not to come forward. Little of the resulting gossip or speculation was published or broadcast, due to the media's legitimate fear of the legal ramifications. But that did not stop the whispers.

Fame has many benefits. One of its costs is that famous people can become the targets of gossip or curiosity on the same subjects that would be dismissed or deemed inappropriate if they concerned non-famous people. Speculation and gossip are hard for anyone, even the famous, not to refute. It becomes virtually impossible to deny something which has yet to be proven. And gossip requires no proof.

Fleury had been scouted by James for the Warriors and played Manitoba youth hockey with his Russell team against Kennedy and his Elkhorn team. For a brief time Kennedy was a Flames teammate. Fleury, who was privately shocked and saddened by the whole affair, adamantly exercised his right not to comment publicly, which in today's world only helped to feed the whispers. "It's a difficult situation," Fleury said. "I know the people involved. I know there's a lot of questions going to be asked. I'm just not going to say anything." As far as Fleury was concerned, the matter was closed.

Additionally, Fleury was preoccupied with the at-times troubled pregnancy of his wife, Veronica. That pregnancy ended successfully on May 26, 1997, with the birth of a son, Beaux, who at four pounds, thirteen ounces continued the Fleury family's tradition of diminutive physical statistics.

But by then the Flames had not made the playoffs. They were watching the playoff games from the worst seat in the house for pro hockey players: an easy chair in front of the TV in their own house. Little did the Flames know there was even more off-season turmoil just around the corner. And this time it involved coach Page.

But another former Flames coach had one more story to share about Fleury. "In 1991," said Coach Crisp, "I left Calgary. Actually, I was fired. You know, coaches are not the most-loved people in the world. Before I could get out of town, Theoren called me and he thanked me for what I had done for him. He wanted to wish me luck in the future." The coach pauses to swallow at least twice. "Not many players will do that." Another pause. "Theoren's call will stick in my mind long after any of the super stats he'll ever pick up on the ice."

<figure>◆</figure>

Benny Ercolani watches Theoren Fleury's hockey games through a computer in the basement of Benny's home just outside Toronto. "Theo's a player," he says. "No one has more determination. My boy's got one of his sticks upstairs hanging in his room, right next to the Gretzky stick. They're both signed."

Benny is the NHL's stats man. Every morning during the hockey season at five-thirty, unless someone has telephoned sooner, Benny's bedside alarm wakes him. In his slippers and dressing gown, with a mug of coffee (cream and sugar) in hand, and his dog, Homer, traipsing alongside, Benny descends into the basement work area of his home on Coulson Avenue.

While Donna, Phillip, and Erica sleep peacefully, Benny logs onto the NHL's mainframe computer in Montreal, an IBM AS 400. The computer's massive memory contains everything anyone could conceivably want to know about the league or its players, historical game stats, every clause in every player's contract, and which Detroit draft choice three years from now the Stars have acquired and retraded to Tampa. But Benny is beginning a 120-minute numerical shuffle through all of the statistics from the previous night's games. By eight a.m. Benny punches a button and the statistical stories of every game are instantly available to all teams and media. That night's hockey history is official.

"This is a fun job," says Benny. "I couldn't think of anything better to do, next to playing hockey, of course." Not a bad occupational rise for a teller in the Bank of Montreal's New Westminster Street branch in Montreal. When Benny joined the league in 1977, his first job was to enter hockey data into the computer from telexed team reports. In the wee hours of every Monday morning of the hockey season the league's statistical summary was released by Teletype.

But the perceived demand for information has been growing and so has the technology. As a result, Benny's basement world and everything it connects to, like most things involving computers and information these days, is changing drastically. The NHL, in partnership with IBM, is pioneering the move into a world of virtual statistical reality.

The league has added two more officials to the twelve-person crew at every NHL game and rewired virtually every league arena. Five of these officials will sit at every game with laptop computers and quietly enter, in real time, a vastly expanded array of game data.

There will be information on the precise length and duration of every player's every shift, who made every shot and from where, who blocked every shot and where, the distance of every shot and where the rebounds went, who hit whom when, who took the puck away and who lost it every time and where, who won and lost every faceoff and where it was and what, if anything, happened as a result.

The goal is to give fans, teams, and media more information more quickly and to produce statistical portraits of a player's activities. Already, anyone with a suitably equipped computer can access the live radio reports for every game as they are broadcast. In the very near future, someone will be able to dial in by computer from their basement and, basically, follow the actual action of the game statistically on their screen as it is happening, including at what time from where on the ice Fleury took a thirty-foot shot and where the rebound went, on the odd chance Theo misses. If all of this helps attract or keep hockey fans, well then, that's okay, too.

But this sports information revolution is not just to allow on-line aficionados to monitor a real-life computer game in real time. These statistics will provide the media with a mountain of new material to expand and refine their reports to readers and viewers whom the league would like to become hockey addicts. "We'll provide the info," says Benny. "The media can write their stories."

Cross-referencing these statistics also will enable every team to compile an amazing array of revealing information such as which players perform which skill best under what circumstances at what point in each period where on the ice and opposite which opponent during a power play or penalty kill or at full strength at home or on the road.

"Baseball has time between pitches," says Benny. "Football has time between plays. But hockey is so fast that humans can't keep up with it. Some player may have not a single shot on goal, which is what we can measure now. But maybe he blocked four shots, one with his stick and three with his body, and then he won 95 per cent of the faceoffs in his defensive zone but only 40 per cent of the faceoffs in his offensive zone. And he got better in the later periods. Now, those statistics are beginning to tell a coach and management which player is producing and whom to play where and when. They'll be able to determine which players on which lines play best against every other player or line in the league.

"This is exciting to me. It opens so many more creative avenues to tell the story of this sport than when our stats operation was pen and pencil. The league used a regular adding machine until 1970."

SUNDAY AFTERNOON – Mike Burke is using his Paper Mate pen to check off the computerized list of players' names at the Calgary airport. By the end of this hectic week Mike will have lost that inexpensive office-issue pen (he prefers blue ink, Coates likes black), as well as its replacement. So Mike will be using a promotional pen from the bedside table of a Westin hotel. Canadian Airlines flight number 970 will not leave for more than an hour, but Mike has been at the airport for longer than that. He is checking in players, tagging bags, and handing out about sixteen thousand dollars in cash in per diem envelopes.

Brenda Koyich is at home with her family this sunny afternoon. But she well knows from her work the previous summer that planning to move a pro hockey team of forty people, sixty bags, 2,500 pounds of gear, and unquantifiable hopes is a major undertaking. Actually executing those moving plans is a grander task, even if the weather is good.

Now for the next six days on what is the Flames' eleventh road trip of the season, it is Mike's job to shepherd smoothly all of those people, ambitions, and fears, and that gear according to Brenda's meticulous plan on and off of five airplanes, fifteen buses, and into four hotels in three cities, passing through customs and immigration twice with players from five countries – and handling an unexpected controversy.

Mike knows two-thirds of the players prefer aisle seats and one-third windows; no one likes middle seats. So he makes special seating arrangements as the players, carrying newspapers, CD players, books, and ample fruit, obediently collect their seat assignments and envelopes. Mike is hopeful about the trip's logistics, though he is uncertain about the Pittsburgh pizzas.

In the tradition of the hockey world, which makes nicknames by adding -y or -ie to many names, Mike Burke is better known as Burkey. A former general manager of the Calgary Expos who also did some public-relations work for a Junior hockey team, he's another Calgary resident who migrated west from Saskatchewan,

Plato, to be exact – summer population, 12; winter population, 5. That's not enough people for a real hockey game, so Mike played pond hockey.

It's Mike's job now to attend to many of the details that make the Flames' hockey operations work. This week that means becoming group leader. Al Coates, the Flames' general manager who becomes Coatesy in his hockey life, recalls his own group-leader experiment years ago, when he led a team round and about an airport, down corridors to other concourses, and back to check-in at the gate next to where they began. "No one noticed," he reports.

Assistant coach Kevin Constantine is worried about this trip's three games, in Pittsburgh on Tuesday, Toronto on Wednesday, and Ottawa on Friday. Due to the NHL All-Star break, the team has not practised in five days. "I've been in this league a few years," Kevin says, "and I have never seen a team play well after more than a three-day break." Kevin has no inkling on this day about how Pittsburgh will soon loom large in his life.

The team seems jovial. "The good news," says Trevor Kidd, the longhaired, semi-eccentric goalie, "is that we just had a little vacation. The bad news is, we're playing Pittsburgh and they're on a fifteen-game winning streak with the hottest goalie in the history of hockey."

Indeed, Gary Taylor has given Kevin several game tapes of Patrick Lalime, an unknown from the IHL called up recently. Calgary has never played him. "In the regular season," says Kevin, as the plane cruises high over the Canadian prairies, "it's 90 per cent what you do and 10 per cent the opposition. In the playoffs, it's more like 60:40. But it's still up to us to play our own game."

There is a surprising amount of down time on road trips. We see these players skate into the bright lights and, later, skate out of the lights into their presumably glamorous off-ice lives. But in between public appearances there are countless hours of decidedly unglamorous activity waiting for and boarding buses and planes, sitting for thousands of miles, getting off and waiting for bags, and buses, and meals, and games.

The travel grind, which is too short a word for such long ordeals, requires its own physical and emotional pacing with requisite reminders that the point is not to endure the travel, the delays and boredom; it's to play a demanding hockey game sharply at the end of it all – and then to move on to the next city and game ready to compete again, regardless of the outcome. "In my six years with the North Stars," says Dave Gagner, usually Theo's road roommate, "I had two hundred thousand frequent-flyer miles just on Northwest."

The plane leaves the Calgary gate at 4:10. Dragging their own bags, the Flames players straggle into Toronto's Pearson Airport hotel at 10:44. Their room keys wait on a lobby table. "Everyone," says Burke, "eight o'clock tomorrow morning at the USAir counter."

MONDAY MORNING – The airport lines again to get tickets for the sixty-five-minute flight to Pittsburgh. Lines for juice. Then lines for security. Then lines for U.S. customs. Then lines for U.S. immigration. At the gate, Jarome Iginla, the rookie, can never resist a coin-operated game. This one is hockey. He challenges Kevin Constantine, who wins and does a mock championship dance. "Okay," says Jarome, "two out of three." Eric Duhatschek is the beat reporter for the *Calgary Herald*. He's mumbling. His laptop swallowed an entire story. Some good quotes from Steve Chiasson were lost forever.

"For me," says Brian Patafie, who enjoys travelling, "professional sports allow me to prolong my childhood. On the road with my family I'm a daddy full-time. On the road with the team we can all be kids all the time. My duties are clear and simple. I think of nothing but work. No electric bills, lawn, or credit cards. I love the road."

In Pittsburgh, the veterans disappear on the way to the baggage pickup area. They've seen the schedule. The wait for bags is the only time for lunch. The rookies wait idly at the carousel. One is Dale McTavish, a tall, lanky defenceman from the Saint John Flames. After an AHL game in Newfoundland three weeks before, McTavish went to a Sylvester Stallone movie, *Daylight*. When he returned to his motel room, the message light was on. The coach told him, "You're going up."

McTavish set off with one set of clothes for a Calgary hotel room and his first shot at the big time. Now he is seven games into his NHL career and worried about losing it.

"It's pretty exciting," he says. "They told me I'm to be a spark, bring some new energy to the Flames, be a little physical." McTavish is from Eganville, Ontario, not too far from Ottawa. More than a hundred friends and relatives have bought tickets for Friday's game there to cheer their town's first NHL player. "I hope I'm still here," says Dale, not smiling.

The bus – players in the back, media in the middle, coaches and management in the front – eases into town, its tires hissing along the wet pavement. Someone asks why Pittsburgh seems so quiet on a Monday at noon. It's Martin Luther King Junior's birthday, a national holiday in honour of the slain black civil-rights leader. "Hey, Iggy," someone calls to the rookie Iginla, whose father is black. "Do you observe Martin Luther King Day?"

Gagner pipes up. "Only until noon." Guffaws abound.

The bus arrives at William Penn Hotel at 12:19. The veterans were right about lunch; the bus departs for practice in twenty-six minutes. The convenience store has a run on cookies and juice. When they reboard the bus, coach Page sits sternly in front. "Pierre," each player says with a nod. Page and Coates confer. Aaron Gavey, a young centreman from Sudbury, Ontario, has brought a Don Cherry videotape for the bus VCR. The players watch hockey en route to practise hockey, cheering the big hits.

Fleury won't arrive until evening. Page gave him an extra day in California to golf with his wife, Veronica, and brother, Travis.

Tommy Albelin, a Swedish defenceman, is thirty-two years old, twenty-eight of them invested in hockey. Like many European NHL players, he sits apart or with other Europeans. Tommy thinks about Fleury a minute. "He's a dirty little player," Tommy says with a smile. "I played against him a few times with the Devils. He's got to do all kinds of stuff out there to make up for his size. It is definitely better to play with him than against him."

Watching pros practise, you realize that NHL players do not play hockey. Kids play hockey; for kids, it's a game. For NHL players, hockey is a business, a very physical business. They do have team meetings, where players sprawl all over chairs, couches, and the floor in various stages of undress, and no one takes notes. But their meetings are to discuss what will soon be done physically. There are lighter moments on ice, playful shoves, friendly taps, or affectionate digs. But they pass quickly and any laughter on ice is quickly smothered, especially when coach Page is around.

His practice gaze is so intense he must keep his eyes in constant motion or just his look could bore holes in objects. "This is a very complicated trip for us," says Pierre. "We want to have a good hard workout and get some battling for the puck going, get back in the groove, scrape off any rust. Handling the puck comes natural to most of our guys. But battling for the puck, now, that is not natural."

The coaches get their own small room down the hall. But there is little room for formality or privacy in the cramped locker rooms the players inhabit on the road, comfort for the opposition not being high on many home teams' priority list. Steve Chiasson walks around wearing a heating pad on his back. Kidd does leg stretches in his underwear on the wet hall floor. "I can't believe

Theo doesn't really warm up," he says. "He suits up and goes out to play, just like that." Theo and Trevor were roommates for three years. "I like to drive Theo crazy. Me and Cale Hulse are in charge of locker-room music. So we put on loud rock and Theo just shakes his head. He's a country-music fan. One time I got in his truck with him. I was going to switch the radio to a rock station. But Theo had set every button to the same country station, Country 105. Now, how'd he know to do that?"

While Trevor stretches, others in ripped but lucky underwear step over and around him in bare feet or sharpened skates. Kidd has just learned from the coach that he will start the next night. "The only trouble with hockey," says the goalie, "is the pucks."

"Hey, Bobby, where's the black tape?" Terry Kane rubs ointment on Gavey's new right-shoulder tattoo, a little green four-leaf clover. "It's lucky," Aaron explains. And it will be come Thursday. The rink manager wants his two-hundred-dollar cheque for ice-time. Jamie Huscroft wants some aspirin.

Some Pittsburgh fans have lingered to watch the opponents. "Look at the size of them!" says Ray McKinney. Ray is eleven years old and better known as Putzie. He's a Penguin fan, but he is waiting to see Fleury. "Theo is my all time favourite," says Putzie, who is also short. Putzie is told that Fleury at that moment is on an airplane flying from San Jose.

"What?!" says the youngster. "He's the one I wanted. That sucks. He's so gooood, man."

Doug Barkley has been involved with hockey for fifty-five years. He's sixty now and the colour commentator on Calgary radio CFR Flames broadcasts. Sitting in the stands at practice, he thinks the Flames look sluggish after five days off. He thinks there are too many NHL teams for the available talent. "Teams today have a couple of good lines," he says, "and everyone else is the same as everywhere else. If your six guys are better than the other's six guys on any given night, then you win. This year with all the young guys it's hard to tell which Flames team is going to show up, the one that beats the champion Avalanche or the one that gives up ten goals to Edmonton. But Fleury, well, you know he's going to show up. He's got such talent, determination, and strength and you know what else? He's got great balance. With that low centre of gravity, it's hard to knock him down."

At rink's end Al Coates is chatting with Eddie Johnston, the Penguins coach and an old friend. "Fleury makes everyone play harder," says Eddie. "He was unbelievable in the World Cup. He comes to play every day, takes coaching well, and he doesn't give a shit. He plays seven feet tall. I tell our guys to keep their composure around Theo. They take a penalty, he gets a power play and bites you hard real quick."

For some players an hour's practice is enough. Others stay for extra shooting or skating. Mike Sullivan, one of the few Americans on the Flames and the only Boston University alumnus, pops open the door off the ice and immediately confronts a mini-mob of Pittsburgh youngsters, seeking souvenirs like hungry baby robins in a nest beseeching an adult bird. "Hey," Sully says before one person can start begging, "does anyone here have a hockey stick they can give me?"

Stunned, the youngsters stand silent for a moment. That is their line. Mike winks at the parents in the background as he wades towards the locker room. Then, he turns at the door and hands his stick to one quiet boy in the back. "Now you don't have to ask anyone else ever," he says, smiling. The boy runs off holding his trophy high.

Players shower. "I thought we practised as well as any Peewee team," says a disgusted Constantine. Bobby, Brian, and Terry pack the sixty bags again. In one hour all the gear is on a truck bound for the Civic Arena where the same trio will unpack all the gear to dry, place Velcro nametags on each stall, and arrange each player's gear just the way he likes it for the next morning's short practice.

Back at the hotel the team scatters – coaches and Coates to a sports bar to watch the Leafs, Wednesday's opponent, and players subdivide into groups according to restaurant preference. McTavish is left alone, having announced a queasy stomach, possible precursor to a teamwide flu epidemic.

TUESDAY MORNING – Home team practises first. A few Flames watch closely. From one section Coates sits silently, chin in hand, watching the Penguins and admiring the arena's many no-doubt lucrative advertising signs. Below him, Page watches this new Lalime guy. "Why does black make everyone look so much larger?" the coach asks no one in particular. Page notices something. He thinks the goalie looks a little weak low on the stick side. Two aisles over there's Fleury, tanned from golfing, his hair cropped closely. "How do you like my new do?" he asks.

The Penguins depart. The ice is resurfaced for the Flames, who huff and puff for twenty-five minutes. "Is this ice level?" Tommy Albelin asks in jest. "It's your legs," says the coach, who has his players practise shooting low on the stick side of Kidd. In the stands Joe Hanke is mopping up spilled beer and peanut shells from past games. He's earning money for college and gets two free tickets per year. "Never been to Calgary," he says. "Closest I've been is Niagara Falls once."

Showers. In the hall Mike Burke introduces Fleury to Patricia and Bobby Bridges. They are from Nashville. Bobby has admired Theo from afar for years. This trip is his birthday present from Patricia. She worked overtime to earn the money. Neither can believe they are actually meeting Theoren Fleury, whom they've seen on TV so often. But they have seen him so many times they feel comfortable using his first name instantly. Fleury does not object.

Suddenly, coach Page, gripping a piece of paper, storms down the hall and into the coaches' room. He slams the door.

Bobby has bags of Flames hats and dolls and different Fleury hockey cards to be autographed. "For sure," says Theo. "How many of these cards do you have?"

"Just six," says Bobby.

Theo signs them all. "You know there are two hundred of these out now? Yeah. My wife gave me one of each in frames for Christmas." They talk country music. Theo would like to visit Nashville someday, maybe when they get an NHL team.

The couple takes pictures of each other with Fleury. "Thanks so much for this, Theo!"

"Hey, no problem," says the captain. "Enjoy the game." Then it's time to tape a TV interview. The camerawoman focuses on Theo's face and then sighs audibly. "Will you look at those green eyes," she says. Fox Sports wants to know about the burdens of being captain. Fleury explains he's the on-ice spokesman for the coach and knows that all rookies look up to the captain as an example.

Fleury is free now. He has thirty-five minutes to make the ten-minute walk to the hotel and pregame meal. Just about right, he says, knowing what's ahead.

Fleury knows every NHL arena by heart. "We can get out this shortcut," he says. He walks outside past the stinking dumpsters and the janitor hosing the cement and up the ramp into a surprisingly sunny day. A lone civilian sentinel stands at the top. Fleury has never seen him before. A flicker of recognition and understanding passes between the two. The man runs for his car. Fleury slows his walk. The man pulls out a Titan stick. "How ya doin'?" says Theo.

"Hi, Theo. Hey, would you please sign your stick for me?" The man produces a silver marker.

"Sure. Where'd you get this one?"

"You gave it to me."

"Really? When?"

The man cannot find the voice to speak. Theo turns the stick over and looks at a code. "February 1993," he announces. "You're lucky, man. I don't give many away."

"Thanks a lot."

"For sure." Fleury turns to leave. But word has spread. A small crowd of men and boys is running up the hill from the front door. Fleury stops to permit the encounter. They open three-ring binders, some with entire pages of Fleury cards. Why would a youngster in Pittsburgh have a dozen Fleury cards? Players know professional collectors use children to obtain autographs because collectors know it's virtually impossible for players to refuse kids. The players shrug. What are you going to do? Fans buy the tickets.

Everyone politely thanks Fleury when he hands back the newly signed item. They hold it reverently while it dries. "Nice coat," one man says. "Thanks," says Theo. "It's wool. Real warm."

Theo will sign three-dozen items at this encounter. To pass the time while signing, he asks the eager crowd a question: "So where do you guys think I should shoot on this Lalime guy?"

Laughter breaks out. Theo shrugs. "Worth a try, eh?" he says. Other Flames players walk by unnoticed.

Satisfied, the crowd breaks up. Fleury moves on. There will be three more sidewalk group encounters with fans who know the route to each team's favourite hotel. At the last one a little boy looks up at his hero, but not too far up. "Hey, Theo," he says, "I tell all my friends you're My Man." The crowd chuckles.

"Well," says the player, "you're *my* size, that's for sure."

Three blocks and precisely thirty-five minutes after leaving the locker room Fleury walks into his hotel for the game-day meal. Some players grab armloads of fruit to take to their rooms. Fleury still has the same six-pork-chop-sized appetite that Ede Peltz noticed. He has a large caesar salad, a pasta salad, spaghetti and meatballs, and milk. Then, it's up to room 1217, into bed in his underwear for forty-five minutes of TV, though it's too late for "All My Children" today. As the rest of the world returns for an afternoon of work, the hockey gladiators take a two- or three-hour nap before becoming the evening's entertainment.

Each player has his own game-day routine and rituals. It's not so much *what* these pregame rituals are; it's *that* they are. If you are going into a battle where everything happens fast and nothing is predictable, at least you can gain some comfort and focus by rigidly controlling the few things you can control. Fleury's routine involves fussing over his sticks, heating the blade, cutting and rounding the handle, taping both just right, testing the stick's resilience on the floor.

Tommy Albelin's routine starts the previous night by reading the opposition's roster and recalling their moves and tendencies from past games. He wants to have a smooth morning skate, a good meal, reread the opposition's roster, perhaps imagine scoring a goal and, if possible, ignore the developing butterflies and sleep.

Trevor Kidd starts to drift away from any social interaction at the morning skate. "Life is all about focus," he says. He learned that way back when he was seven and goalie for the Oakbank Winterhawks in Winnipeg. "I think about the good things I've done," Kidd says. "Sure, you hear the critics. They buy tickets, too. I try to remember you still have fans, maybe silent ones, out there who still like you, win or lose."

In fact, on this night as he waddles down the ramp to the dressing room after the pregame warmup, Kidd will look up into a sea of yellow-and-black-clad Penguin fans. He will see a lone youngster in a red Calgary jersey waving. The goalie will stop. And he will hand his bright yellow TPS stick over to that youngster, whose eyes will grow instantly to the size of hockey pucks.

The bus leaves the hotel at five sharp. Until 4:59:45 Kidd stands on the sidewalk by a lamp-post. Fleury is signing autographs. Kevin Constantine, his red crewcut freshly brushed and a fresh wad of bubble gum in his mouth, goes to board the bus. "Are you famous?" one youngster asks.

"Nope," says Kevin. But he will be soon. Five months later, almost to the day, Constantine would be named Pittsburgh's new head coach.

Almost surreptitiously making the rounds of each bus seat is a piece of paper, a fax from Calgary that resembles the paper Page was clutching when he stormed down the hall that morning. It is a copy of a column from the *Calgary Sun* by Mark Miller, a sports-beat writer. On page one of that morning's *Sun*, in huge World War type was the bold headline: "THEO'S AGONY – Flames Star reveals to Sun why he's so troubled."

It seems that Mark happened to get on the same flights from San Jose as Fleury did the previous day. Mark happened to get seats next to Theo. And the reporter happened to have handy his little tape recorder. For hours he asked Fleury questions and Fleury answered his sometime summertime golf partner. Fleury did not use the word "agony." But "frustration" or "tired" do not sell as many papers. And those words would not have fit on one line in mega-type.

Miller listed the allegations about Fleury: the poor results on a recent stationary-bike test, late nights out, and possible role in the Graham James affair. Fleury was quoted as denying that he lacked dedication and complaining instead about the Flames' hard travel schedule, the lack of charter flights, the long and demanding practices ordered by coaches, and the overall lack of consideration for their impact on the team's star, who wasn't as young as the many rookies.

"I don't know what's going to happen," Fleury was quoted as saying, "but I don't want to leave Calgary. I'm just real frustrated with the whole situation. Maybe it's time someone listened to me."

Miller wondered when he learned the front-page headline on his column went from "THEO'S PAIN" in the first edition to "THEO'S AGONY" in the second. But Mark had known he had a major story and since Eric Duhatschek, the *Herald*'s veteran reporter, had not been sent to the All-Star Game, Mark had Theo's comments exclusively. In the competitive world of daily newspapers, that is like a playoff hat trick.

Fleury was as yet unaware of the developing tempest. Chided by his editors for missing the story and driven to match it, Eric waited for the star in the hotel lobby. Theo's first reaction was: "My agony? What agony?" In fact, that was the headline in the next day's *Herald* with the subhead: "Reports of Theo Fleury's demise have been greatly exaggerated." Perhaps naively, Fleury had trusted Miller not to embarrass him. He was blithely unaware of the competitive dynamics between newspapers. "Hey," Theo shrugged. "I'm a high-risk kind of guy."

So Theo talked with Eric too for the next day's paper, which, of course, satisfied Eric's bosses for a day but kept the controversy brewing. Theo said, yes, he was feeling tired but he wasn't the only one who needed to play better. He dismissed the bike test, saying hockey is not played on a bike. And he pointed out that some teams give their stars *carte blanche* on skipping practice, especially during the season's last third when the accumulated physical punishment takes its toll.

When Eric had walked past Mark that first day, he said, "Thanks, Mark. You've sure made my day hell." That's a compliment to a competing reporter.

"Hey," Mark replied, "all I did was turn on the tape recorder."

"I didn't say you did anything wrong," Eric added. "I just said you'd made my day hell."

Reporters, especially newspaper beat reporters, are sometimes in a difficult position. The teams need them to generate continuing interest in the game and their business. And the reporters need the teams for access and convenient travel. Although it gets stale sooner for reporters with families, it also does not hurt their careers or egos to be flying all over the continent with a professional outfit, free of close direction by editors, mingling with stars, at times interviewed on TV or radio for their hockey expertise, and, once in a while, even recognized by a fan as something of an adjacent celebrity.

The reporters travel and eat with the team, but they are not of the team. They do pay their own way; their employers are billed by the team for hotel and airplane costs. But, seeing them every day, players come to think of the reporters as part of the Flames entourage, which is great for eavesdropping but not so great when controversy erupts.

The professional reality is that radio and TV reporters have broadcast contracts and substantial business relationships with the team. But newspaper reporters see themselves as totally apart from the team, like watchdogs over government. In fact, to a man they say they do not care if their team wins or loses and, frankly, aside from the awkwardness of interviewing defeated players in a locker room, they think that losses make for better stories.

"I'm a professional," says Mark. "After six losses, you know, you're tired of writing, loss, loss, loss. And you'd like for the guys to win just for something different to write. But it's all just stories for us. Eric and I are friendly. I hear from my boss about his stuff, too. But our stuff is all pretty much the same unless you happen to be on a plane all day with the star."

A coach and star player feuding while losing is an irresistible story for newspaper reporters anywhere. The reporter's role as occasional instigator ("The coach says he thinks you're not working hard enough. What's your reaction to that?") is less closely chronicled by the same reporters. The seesaw rhetorical conflict, the verbal ping-pong of "he said" and "he said" in the media, is as predictable in public dialogue these days as the appearance of tomorrow morning's newspapers.

To save money, the Flames team does not send its public-relations people on road trips. In the summer of 1997 the league's board of governors voted that a media-relations person be required to go on each road trip. But this time it was left to a harried Mike Burke to add media relations and media mediation to his job description. He announced that the coach and star would meet soon. And that was reported like a political peace conference until the steam of the incident slowly ebbed.

Coates, a longtime personal confidant of Fleury's, was puzzled and annoyed that Theo would not talk to him before going public with his complaints. But the general manager is experienced enough to know reporters' tactics. "I think," Coates would later say, "I could get O.J. Simpson to admit to anything, if I had him alone in an airplane seat for six hours."

Page knew nothing of Fleury's Moose Jaw "beaking off" incidents. But the coach had complained to Fleury about his physical conditioning and practice attitude. Privately, Page had wondered whether his captain had the mental strength to continue to want to get better, a basic requirement in the coach's book of character traits. Page had told Fleury he could practise only twenty minutes a day if Theo went all out those twenty minutes. But perhaps most inflammatory to Page was the fact that the reporter's interview and the star's complaints about needing time off came on the extra day off that the coach had given him.

That caused Page to reply in stronger terms in Pittsburgh than he would have wished later. "Being a coach is like being a player," he would say in disgust over his own performance. "Sometimes you forget first what you know best. These things should be handled in private."

Page is known as an emotional coach. For years behind the bench he would say whatever he was thinking. That led to some bench penalties and hurt feelings. Page had gone through some therapy to ease his emotions. The result was that he now rarely exploded during a game and, a point of real pride, had received no bench penalty in two years. Between periods the coach had taken to walking into a small room and sharing with the walls his strongest feelings about recent events. "You have to vent, to get these things off your chest," he would say. And this way the only people who heard the coach's comments were the assistant coaches or Gary Taylor, the video man.

Page did not know the circumstances of the Fleury interview. It sounded to him like a full-blown press conference. And the story would be all over both papers back home for days. The *Sun* initiated a poll of readers to see if Fleury should be traded: "Coaches riled at Fleury. What do you think?" Apparently, some readers thought this guy getting about thirty thousand dollars every game was spoiled and should be traded.

"Fleury traded?" said Doug Overton. "I doubt that. But we'd be interested." Doug is a scout for the Dallas Stars. "We scout everybody all the time. Fleury's play sure opened the door for other small players. Some guys start out their career with desire like his, but it seems to fade or come on and off. Fleury's desire makes him seem a whole lot bigger than he is physically."

"I can't believe what they are saying about Theo," said a distressed Veronica Fleury, who shared the articles and her dismay during daily phone conversations with her husband.

For his part, Fleury vowed privately to be more careful with reporters. Publicly, he said he'd just go out and put the fun back in the game. That was the way to win.

But not in Pittsburgh. Despite the fervent cheering of the Nashville couple, who were two dots of red in a sea of black up in Section B6, Row D, Seats 5 and 6, despite knocking Mario Lemieux out of the game and twice scoring on Lalime low on the stick side, the Flames lost 4–2. "Once again," said Coates, watching from a box on high, "we were close but not close enough."

The Flames' locker room was littered with sticky liquid and pieces of a bright yellow goalie stick that had been smashed against the table holding dozens of cups of Gatorade. This is why players' street clothes are always hung in a separate room. Reporters chose not to interview Trevor Kidd about his game that night.

At 10:15, Mike Burke announced that the bus would leave for the airport in thirty minutes. Right on time, the truck delivered fifteen large pizzas to the back of the bus. Mike thought the food would hold the players until their special double-sized meals on the charter flight to Toronto, and that things were going pretty well.

He was correct about the food anyway.

Neither Veronica nor Theoren were supposed to be at the Longhorn Bar on August 11, 1994. Veronica had decided to stay at home that night and Theoren was supposed to meet a friend elsewhere. After considerable coaxing, Veronica went out for a few drinks and maybe, hopefully, someone would ask her to dance.

Then this guy sent some drinks over to her table and she asked him if he could two-step. Her favourite song, "I'm in a Hurry" by Alabama, came on, and he was a really good dancer. He even got up and sang with the band. Her friend said, "Do you know who that guy is?" And Veronica said, "Theo Fleury."

Even when her friend said, "He's *the* Theo Fleury," Veronica remembered only that she had watched him play with her father on TV in the 1989 Stanley Cup finals. Having recently lost her mother, Veronica was not seeking an emotional relationship. But this guy was such a good dancer. He was just so much fun and the next day at work her friends said Veronica was walking around like "a little glowball."

The guy did call. He proposed a drink after work. She waited. And waited. Ninety minutes late, Theo showed up not so fresh from a round of golf. That was the fall of the lockout, an awful time for a hockey player like Fleury. "I was lost without hockey," Theo admits. "I'd just drive around all over Calgary with nothing to do." But hockey lockouts are a terrific time for a couple to come to know each other better, as a man and a woman, not as a famous man and a woman. Veronica had not thought much about hockey players, but when she did, she did not think of them as having a soft side, a side that would lead him to video-tape himself singing a love song and give it to her as a gift. And Theoren liked the way he felt around her. "I never saw him as a hockey player," Veronica recalls, "until months later. Even then, it was the man I loved, not the hockey player."

Finally, Fleury told his agent to get him a job – anywhere. He flew to Scandinavia and played for a Finnish team, which wasn't doing well, but whose fans discovered that Fleury's enthusiasm could cross political and language boundaries. Veronica followed Theo to Finland, where for weeks they only had each other.

Theo's relationship with Shannon had long been crumbling and finally died. Theo gave a shattered Shannon their house and car and a support agreement for Josh and they remain friends. The next summer, to avoid making it a media event, Theo flew his entire family, numerous friends, and Veronica's family to Las Vegas – twenty-nine people in all – to witness their marriage one year to the day after the meeting that Veronica felt was sheer destiny. That trip was Donna Fleury's first airplane ride. She was so nervous she went to the bathroom six times in the two-hour flight. Now, she loves flying so much she wants to fly overseas, say, to Japan for the Winter Olympics.

There is something striking about the wives of hockey players. They are usually pretty and almost always dressed far more expensively than other women their age. They bask in or suffer from the same fame as their husbands; if there is a contract dispute or trade rumour, they are involved, too. They must watch – and be watched watching – their husband targeted by enemy players or criticized by reporters. And like Veronica, they become fiercely protective of their man. Frustrations at work bring fall-outs at home. "How's it going?" Veronica would ask one wife whose husband had been sitting out game after game and had demanded a trade. All the wife did was roll her eyes. "It's tough," she said. In unity and sympathy, Veronica touched the arm of the wife, who could not know that Coates was discussing a trade, even as the two women spoke.

There is always a newspaper or TV station that wants to visit the player's home to get pictures of the happy couple in the kitchen cooking together. Many readers like to read that their heroes are all-round guys nowadays. The league likes that too; it helps counter any bar assault stories. Family feature articles please Flames management and may help sell the Flames favour-ite recipes book that Veronica Fleury helped organize to raise money for a women's shelter. The photographer will want to include the couple's children as well, which causes some protec-tive players to balk. When the newspapers run out of wives' lives to chronicle, they'll do a feature on the less tastefully decorated apartment shared by three Flames bachelors. Most players' phones are unlisted and addresses usually are kept secret, although word somehow seeps out.

After Flames games the women gather outside the basement dressing room waiting, always waiting, for their players. It's not easy being married to a celebrity and always having to take second place. Even when hockey player and wife are standing together talking, she must step back when someone approaches for yet another autograph. And when the men emerge from the dressing room, one by one, their hair wet and shiny and their ties not quite in place, the wives must always wait some more. In one game with seven seconds remaining Theo was flattened near the goal. Blood was visibly pooling on the ice. Theo was helped off. He was yelling at the opposition, a good sign. But Brian was holding a towel to Theo's face. Near his eye.

Veronica had, of course, been watching every second of Theo's shift. She does this naturally, but after one game he mentioned he had seen her talking to Josh when he scored. So now Veronica's eyes must always be on the ice when Theo is. Right after the facial injury, Veronica rushed downstairs from her regular seat. There, she waited. And waited. And waited. Hockey wives are not supposed to fuss in public over injuries. But it's hard to worry and not show it.

One emerging player gave Veronica the thumbs-up signal, which was good but, knowing hockey players, could merely mean Theo was still breathing. Even the doctor did not emerge from the dressing room.

When Theo finally did walk out through the red doors, the last player of the night to do so, he could not get to his wife for the longest time because of the friendly autograph crowd, youngsters mainly, that clamoured for his attention. They were oblivious to the physical pain he was working very hard to ignore himself. As always, Theo signed his name and number for as long as anyone was asking. When they touched his coat and hand, just so they could tell themselves they really had done that, he ignored it. When any one of the little people said, "Good game, Theo," believing in their heart that it was because they were there and saw it, Theo still said, "Thanks, bud," knowing in his mind – as well as on the scoreboard – that it was not.

Veronica saw right away that he was blinking oddly. But then some German students wanted a bunch of photos with Theo and, of course, he complied. It took twenty minutes for him to cross the last twenty-five feet to his wife.

He had eight stitches under his eye and the anaesthetic was keeping Theo from blinking properly. Ronnie Stern, a team jokester, walked by. "Nice stitches," he said. "They look nice and tight." In hockey, that's a compliment.

Veronica must work at controlling herself at times. Whether her husband is hurting and wants to get to their house or merely seeking to have a quiet dinner out with his wife, there is always someone, often several someones, who want to compliment him, which is nice but also inevitably the prelude to an autograph request. "Theoren always complies," Veronica says. "He is the most generous, unselfish, and courageous man." Fleury shrugs. It all comes with the job of public hero.

"There are times in hockey," said Lanny McDonald, "when you'd just like to be yourself or a husband or a daddy. But people – it's their first time ever around a celebrity though it's number twenty-eight of the day for you – they don't think you're human any more. They think if they get near you, something magical happens. So they put you on a pedestal and make you into something you're not, some kind of god. I just tried to be gracious all the time. But sometimes you can't live up to what they want you to be."

The famous person learns what's acceptable or what's acceptably outrageous. They learn what works best in a crowd, when a wink makes that link, or a handshake or a compliment on a piece of the beseecher's clothing. The person complimented will remember it forever. Lanny still has adults come up to him and say, "I met you when I was ten and you called me 'Blondie.'"

Sometimes after a while we come to resent a famous person, who no longer seems to be what we have tried so hard to make him be. Sometimes the feeling is mutual. Sometimes fame can be fickle. Sometimes the reason for a famous person's original fame gets lost and he or she becomes famous merely for being famous. But there is no doubt that fame changes its captives as well as its captors. And both sides know their role and lines by heart.

Whatever exactly fame is, however, it can generate an awful lot of dollars both for the famous person and wherever or whatever he or she touches or endorses. When hockey equipment like elbow pads or stockings on some pro hockey teams becomes so old, so taped and darned that it is essentially useless, the team does not throw it away. People are willing to pay substantial sums for almost anything worn in a game, more if it is autographed.

At first anyway, there are few people who do not enjoy seeing or hearing that flicker of recognition that confirms their specialness, their fame. And there are today so many more ways people can become famous by design or by chance. Instantaneous communications may substitute immediacy for insight. But they are ubiquitous. Think for a moment about ancient times when fame was achieved only by word of mouth. Alexander the Great could have no agent to promote him. There could be no newspaper stories from Alexander's home town, quoting neighbours, teachers, and swordfighting coaches who just knew he would conquer the known world someday. No grainy yearbook photo of Alexander with a terribly dated hairstyle. No women's magazine articles on how Mrs. Alexander survives her husband's long absences and what she cooks his first night home. No *Maclean's* articles analysing his military strategy. No *Globe and Mail* pieces from Greece explaining how Alexander was almost born in Canada. No *Cosmopolitan* article on "How to Attract a World Conqueror." No CDs of Alexander's Favourite Marching Songs, no Alexander's Trail Mix, no Alexander's Campaign Chair or Hiking Sandals, no Tim Hortons Alexander Coffee Mugs to Conquer Rush Hour Traffic. And there were no competing tabloids to duel over publishing the alleged confessions of Alexander's concubines – "I Slept with the World Conqueror!" and "Alexander the Great Was Great!"

Fleury does have a few endorsements – a friend's restaurant, No Fear clothing, Jofa equipment, maybe Nike some day. He runs his own hockey school and works for juvenile diabetes. The Flames use his gaptoothed smile on billboards to attract season-ticket-holders – room for a few more. But Theo does not often try to figure out the fame deal. He does at times resent the judgemental side of fame, the part that allows people to sit in the stands and so easily pass judgement on his night's effort on the ice as if he were not human. But he will never talk about it publicly. And fame does make it harder to hear the truth. Famous people are to sycophants as porchlights are to moths. Which explains why so many famous people rely more on the people who knew them before fame struck and the money arrived. They somehow seem truer.

But most times Theo seems just to shrug and accept fame. "I don't think I've ever turned down an autograph request. I kind of think of it as a reward for all those nights in Junior sleeping on the bus with my coat for a pillow."

There is no fame in his home, however. That is his sanctuary where he can watch soap operas and movies with Veronica, play with his dogs, his baby, Beaux Destan, and older son, Josh, and all of his TV and stereo gear. Theo has trained Hat Trick to do a high-five. Ditto, Theo says, is hopeless at tricks.

Fleury has a two-car garage to protect his red Dodge Viper. He bought a snowblower for the minuscule driveway and ended up offering to clear neighbours' driveways as well. Then, he used it to clear off an ice rink out back on the lake for a Christmas Day game of shinny with his brothers. When he awoke Christmas morning, Fleury got a great gift – the manmade lake's maintenance people had Zambonied his rink, making the ice almost as good as George Greenwood's at the Saddledome. "When we were young," Theo says about his siblings, "I was away so much of the time. It's really great to get to know these guys finally. We have a blast."

Both brothers play for the Russell Senior team, the Rams, as did their father, wearing Flames hockey pants though the colours do not match Russell's. Ted had a brief tryout with a minor-league team in the American South. He has married, has a young daughter, and coaches youth hockey. He has been employed tearing up tracks for scrap from abandoned prairie rail-lines. Travis landscapes in the summer and lays carpet come winter.

Both men are chronic sports fans – and usually try to "borrow" Theoren's free No Fear clothing whenever they visit Calgary.

Theo takes a book on road trips, but at home he largely watches sports every day. "I can watch almost any sport," he says, "even bowling. And I went to an NBA game and saw Michael Jordan. He's great. Basketball is okay, I guess. Both teams scored a hundred points. Where's the D in that?"

Theoren also attends many of Josh's lacrosse and hockey games and cheers vocally. "Good pass, Josh. Now, go! Go! Now, rip it, Josh! Rip it! Yes! I knew he would score. I got him a new blade today and I taped it. I said, 'You're gonna score a goal tonight.'"

But Theo misses some games because of his own, especially the forty-one on the road.

◈

WEDNESDAY MORNING – The good news, when the Flames board their Air Atlantic charter at the Pittsburgh airport, is that the special meals are already on board. The bad news is that Toronto's Pearson Airport is closed due to an ice storm. They sit in Pittsburgh. They circle Toronto. They land. They skid and skid and skid.

Glare ice, an inch thick, coats everything. A planeload of guys who earn their living on the ice is quite quiet while their airplane tries to stop on the ice. The plane creeps off the main runway and parks. Seventy-five minutes later the bus creeps near the plane and skids. Players fetch their bags from the airplane and shuffle gently across the black ice. "Hey, Bobby," one voice shouts in the darkness, "break out the gear and let's have a practice."

"Gentlemen," says Steve O'Donnell, "watch your step." Steve is a veteran bus driver and hockey fan. He loves hockey people.

They can tell. So Pacific Western Transportation routinely assigns Steve to ferry visiting hockey teams. "Hockey people are great," he says. "The Rangers are a little grumpy. But most of them treat me good. And you can see in their faces when these famous players get on my bus, they remember me."

Steve inches his bus and the Calgary Flames across the tarmac and around the hangars and, slightly faster, on the slow, slick drive to the Westin Harbour Castle on Toronto's lakefront. "Good night, gentlemen," says Steve.

Or good morning. It is 2:40 a.m. when Steve pulls up to the hotel. The morning skate is cancelled. Team meeting at noon. Players lumber through a deserted lobby to get their keys. Theo watches a movie until 4:00 a.m., then sleeps until 11:30.

LATER WEDNESDAY – Mike Burke spends the morning double-checking arrangements for the rest of the trip and trying to find extra game tickets. Each home team guarantees each visiting team the chance for players to buy a total of fifty tickets. In Pittsburgh, the Flames wanted none. In Toronto, close to home for many players, including Dwayne Roloson, that night's starting goaltender, Burke has to find seventy tickets.

After the team meeting Theo and coach Page meet privately. They are friendly – well, professional. Each repeats his position. Theo says he will work hard. Page says that's all he wants. Mark Miller, the *Sun*'s reporter, is ecstatic with the play of his stories on this trip, better even than a political scandal. "This has to be the best job in the world," he says.

The next day's *Calgary Sun* has both men face to face – "WAR OF WORDS – Agony continues for Flames." On Theo's picture the quote: "I was just saying what everybody on the team feels. Lots of guys are frustrated and feeling a little bit tired." On Page's photo: "I've been trying to save him all year. . . . It looks like he doesn't want to be saved."

Inside the paper, page after page of coverage, including long vituperative fan quotes denouncing Fleury as a whiner.

"I try to get through to him," Page mutters over coffee. "I said, 'Theo, you can't be a hero without paying the price.' I'm not sure he wants to get better. Getting better is what life is all about, no matter how good you are already."

Steve O'Donnell has the bus in place for the five p.m. departure for Maple Leaf Gardens. The autograph boys hang around the door. Steve makes conversation with coach Constantine. "It looks like Wendel Clark is coming back from his injury tonight," Steve says.

"No," says Kevin. "I heard not till Friday." Steve nods. He hangs around the Gardens. He hears a lot there and on the buses. But he's not going to argue with a customer.

When the Flames arrive at the Gardens, they get the starting lineup. Clark is in it. And he will score Toronto's fourth goal. Felix Potvin will start in goal for the Leafs.

Philosophy might be too formal a word for such a physical game, but there are two lines of thinking about visiting goalies and home-town crowds: one says they will play better in front of family and friends, one says they'll be distracted. Page on this night hopes the former line is true and goes with the earnest rookie Roloson. Since they traded Rick Tabaracci to Tampa for Gavey earlier in the season, the Flames have leaned towards Kidd with Rolly as backup.

Page likes the intensity of Kidd, who was the Flames' first draft choice in 1990. But the goalie's long hair, goatee, and erratic locker-room behaviour have brought the words "weird duck" to Page's lips. The coach has also noted that Kidd has a bad game every six or seven outings. "Everyone has a pattern," he says, "goalies, pitchers, coaches." He can't control much of a game, but Page picked the quiet Roloson over Tabaracci this season and this night he chooses Roloson over Kidd to play. "They tell me they won't trade me," says Rolly, "but, of course, you never know."

What Page can't control is revenge. After Cliff Fletcher left the Flames to run the Leafs, he engineered a trade with his old team to bring Doug Gilmour to Toronto. Gilmour's game pattern is that he always plays well against the Calgary franchise that let him go. That pattern will hold on this night, with Gilmour racking up the points.

Signed as a free agent, Dwayne Roloson is a twenty-eight-year-old Ontario native and U.S. college graduate who could have played pro soccer. Rolly has invested twenty-four years learning hockey, the last two trekking across the Maritimes and New England states putting his body in front of rapidly moving pieces of rubber for the Saint John Flames. When Page likes someone like Gavey or Roloson, he says they have "character." Page has seen Roloson studying Gary Taylor's tapes of the league's best shooters, watching, rewinding, and rewatching for their propensities in different situations. "Theo has one of the toughest shots," Rolly says. "When he gets the puck in the curve of his stick just right, he doesn't just shoot the puck. He launches it."

Rolly does a lot of thinking and studying off the ice. "But out there in a game I don't want to think," he says. "I just need to react." How does he react after a goal? "My reaction is not to react. I work very hard at blocking everything out – the goal, the crowd, the horn. I have to refocus for the next shot."

By the time the Flames' bus arrives at the Gardens' side door for the 601st game of the National Hockey League's season, Calgary's channel 7, CICT, has already been in the building for hours, setting up the broadcast so that viewers across southern Alberta, northern Montana, and southern British Columbia can sit down with an early dinner and their team and yell at their TV screen.

The independent Calgary station has bought the rights to fifteen home games and fifteen road games every year. The CBC gets first choice of games, TSN second, and channel 7 gets thirty mid-week games. "We promote ourselves as community-involved," says Kim Corrigall, broadcast manager. "And what better way to show involvement than with the community's team?" The station and Flames have even done some cross-promotions, a feel-good civic-spirit promo showing four Flames players stopping their car to fix a stalled school bus and settle down the children.

The station pays the team a rights fee and sells three hours of advertising. "It's a very popular package," adds Kim, who plays only recreational hockey now, leaving the more competitive brand to his teenage sons, Tyler, a Midget, and Lanny in Junior B.

"When Fleury arrived," Kim says, "it was an instant big deal. He just connects with the fans. People want to see him. Sometimes it seems hockey is no longer a game of heroes, just businessmen on skates. That can make it a tougher sell to the fans. They want to identify with a team and someone on that team. For the Flames, Theo is it."

Ed Whalen has done the play-by-play on CICT for nearly two decades. Grant Pollock is the host. Ed is sixty-nine years old and one of those jovial, longtime local TV announcers whose voice and face grow so familiar in our homes over the years that he becomes a walking institution affectionately greeted everywhere. He is often kidded about his age. When Fleury left the ice at that practice in Pittsburgh, he spotted Ed up in the stands. "Hey, Ed," Theo said, so everyone could hear, "you sleep in a pickled waterbed."

Ed laughed harder than anyone. "That's the old Theo," he said. "I've worked in the belly of this TV beast for forty-eight years. I remember one game long, long ago, I looked down at my sheet to get a player's number and when I looked up, the puck was in the net. I said, 'Eddie, my boy, you better smarten up.' So I've memorized the rosters for every game ever since."

Since Ed's listeners are seeing the game as he speaks, he must work at describing the scene without sounding redundant, a harder task than it seems. "People love sports," Ed says, "more so today, I think, than ever before. Sports are simpler than most of life. The nice thing about sports is the score is final, win or lose. The bad thing is, the score is final, win or lose. That intrigues people."

The Flames' dressing room in the Gardens is far from intriguing. It's a cramped, angled basement corner beyond the parked Zambonis. Rock music blares beyond loud. Fleury rolls his eyes. "HEY, KIDDER," he yells, "WHY DON'T YOU TURN THAT THING UP LOUD?" Kidd is in a loose mood, thinking he is not playing tonight and taping new sticks the way as a child he saw Brian Hayward of the Jets tape his back in Winnipeg.

Fleury appears pumped, even in his underwear and rubber bath sandals. "Had a good talk with Pierre," he says. "Gotta get me a good stick tonight."

He selects a new Titan from his pile. He heats the blade, curving it just so. He files the edges. He saws off the top down to two inches below his chin. "Josh's stick is too long, but he won't let me cut it." Then he files the handle round at the top to fit in his small hands. "Good thing I took shop in Russell." He tapes this newly created masterpiece. Then he pushes it against the floor, bending it and seeming to flick a wrist shot.

"Whaddya think?" he says. "Looks like a shooter to me. Yes, this is a good one. Watch out, Felix. Here we come."

In fact, all the Flames seem in high spirits. Many of their families are present. It's a TV game back home. It's Maple Leaf Gardens. The Flames have not won in Toronto since 1994. But if pregame chatter could win a game, they'd be three goals up before "O Canada."

Jonas Hoglund, a Swedish rookie, does put Calgary up first. The Flames take ten shots before the Leafs get one. Unfortunately, Robert Reichel takes a hooking call. Twelve seconds later, Doug Gilmour scores against his old team, his first of five points this night. With fifty-four seconds left in the first period, Toronto scores again. Page wants to pull Roloson. "He's too shaky," he says. But his assistant coaches, Guy Lapointe and Kevin Constantine, talk him out of it.

Early in the second, Tie Domi goes off for hooking. Thirty-eight seconds later, Theo scores his twentieth of the year, the first with his new stick. But the Leafs quickly score twice. It's 4–2. Moments later Fleury buries another one with the new stick, high on the glove side. That's his 299th career NHL goal.

For the third period, Kidd skates out to tend goal. As usual, Leafs fans and the Gardens are full of noise. The Flames are excited and hopeful. Theo is definitely in this game. With 19.7 seconds left, Theo steals the puck at centre ice. He starts to weave towards the goal on a breakaway. The crowd leaps to its feet as one, screaming. Can he tie the game in the closing seconds once more? About fifteen feet out, a lone Fleury lets it rip high on the goalie's left side again. Potvin gloves it. With a half-second remaining the Leafs get an empty-netter. Final: 5–3.

The locker room is a sombre place. The reporters zero in on Fleury; somehow, instead of being the hero for tying the game in the second, he's the goat for not tying it in the third. Never mind the lapses of everyone else. "You don't have a lot of time to think out there," he says. "I shot it into his glove. It's just reaction by him and me. I guess he outguessed me that time. He's a good goaltender. But we gave up two power-play goals tonight. We hurt ourselves. A loss is a loss and you gotta move on."

Fleury spots relatives consoling a downcast Roloson, pulled from the game in his Gardens debut. Fleury walks over to introduce himself to them. He is holding his new, almost-hat-trick stick. He looks at one youngster. "Can anybody here use a used stick?" Fleury says. Suddenly, smiles break out all around.

Fleury goes to dinner with his old teammate, Gilmour. Others seek out family. The return bus is nearly empty. A disgusted Al Coates walks alone all the way back to his hotel room in the rain.

There, his message light is blinking.

THURSDAY MORNING – With bags over their shoulders, players straggle out to the bus again, except for Steve Chiasson, who runs through the cold wearing only a sports coat. "Some son-of-a-bitch stole my coat at the restaurant last night," he says. Chiasson missed part of the Leafs game. He blocked a shot with his jaw. "All I remember," Steve says with a half-smile describing the puck flying at his face, "was seeing 'National Hockey League, Gary Bettman, Commissioner,' over and over and over." On his jaw this morning Chiasson has a bump the size of a golf ball. This prompts everyone to call him Gopher for the rest of the trip.

The bus is quiet until Trevor Kidd leaps aboard and exclaims, "Look, everyone, the sun came up again." No one laughs. This is the Flames' first morning-after since their latest loss, since they did everything they could, invested all of their emotion, thought they might pull out a tie, maybe even a win, came within a tantalizing inch or two, but lost badly in the end to the league's worst team.

As he does after losses, Fleury has lain in bed and replayed the game in his mind, shift by shift. Now, every Flame must forget the entire evening, discard all of that emotional and physical investment as if it were a dirty paper cup, and focus immediately on this morning's practice at the Gardens. Then comes tomorrow's game in Ottawa. It takes a surprising amount of will to focus on forgetting something so recent and painful.

Tommy Albelin sips coffee outside in the cold, ignored by the autograph-seekers. He played two years in Quebec and seven years in New Jersey before being traded to Calgary. "New Jersey, Calgary," he says. "To us, it doesn't really matter. I have my gear and my family with me. We go home to Sweden for the summer."

But mistakes do matter to Tommy. Too many of them could threaten his six-hundred-thousand-dollar salary. He has learned the hard way that the fastest way to make new mistakes is to think a lot about the old ones. "If you make a mistake in a game," he says, "you better let it go real fast. Because if you sit on the bench and think about it, things can go real bad for you. So you forget as quickly as possible."

Tommy flips his long hair back. He has opted against shaving this morning. Didn't feel like it. He's thinking about practice now. By tonight, he'll be poring over the Ottawa Senators' roster remembering past encounters and moves. The anguish of another avoidable loss in the playoff stretch is already ancient history just nine hours later.

Tommy smiles down at a fellow traveller who is new to forgetting fast. "So you want to be a hockey player?" he inquires. "There's a lot more than you think to the backside of this life, isn't there?"

Practice goes well in the deserted Gardens. The Flames were slow to suit up beforehand, which prompts Page to walk through the dressing room clapping his hands and uncharacteristically chanting, "C'mon, boys! Let's put a sprint on." Behind his back several players exchange quizzical looks. But out on the ice they are all business for nearly an hour. A few Leaf players chat with Flames friends; no one discusses the game.

In the dressing room a TV shows "The Price Is Right." "Oh, I love this show," says Theo, turning up the volume. "I watched it all the time when I was this high." Soon, a band of professional hockey players, grown men in their underwear, is standing in front of the television loudly cheering a woman contestant. The bus is waiting. Soon, the plane will be waiting too. The players remain there rooting and shouting advice at the woman on the taped show. She does not listen. Together, the players groan when she loses. Someone even throws a dirty sock at her. "Loser!" Fleury yells.

Bobby and Brian hurriedly haul the gear to a truck, bag by bag. As the bus pulls away, coaches surreptitiously pass around the latest newspaper fax from Calgary. At the airport Steve O'Donnell, the driver, waves. "See ya, guys!" The Leafs are on the road the next night, but Steve will be picking up the Dallas Stars then for their Saturday night game at the Gardens.

Inside the terminal, Mike Burke is handing out boarding passes for Canadian Airlines flight number 812 to Ottawa to every Flames player, save one.

"Oops," says Kevin Constantine when he spots Al Coates across the concourse talking with Dale McTavish. The other players see them as well but pretend not to. It's like a squadron of bombers on its way to a target when enemy fighters pick off one of their number and it starts to fall. There's nothing for the others to do but watch and thank the stars it's not them. One-on-one conversations between a player and the general manager in the airport can mean only one thing.

On the eve of playing in front of his family and friends, after nine NHL games and one goal, Dale McTavish is going back down to the minors.

"It's not my favourite part of this job," admits Al. "You always want to be hopeful at those times. I reviewed with him why we brought him up – to be physical, to provide a spark, to be a presence along the boards, to make sure the puck got out along the blueline. He did the job for four or five games, but I said we saw a fall-off. I told him if he had done this and this and this, those nine games might have been stretched to the balance of the year and he'd have put us in a position of moving a veteran out or trading someone because Dale had taken his place. I told him what he had to do to get back up and said we hoped to see him back up. He took it well, I think."

Dale makes his way alone to the plane back to New Brunswick. One by one, the other Flames players walk through the metal-detectors where the female guards notice something. "Why is it," one asks, "all the good-looking guys live out of town?" The Flames board their flight to Ottawa. They do not notice at first that the general manager is no longer with them either.

◈

Trades are funny things in the professional sports business, unless you are involved. Two or three of them are seriously discussed for every one that shows up on the sports pages as consummated.

They start off innocently enough, with one member of the general managers' club thinking out loud to a peer on the phone. Perhaps he's bemoaning his team's low scoring. Some days, weeks, or months later the peer may phone back and wonder if his pal is still looking for scoring. And, well, he might be, what did the peer have in mind? And so it goes, back and forth barter over the playing skills and contracts of players oblivious to these discussions.

That blinking message light the previous night was from Bob Pulford, then general manager of the Chicago Blackhawks. Coates and Pulford had been talking about a possible trade for nearly a year. It started the previous spring when Chicago and Calgary felt they had a surplus of talent at different positions.

The discussions faded over the summer when Chicago made a deal that sent Jeremy Roenick to Phoenix for Alexei Zhamnov. By late fall both Chicago and Phoenix were disappointed with the goal production while Calgary was becoming disappointed with the scoring of Robert Reichel, a Czech brought back from Europe with a two-million-dollar contract. Calgary was interested in a swap for one of Chicago's young players who was disappointing his Blackhawk coaches.

Coates went to Chicago in November. With Pulford, he watched that young player. Calgary's scouts had advised Coates to make a one-for-one deal if he could. But nothing happened that night. Now, two months later Pulford was seeking to revive the talks. Coates was willing. He was even more unhappy with Reichel's play. While the Flames and Reichel went east to Ottawa, Coates went west to Chicago to watch the Maple Leafs play the Hawks.

He was still willing to trade. However, Chicago's opinion of its young player apparently had improved. The Hawks began talking about Calgary adding a sweetener. Coates balked. The deal went on hold, this time for good. The young Chicago player had improved enough to stay, for now. And he will never know how close he came to changing teams that night. "There was a window of opportunity there," says Coates, "and for whatever reason both teams missed it. And I doubt now if Chicago will ever trade that guy."

Coates returned to Calgary to talk other trades by phone. Eventually, Reichel was dealt to the New York Islanders for Marty McInnis. Brenda Koyich booked them both into the same Toronto airport hotel as they switched teams and sides of the continent. But neither player knew the other was in the same building.

Another road trip soon after saw a trade between Calgary and the Hartford Whalers – Steve Chiasson for Hnat Domenichelli and veteran Glen Featherstone. The two teams actually began talking about Domenichelli back during training camp. Page especially liked the youth – "He's got jump and character," the coach said. Domenichelli played in Junior on the same line as Iginla. Calgary needed goal-scoring and more skating speed. Page and Coates thought the Iginla–Domenichelli chemistry might work. But Hartford was vague about what it wanted in return.

Hartford thought Domenichelli needed more seasoning, so he was left on the Springfield AHL team. As the winter progressed and the March trading deadline neared, Whaler coaches came to feel they needed a good strong defensive veteran to make the playoffs. Hartford's Jim Rutherford approached Coates again at the All-Star Game. They talked back and forth. Other players were mentioned. The trading deadline was looming. They settled on Chiasson for Domenichelli, who brought speed and a potential future, and Featherstone, a big, seasoned defenceman, who brought experience and size to Calgary.

Egos may be invisible but in the National Hockey League they seem to bruise much more easily than those big bodies that house them. Trades can be tough emotionally. Each side is making a conscious, open decision that someone else is worth more to them than someone they already have. "You're always careful in trades," says Coates, "to emphasize that the other team wants your player, not that he's being cast off. This is a tough business. No one and no job is sacred. But these are human beings. Sometimes it's real tough trading guys, especially players with families. My wife has gotten involved in a lot of charity work with players' wives. And you get to know them. But I try to keep it a business. The other team has a need. We both might gain from it. My job is to make our team better."

And the business has an impact on Coates's own family as well. "From training camp through the playoffs," he says, "they know Daddy won't be around too much." And even when he is around, he's got to check his voicemail, watch the sports news, or some player in some hockey game off the satellite.

Coates, like Lanny McDonald, has seen a change in attitude with the big money of pro sports. "The players of today are much more businesslike," Coates says. "And they are hardened by the business side, as much as we try to keep it a game, a simple game that players have fun with. And they need to have fun with this game. But the reality is that they are in a business and the more they get familiarized with the collective-bargaining agreement and the union, the more they become hardened to the business. Then what follows, naturally, is that they must also expect the consequences of a business."

Sometimes the business of trades gets tied into contract talks. In 1996, Phil Housley, a well-liked Calgary defenceman, was set to become a free agent. He made it clear he did not want to stay in Calgary. "You can't let a franchise player just walk away any more," said Coates. "We could have kept him for a couple of months and then lost him for good, for nothing. Or we could trade him and get something for him." Calgary traded Housley to the New Jersey Devils, which is how Tommy Albelin and Cale Hulse came to be Flames.

In 1997, Calgary faced a similar situation when Dave Gagner, Fleury's roommate, was about to become a free agent and could walk away. Gagner and Fleury had developed a genuine affection for each other. When told of the book being written about the diminutive Fleury, Gagner had asked, "Is it a short story?"

Because there were no really tempting offers for Gagner, Coates opted to keep him, hoping his scoring and experience would help the Flames reach the playoffs and that his presence would send a signal to other players about the team's commitment to winning now. Coates hoped that they could negotiate later with Gagner's agent. In the end, Gagner signed with Florida.

Sometimes negotiations are simpler. When Fleury's initial Flames contract expired in 1995, he could have shopped himself around the league not so much to move, but to solicit a large contract offer that the Flames would have to match. Many players have done that to their existing teams. "Good for them," says Theo. "But how do you know the grass is really greener over there?"

Fleury did stay out of training camp, fearing that an injury would ruin his position. But he did not miss a game. According to Theo, the Flames made a five-year offer starting at $2.3 million and ending at $2.8 million. Fleury, who was then earning $870,000 Canadian, said, fine. "That's a lot of money," he says. "Look, when I was playing road hockey back in Russell, I didn't say, 'Someday I'm going to make $2.5 million in the National

Hockey League.' I said, 'Someday I'm going to play in the National Hockey League, period.' And here I am playing in the National Hockey League. How many millions do you need to live comfortably anyway? We didn't want this to get ugly and controversial."

Fleury also remembered that Entry Draft day in his parents' living room when the phone rang. "You know, not that many teams were banging down the door to get at me," he says. "The Flames believed in me then. Why shouldn't I stick with them now? I felt a special loyalty to the Flames. I want to stay here and see my son play hockey. And my wife's family is here, too. Calgary fans have been great. They work hard for their money and they pay good money to see me and my teammates play. It's hard to think when I go out and have a bad night that some people are thinking, 'That damn Fleury is dogging it out there.' You know, there's more to being in the public eye than meets the eye."

Fleury's contract negotiations involved guaranteeing the money. And Theo wanted a no-trade clause, which the Flames opposed on principle. Theo called his father again. They had a fairly brief talk. "I asked him," Wally Fleury recalls, "'What are they offering you?' He told me. I said, 'That's a lot of money.' He said, 'Yeah, but they won't give me a no-trade clause.' I told him, 'You're five-foot-six. Suddenly, somebody comes up and wants to pay you $2.5 million to play hockey in the NHL. Do you want to stay in Calgary?' He said, 'Yeah.' And I said, 'Well, boy, my case is closed.'"

The next day the Flames announced the signing of Theo Fleury to a contract – $2.3 million the first season of 1995–96, $2.375 million for two years, then $2.4 million with a possible fifth year at Theo's option for $2.8 million. So, after four years, Theo could theoretically walk away with no compensation to the Flames à la Housley or Gagner.

In Canada's 48 per cent tax bracket, Fleury's salary works out to about $15,060.97 U.S. for each regular-season game. Of course, when you divide the salary by the investment in "schooling," the practice hours and games Fleury put in developing his skills over the years, the hourly pay is likely less than minimum wage. But that gets overlooked because that's not what heroes do, eh?

THURSDAY AFTERNOON – Aaron Gavey's four-leaf-clover tattoo works like a charm. With a free afternoon in Ottawa many of the players go to a casino in Hull. Gavey wins a thousand dollars. Alone in the hotel elevator, he yells for joy.

The next morning coach Page moans. There on the front page of the *Ottawa Citizen* is a colour photo of Dale McTavish and a big headline: "SHOT DOWN IN FLAMES."

"Party Poopers: Eganville hockey fans were planning a big night at the Corel Centre tonight to honour Dale McTavish of the Calgary Flames – the only Eganville native ever to play in the NHL. All that turned to ashes Thursday when the Flames demoted McTavish to the minors."

The fact was, Flames management was trying to wring some victories from their unsettled team and creep into the playoffs. They knew nothing of Eganville's happy plans or its proximity to Ottawa. "We could have kept him on for a day," Coates says later. "But he wouldn't have played in Ottawa for sure. He makes I think forty-five thousand dollars playing in Saint John. And he makes about three hundred thousand on a pro rata basis playing in Calgary. So how much money does it cost to be a nice guy for two days?"

The plane ride to Ottawa was uneventful. Fleury carried on a small pizza and tried to mooch another piece from Jamie Huscroft, who refused. "You're not my friend any more," said Fleury. "Keep your head up in practice tomorrow." Fleury spotted Mark Miller, the reporter. "Get out of here, trouble-maker," he said.

"Hey, Theo," said Mark, "it was my editors."

"Yeah, right." Theo plopped down in seat 14F and slept.

Tommy Albelin was flicking ice cubes at the bump on Chiasson's jaw. Joel Bouchard made an admission. "It's hard playing with Theo," he said, "because, you know, he's so good and makes everything look so easy."

THURSDAY EVENING – Fleury meets with Mike Trudeau for dinner. He's now a landscaper in Ottawa, but years ago he was a hockey-camp mate in Brandon and was on the other side in that friendly Portage la Prairie game that ended so bloodily. In fact, Trudeau was the only Portage player to visit Fleury in the hospital. That's the kind of thing Theo remembers. The two reminisce while riding in Mike's pickup to Capone's, where Fleury sits unnoticed at a back table. He recalls always being hungry at road games when he was young. Theo orders a shrimp cocktail, full caesar salad, and a large steak with pasta.

Fleury asks for the bill. The waitress returns to announce that Tony, the owner, is so pleased that Theo has returned he wants to comp the meals. Another perk of fame. Fleury tracks Tony down to thank him. Tony asks if the player would meet his kitchen staff, all hockey fans. Another price of fame. On the way out Fleury passes Alexei Yashin, a star on the Senators. They nod wordlessly.

FRIDAY AFTERNOON – Game-day meal is complete. The autograph-seekers are gone; they know the game-day afternoon routine. DO NOT DISTURB signs are all over the ninth floor of the Westin Hotel.

In Calgary, Veronica Fleury is making an early dinner so she can sit by the radio and listen to the game. Theo usually calls her after his nap before he leaves for the game. She'd like him to phone after road games, too, but Theo does not always remember. Veronica gets antsy just sitting during games. When she's in the Saddledome watching, she must put her cold drink down during each of Theo's shifts. Watching the Toronto game on TV Wednesday night, she was eating some hot dogs, French fries, and coleslaw alone and got so excited when Theo scored twice that she spilled her Coke. Hat Trick, who arrived on a day when Theo got three goals in one game, would not stop barking. The Toronto game made for a grand evening for Veronica, even with only two-thirds of a hat trick.

Tonight Veronica will work out on their stationary bike while listening to the familiar tones of Peter Maher on CFR radio. Peter's voice is soothing and authoritative, as befits the son of a funeral director. When Peter was six, his grandfather would drive his car around Campbellton, New Brunswick, making advertising announcements over a public-address system on the car roof. Sometimes Grandpa Maher would let Peter do the bingo announcements. Peter found speaking loudly to be so addictive, he made a career of it.

He has done sports broadcasting from New Brunswick to Indiana and, for a while, was the Leafs' play-by-play announcer. But Calgary is home now for the fifty-year-old broadcaster and CFR is the home to every single Flames game, nine exhibition and eighty-two regular-season, plus playoffs. So important are the Flames to CFR (Calgary Flames Radio) that the station has a separate sales force selling year-long ad associations with the team. Even in the off-season, CFR broadcasts hourly ads for the team and sponsors associated with the team and station.

Every three-hour Flames game becomes a five-hour broadcast package with pregame predictions, Peter's play-by-play, Doug Barkley's colour commentary, and postgame interviews and analysis with Jock Wilson and a shifting squad of guests, spiced with one hundred thirty-second ads. CFR is a fifty-thousand-watt station and has listeners as far north as Edmonton, as far south as Great Falls, Montana, and a hundred miles into Saskatchewan, where CFR's parent company broadcasts one

Flames game a week on affiliated stations. Don Armstrong, vice president, estimates each game draws a hundred thousand listeners, even more than CFR's golden oldies format. "Our intention," he says, "is to be the voice of the Calgary Flames forever."

Peter Maher spends his pregame afternoons not speaking at all. Long-distance airline travel, changing climates from Florida to Edmonton, and winter weather within Canada can wreak havoc on a pro's vocal cords. He drinks his coffee with cream only, since sugar causes coughs.

FRIDAY EVENING – Everyone is ready to board the bus at five p.m. At 4:56, Fleury is sipping coffee in the lobby looking sleepy when someone mentions his wife. "Oh, geez," he says, and rushes to a pay phone. Compared to the Saddledome right next to downtown Calgary, the Corel Centre is on the moon. It is the only structure in sight at a distant highway interchange. Besides cheaper rural real estate, the advantage to building the Corel Centre so far from anything in Ottawa is that it is forty-five minutes closer to Sudbury.

But the Centre is one of Fleury's favourite arenas. A snowstorm rages as the bus backs entirely into the new building. In the dressing room Kidd is anxious tonight; he is staring meanly at everyone and wants Terry Kane to break his Power Bar into three precisely equal pieces. "Goalies are weird," says Theo, who is working on another new stick. "I had good luck with the last new one," he says.

The weather holds attendance to 13,306, but they consume 7,613 hot dogs. Corey Millen scores for Calgary, which holds the lead after one period. Fleury is interviewed on TV during the intermission. "There are nights when you're a little frustrated," he says, "especially coming off the World Cup with expectations so high. I said some things recently I probably shouldn't have said. I don't pull punches and sometimes they get me in trouble. As athletes, we're not allowed to be tired. We have a bad night as a professional and everyone gets angry, as if they don't have bad days. Pierre, Coatesy, and I sat down and talked things out. . . . I need to improve my game and pick up my play."

In the second, Millen scores again. But then Alexei Yashin drills one for Ottawa. After two, Calgary 2, Ottawa 1. The third period starts slowly. During the TV timeouts, Theo skates around tapping his stick in time to the music. With one minute left, Ottawa pulls its goalie. With 29.7 seconds left the puck dribbles past a sprawling Kidd. In overtime, Jonas Hoglund drives one off the crossbar and with 36.8 seconds left, Ottawa smothers a Fleury shot to gain a tie and a point in the standings that proves crucial later when the Senators squeak into the playoffs.

"This was an unacceptable performance," Kevin Constantine mumbles on the bus. "Our goaltending was beyond spectacular. But good teams do not leave games like this without two points." The bus door opens at the hotel at 11:40 p.m.

SATURDAY MORNING – It's 6:30 a.m. Dawn has yet to arrive, but when it does, it will be icy and grey. Bleary-eyed players with wet hair, fruit, coffee, and newspapers dump their bags into the belly of the bus and try to sleep in the back. "Long road trips are all part of the game," says Jamie Huscroft, who will soon be traded to Tampa Bay. "You get home and the wife wants to talk and the kids want to play and you're like, look, I've gotta go to bed, okay?"

Stan Halpenny is not looking forward to this sixteen-hour day, driving this bus to the airport on icy roads and then taking a swim team down to Kingston and back. Precisely at seven, Fleury steps on the bus, having satisfied a pack of hardy autograph hounds standing in the wind and ice. "Seven a.m. on a Saturday in the snow," he says. "Do you believe those guys?"

There is chaos at the airport check-in. The plane will be at least two hours late. Bags are piled everywhere. The youngest players crowd to get their boarding passes first. "As long as the rookies are happy," Ron Stern says loudly, "that's what's important."

At the gate, players claim spots of floor and fall fast asleep.

The travel veterans know to carry soft bags; they can become pillows. Children tote pieces of paper among non-sleeping players who obediently sign. Jarome Iginla nods off in a chair. Brian Patafie scribbles a large sign and Theo sticks it in the player's arms: SPARE CHANGE PLS. All nearby travellers chuckle at this team mischief.

Dwayne Roloson and Jamie Huscroft begin a checkers game. They are atypical in choosing mind games for idle travel time. Not surprisingly for people living a physical life, most players bring CDs or tape players for music. They prefer newspapers or novels to nonfiction, do not seem to carry pens, and prefer phone calls to letters. Later in the day, Jamie and Dwayne will compete through games of Scrabble. "Faa is too a word," Dwayne will claim. Jamie pretends to wipe his forehead and look at his hand. "What does this look like, stupid rubbing off of me?"

"I'm going to play hockey until I get it right," says Joel Bouchard. "And you don't get it right until you win the Stanley Cup." He's planning his Calgary evening alone: a pasta dinner in his apartment and falling asleep on the couch watching hockey for a change.

"What are they doing," Fleury asks as the delay drags on, "building the plane?"

Jonas Hoglund, the not-quite hero of last night's overtime, wanders off to find the men's room; flights in the northern half of North America are always so long. He is standing there, in the men's room, when a middle-aged man, a portly but knowing stranger, waddles in and stands nearby. According to men's-room protocol, both men stare at the wall silently.

"Hey," the man says anyway, unwilling to waste this special moment next to a famous person, "that was a great game you guys played last night."

There is a brief pause. "Really?" says Jonas, not the least bit surprised to be recognized while urinating in an airport 2,236 miles from home. "I thought we should have won."

"Look," says the man, zipping and turning to Jonas with sincerity, authority, and some patience, "let me tell you, that was tough. I know, believe me. But that's professional hockey. You've got to move on."

With a blank face Jonas watches the wrinkled but confident expert walk away. "I see," the professional hockey player says to the wall straight ahead. "Well, thank you very much."

Finally, it is time to board flight 901. The disappearance of players down the ramp is the catalyst for one hesitant youngster at an adjacent gate. He pushes through the crowd to Fleury. "Hi, Theo," he says.

"Hi, bud. What are you doing wearing a Canadiens hat?"

"All my friends have them," the boy explains.

"Well," Theo orders as he signs it, "you tell all your friends to get Flames hats."

To keep this hurried conversation with fame going on this Saturday morning the child wants to know who and when the Flames play next. Fleury looks at adjacent team members. They shrug. "Hey, Terry," says Theo, "who do we play next?"

"The Islanders on Tuesday." The boy nods knowingly.

"Good luck, Theo."

"Thanks, buddy."

For almost five hours the plane drones westward into a headwind, not unlike the whole season. There have been slightly more than 5,500 players in the eighty-plus-year history of the National Hockey League. Of the twenty-four of those players on flight 901 on this day at the end of a three-game, roughly six-thousand-mile week, twenty-one are asleep, sometimes twenty-two. Every fifteen minutes Jamie shakes the shoulder of Chris O'Sullivan.

"What?" demands Chris.

Jamie is concerned. "I just want to make sure you're getting enough sleep," he says.

Fleury is looking out the window and feeling thoughtful. He's wearing a gold bracelet but not a watch. Keeping time or being on time is not always a priority to Theo, as many of his appointments will attest. "I don't like to worry about things," he says, "including time."

"I've got so many memories from this game," he says. "I've had like about six hundred stitches over the years. That's about one for each game. I've got the puck from my six-hundredth game, too. I stole it from the net after the horn. It'll be good to get home. That's the downside to fame. You lose all your privacy outside your house. Sometimes you need a disguise when you go out. Even in your house, you see people driving by slowly, trying to look in.

"I learned something on this road trip. The reporters don't really know me. They might think they do. But they don't. I try to be so accommodating to them. And they use me to sell their papers. I realized for the first time this week, I'm just a commodity to some people. You know, this week was the first article ever talking about trading me from the Calgary Flames. You have one bad game or month or even year and they talk about trading you?"

He looks around the quiet aircraft cabin. "It kinda hurts a little, you know?"

A long while later the plane lands in Calgary. Eighty-eight people stand and stretch their sore and cramped muscles. "Well," says Ronnie Stern, "that didn't take long."

In the baggage-claim area there is one other surprise. Actually, two. One surprise is not too bad: To save weight the airline left all of the Flames' hockey gear in Ottawa, which means practice is cancelled. The other surprise: most of the players' luggage was also left behind.

❖

Watching professional athletes play hard can make spectators very hungry. And thirsty. Which pleases Nancy Cleveland to no end.

Nancy is food-services manager for the Saddledome. She began learning the specific business of feeding spectators by selling hot dogs in Houston's Astrodome. Then she ran food services in Denver's McNichols Arena and then in Mile High Stadium before moving on to be assistant general manager at the America West Arena in Phoenix. What began as a consulting trip to Calgary for the 1988 Olympics ended with her returning full-time in 1995, just in time for nearly fifty million dollars in Saddledome renovations, which meant her business attire for months included a hardhat and steel-toed boots.

Eating at NHL hockey games may once have been more of a refuelling stop between periods. But today catering is an increasingly important aspect of making every game an entertainment – and sensory – experience, and a major revenue stream. The assignment for Nancy, her twelve full-time staff members, and seven hundred part-time food-service workers includes everything from moving the pop machines from the back of each stand to the counter to save employee time and movement, all the way up to overseeing the chef for the fancy buffets that precede most games in the Chrysler Club.

The Flames want the Saddledome's operation to reek of classiness. So Nancy disposed of the disposable plastic dishes that dominate luxury boxes in U.S. arenas and substituted real china. She put linen skirts around the buffet. Since Nancy is a real popcorn fan, she insists on fresh-popped and real butter at those stands. She has also expanded food and drink varieties, adding salads, premium beer, and wine coolers, as well as relish and chopped onions to the condiment trays, and the Saddledome has increased all portions (prices, too, at times). The customers might not eat everything, but no one should ever feel they didn't get their money's worth. Thus, sixteen-ounce drinks became twenty ounces. And she added special nozzles to reduce time waiting for the carbonated fizz to fall.

For the circus and travelling Disney shows, she added cotton candy and smaller drinks for smaller bladders. Unlike American arenas, Canada's feel they must be able to exchange foreign currency. Nancy insisted on a standard exchange throughout the Saddledome so no one would feel, well, shortchanged. The napkins she had printed with the Saddledome logo rather than the Flames symbol, so they could be used at any event. That earned her a larger volume discount from the printer.

Nancy and the Saddledome staff installed brighter lights and have opened the concourses to ease fan movement and provide a feeling of airiness, no minor decision since it involved moving walls and pillars. She's adding one food section with garden tables and opening it for birthday and anniversary parties. "We want," Nancy says as she breezes through one last pregame inspection tour with one ear to the radio in her hand, "this place to be a friendly, comfortable place that people want to come to."

She also quickly adjusts service to suit changing Canadian tastes. Canadians love ice cream, even in winter when the ice cream grows harder outside the store than in the freezer. So she added more ice cream machines. Likewise, she would sell 1,600 pretzels at a Phoenix basketball game, but Calgary hockey fans buy only 400. And restaurant smoking sections need to be larger in Canada than in the U.S. She's working on more ice machines and ATMs.

To spread concession sales out a little, the Saddledome installed TV monitors over each stand, so customers in line need not fear missing any action. Sometimes Nancy even gets to watch some of the game. "The first one I saw here – this is a true story – I turned to my friend and I said, 'Who's that little 14 guy?'"

Customers in the Chrysler Club section need never even leave their seats. Waitresses keep running tabs for them and transmit orders by radio to the food stand, which saves time and staff traffic. Having read the customer's name on the credit card, the waitress is encouraged to address them by name throughout the game.

Noticing that beer-buyers will stand in long lines at beer stands rather than buy brew at a food stand with a few families, Nancy invested in several portable beer units that can be rolled anywhere. Those units cost ten thousand dollars each to build and now do four thousand dollars in business every game. To save on refrigerating costs, much of the beer in the building is stored in five huge, efficiently chilled rooms and siphoned from there through cooled pipes like fuel lines.

To avoid potential accidents and public-relations problems, she improved staff training so those who sell alcohol will spot intoxicated customers better and have them removed if necessary. The Saddledome has even paid for taxi rides home.

Nancy is a big supporter of weekend matinee Family Days and Family Packs, which the Flames will increase. "Families are our future," Nancy says. "Families are always more excited and refreshing." And she likes games against the original six NHL teams; they're more likely to sell out. For one Toronto game the Saddledome sold 5,300 cups and 1,754 cans of beer, 4,800 portions of Coca-Cola, 2,500 popcorns, 601 candy bars, 1,200 orders of nachos, and 942 hot dogs and Polish sausages. Fans also downed 477 small, 1,081 regular, and 1,047 large ice creams.

Sunday games are bad for beer sales but great for popcorn. Besides weekend matinees, the best sales games are weekday evenings, especially Thursday and Friday, presumably because fans can already smell the weekend. Tuesday or Wednesday evening games can be good or bad, depending on the visiting team and the weather.

"I always dreamed of being in the NHL," says Brad Andrews. "I got there all right. I'm just not playing." Brad loves hockey, also skating. "I feel so free when I'm skating," he says. "Even when I come off the ice, I'm still glowing."

Brad's dad, a postal worker, used to let his boys flood the entire backyard every winter at their Calgary home on Richmond Road, even though that meant their father's first challenge every day was to negotiate twenty feet of ice just to reach his car. Today, in his free time, Brad scouts for a Calgary youth team. His brother, Wayne, coaches youngsters. "Hockey isn't so much a game," Brad says, "as a way of life."

For Brad, hockey is also work. He started out as a Flames usher. Now, he is the ticket-office manager. Calgary is notorious for its late-ticket-buying clientele. That complicates Brad's sales predictions, which are relied on to order and make food. He knows the Rangers, Leafs, and Canadiens will sell out in Calgary. The same is usually true for the Blackhawks, Red Wings, and Boston. But this next game is on a Tuesday and the Islanders are harder to predict. The Flames did not win on the previous week's road trip. There was the controversy over Fleury. The weather forecast calls for snow. So Brad estimates around 16,500, 2,388 shy of a sellout.

He's been in since mid-morning. Walk-up sales are steady, especially in the lunch hour, but smaller than desirable. He might not even make 16,500, especially if it starts snowing at dinnertime.

Pat Halls has had to make his sales predictions well ahead of time for a print order. Among other things, he edits the Flames programs, sells ads for them as well as ad signs all over the building and even beneath the ice on the rink floor; a corporate logo, painted and entombed there, will cost you about $110,000 a season.

The Flames sell about 1,600 programs for each game. Actually, the Calgary Figure Skating Club sells them as a fundraiser and keeps 10 per cent of the four-dollar price. Fleury's photo on the cover will sell more programs; that's a given. But there are a lot of variables – the weather, if the game is on TV, which team is visiting, and how close is payday.

Work on dinner began around lunchtime in the Saddledome, starting with the salads and the arrival of chefs Michael Kelly and Steve Langley. At that time Fleury was at home downing plates of pasta. Theo fell asleep with the soap operas on TV.

Theo likes to arrive to the Saddledome about two hours before a game. He used to get there perhaps four hours early, but these days two hours of fussing is sufficient. Now it's going on five o'clock, the end of the work day for most people and the start of the work day for Theoren Fleury and his teammates.

Soon, the headlights of Calgary's commuters will be streaming out from downtown. A few flakes of snow appear as darkness chills the air. But Fleury is headed towards downtown, sipping his Tim Hortons coffee, listening to country music. "I met Garth Brooks at the World Cup," he says.

On the few game days when Veronica does not take him, Theoren drives himself to work. He turns his white pickup off the highway a little early for the Saddledome, eases knowingly up the hill into a quiet residential neighbourhood, and cruises slowly down Salisbury Street.

This is not the route to the Canadian Airlines Saddledome. But it is the route to look back and see the Saddledome. Fleury knows exactly where he is going. He goes there all the time, whenever he wants a private reminder in a public place. Fleury parks the truck. The driver's window opens. The motor goes off. All is winter-quiet save for some distant traffic over on MacLeod Trail.

Fleury gazes out at a spectacular vista on this late-winter's early evening. The immense, brightly coloured Saddledome, Fleury's home, sits there, awaiting thousands of people. Amid countless lights, the Saddledome looks like some futuristic sleeping beast with steam rising from various ports. Fresh snow drifts down through the lights, giving everything a strangely warm glow in the cold air. Behind the Saddledome stands the dramatic, well-lit skyline of Calgary and, beyond, the snowy peaks of the Rocky Mountains, felt but unseen. Both the towering skyline and the mountains seem that much more dramatic because everything else is so flat, as it was back home in Manitoba.

Beneath the Saddledome's curved cement roof, the cooking underway is quite furious by now. Brad Wetzel is opening the Chrysler Club bar and Michael Alexander will soon be on condiment patrol, refilling every container and erasing each spill and splash as customers rush back to their seats. Mike Duben and the boys are touching up the ice. The TV cameras are warming up as Karla Piper meets with her entertainment crew and Grant Kelba starts getting inside Harvey the Hound, literally and figuratively, trying to think like people think a dog thinks. Stella Gendron has all of her radios set on CFR, where the pregame talk is already intense. The Flames, everyone notes, have not won since beating the Mighty Ducks nearly two weeks before.

Liz Ripak, a high-school guidance counsellor by day, is donning her Saddledome usher's uniform. As always, this night she is in charge of section 109. The Flames want ushers to come to know their regular customers, so Liz is permanently assigned up behind the penalty boxes. "I get paid to watch hockey games," she says, still not believing her good fortune. One by one, and later in fours and sixes, fans will be walking over the crest from the concourse, stepping down the stairs, and out into the arena that seems larger than life.

Two of the fans taking their seats are Keith Shaw and Kim Paterson, both prison guards and both longtime season-ticket-holders. They have the self-assigned task of hassling opponents off their game. They yell mean things – not crude, but mean.

After years of hassling, Chris Chelios of Chicago leaned around the glass and said, "Isn't it time we became friends?"

"Okay," said Kim, "give your friend your stick."

And Chelios did.

Liz Ripak has ushered every Flames home game since 1989 and witnessed every home game of Fleury's. "He's a gutsy guy," she says. "You know, he could have gone somewhere else for more money, but he chose to stay with us in Calgary."

Mike Board also covers some Flames games and trips for the *Herald*. He likes Fleury and hockey, but tries to keep a professional distance from the team and remain more like a privileged representative of his newspaper's readers. He's planning a story soon on Fleury's new Nike skates. When the *Herald*'s photographer lies on the floor to shoot the skate and up at Fleury's face, Mark Miller of the *Sun* walks by. "What's this?" he asks.

"It's a feature for my favourite newspaper, the *Herald*," Fleury responds coldly.

Mike watched from home the *Sun*'s coverage of the recent Theo flap and his paper's response. "Sure," Mike says, "controversy always sells more. But you've got to be careful not to blow anything out of proportion. You've always got to be fair." He has found Theo invariably available for interviews but noticed the player seemed somewhat more cautious the last time they talked.

Irv McDougall is on his stool by the loading dock. Irv got bored with life when his wife died. He's not exactly security, being seventy-five years old. But his job is important. He checks the passes of everyone entering the northwest basement door on game days. "You wouldn't believe the people, even kids, who try to get inside here," he says, "just to get a peek at someone famous, especially Theo." Irv takes routine pride in recognizing Flames players, even the many new young ones streaming through nowadays. He waves each player past free of formalities, thinking this might help their concentration just a touch more. Soon, even the youngest seems to expect that treatment.

But Irv never gets to see a single home game. Which is okay, since he's not much of a hockey fan.

Outside, still up on the hill to the east, Fleury is watching. "Whenever I come here," he says, "I'm always amazed. All that's happened is so unbelievable and wonderful at the same time." The little boy from the little prairie town, the one who started off to the west down Thacker Street in a snowsuit with a heavy pillowcase on his shoulder, simply to go skating with a friend, has travelled a very long way to this personal overlook. And who knows what's yet to come in hockey, in singing, in acting off the ice?

Shortly, Fleury will drive his truck around the corner and down the hill to park behind the Saddledome. With his cap pulled down tight on his head, he will walk past the friendly old guy on the stool, who has been there since that first game when Fleury came up from Salt Lake City. "Good luck, Theo," is the ritual pregame greeting. "Thanks, Irv," is the required reply.

Theo will walk near the Jumbotron control room, where millions of dollars in equipment is being readied to send this game all over the building and out to outer space and back down to the inner space of Long Island, where scores of businesses have invested thousands of dollars to sell cars and newspapers and legal services. In the hall, Theo will pass wordlessly by some people who will nod to him and then turn, point, and whisper after he's past.

He will walk near the visitor's dressing room. The Islanders were Fleury's favourite team throughout childhood; Clark Gillies was why Theo chose number 9 in the first place. Today, number 14 doesn't even think of that. The Islanders are just another of twenty-five, soon to be twenty-nine, opponents, including Nashville. So Theoren Fleury, the wannabe singer, will likely reach the capital of country music one way or another.

Theo will hang his leather coat and clothing in the Flames' second dressing room. He will shower and then don his hockey underwear. He will wince at the loud rock music blaring from

Kidd's corner. Only when Theo initiates the first conversation will others talk to him. Fame also carries extra space.

Theo will fuss with two new sticks, probably singing to himself all the while, but actually picturing the upcoming game and some of the moves he might try. He will watch some TV, witness Trevor Kidd go through another nervous pregame visioning experience, imagining his moves in the upcoming game, don his own gear one more time, left side first, of course. And he'll be ready by the door after the warmups for the trek to the big bright ice across the hall. There, waiting to go on, the entire team will be chattering and tapping gloves. Some of the words chattered would melt the ice, if the boys were on it already. But each player on both teams has gone through his own lifelong struggle – of dreams, of endless practices, of games, of injuries, of disappointments and losses – to get to this dramatic place and this exciting moment and to have so many people watching. Tonight, they will tap the same teammates in the same order with the same glove and surely say the same ritual reassurances as they do before every game. If they cannot control what's about to happen, then, by God, they will control the rituals beforehand.

The Saddledome will be pitch-dark by then. Even from beneath the stands, Theo can hear the sound of a comet on some scoreboard video he has never seen. Suddenly, there is an explosion. "Let's go, boys!" The lights flash on. And here comes Theo's favourite part of the game. Theoren Fleury and the Calgary Flames, clad in white and red for the good guys, leap onto the ice, professional athletes onstage now about to do their violent, beautiful, unpredictable business for 16,072 screaming fans in the building and many thousands more watching elsewhere.

Theoren will look over at Veronica's seat as the lights come up and they will exchange a signal. Theo may even make a funny face. It is bad luck, requiring an apology, if Veronica is not in place before the warmups. The Jumbotron will be busy all evening stoking and revisiting the excitement and showing Flames fans – and even some lost soul in an Islanders jersey – having an entertaining time. Harvey the Hound will hug a little girl and shoot T-shirts into the upper deck. Coach Page will pace behind the bench, his eyes seemingly about to explode from his head. Wearing a headset that connects him to Al Coates and Billy Hughes, a third assistant coach, up in the press box nearly ninety feet overhead, Kevin Constantine will chew his bubble gum at a speed that matches the pace of play on the ice. Gary Taylor will tape this game plus the Phoenix–Philadelphia and Montreal–Florida contests.

A few fights will break out in this Flames–Islanders game and Marty McInnis will get an assist for New York against the team he will soon join. On this night again, Theoren will not score. But Steve Chiasson, Mike Sullivan, Aaron Gavey, and Corey Millen will, breaking the Flames' winless string and winning, 4–3. Throughout the night skies, the mellow tones of Peter Maher will carry the action for radio listeners in cars and homes across Western Canada.

An hour after the final horn, hardly a person will be left in the Saddledome until two-dozen cleaners descend on the littered stands. Soon, the place will be ready for Thursday's game against San Jose – and 3.5 tons of new garbage will be out in the dumpsters, freezing already.

But all of that is yet to come. For now, Fleury is still parked on Salisbury Street overlooking the Saddledome. It is a short street. But it has been a long road. Many people have touched this player's life and he remembers most distinctly. Many have been touched, pleased, disappointed, even hurt and inspired by this player's life, though Theo cannot know them all. During warmups one night a youngster will stand by the glass waving at Fleury as he circles the Flames' end. And waving and waving. Then the child will walk away, proclaiming with juvenile certainty, "He saw me. He saw me."

While Fleury's career has moved on, so have those from his past. Coach Kvisle from Moose Jaw is back farming now. Coach Fowler still runs his autumn hockey camps but no longer coaches youth hockey and has turned over the Major Pratt high-school hockey team to Theo's Winnipeg linemate, Mike Rolling. Len and Ede Peltz have sold their motel in Russell and are methodically selecting a retirement location.

On the Flames, Ian McKenzie still voyages from rink to rink, more of them in the States now, it seems. "In my career as a pro scout," Ian says proudly, "Fleury will always be my gem." Brian Funfer has moved on to another job and within weeks Rick Skaggs will follow, as will all of the Flames coaches. Come summer, Nancy Cleveland would take her catering expertise to a new job in a major Las Vegas hotel.

It had been a very frustrating and puzzling season for coach Page. So distracted did he become near the end that twice in the same month he let his jeep run out of gas in Calgary traffic. A few months after the season, coach Page would demand a two-year contract extension. Al Coates, his friend of seventeen years, would counter with a one-year extension, and when that was refused, the Flames would release Page to look elsewhere, like Anaheim, where a former Flames colleague now is general manager. Fleury would shrug and profess shock. "How do you know the grass *is* greener over there?" he would say again.

Then days later, reporters called with rumours that Theo himself was on the trading block. The Flames said no, San Jose had just asked. Fleury said he wasn't sure what to think. Of the eight players drafted by the Flames ahead of Fleury in 1987, none became stars and only one (Matteau) remained in the league. But whatever happens, Fleury says, he'd like to be remembered "as someone who loved the game, worked hard at it, had fun, and brought others fun from watching."

One summer Wednesday Theo would announce that he was resigning the team captaincy, which he had accepted reluctantly in 1995 during the contract holdout of the previous captain. Theo said he wanted to concentrate now on improving his play and give a new head coach free rein to choose a team leader.

The next day Al Coates introduced the Flames' new head coach, Brian Sutter, a member of Alberta's legendary hockey family. Fleury was the only Flames player to attend that news conference, where he applauded heartily.

When Mike Sullivan's future appeared uncertain with the Flames, Coates did shop him around for a trade. He received a few essentially equal offers of future draft choices but accepted Boston's bid so that Mike could return to his home town. Come summer, the Flames would send a future draft choice to Tampa Bay to get goalie Rick Tabaracci back, sending ripples through the minds of Kidd and Roloson, who was soon traded to the Carolina Hurricanes.

Back in Saint John, Dale McTavish would try to play hard more consistently as Coates and Page had suggested and would break his right foot in the process. That cost him a month of playing time. And then the Saint John coach was let go. Dale made plans to marry his girlfriend, Christine Eng, and was thinking about playing for bigger money in Europe. He would still like to restart his NHL career that lasted twenty-five days and nine games. "It was awesome," says the twenty-five-year-old. "It's where you want to be." He still has the puck from his sole NHL goal and the videotape of the goal that Gary Taylor gave him.

Every few days Dale watches the tape. He finds himself wondering often if Theo's breakaway shot in the closing seconds of the Toronto game had gotten past Felix Potvin and the Flames had won that game, would the team have been less eager to make a move and send Dale down? He will never know.

Soon after that Maple Leaf win, Toronto general manager Cliff Fletcher would trade an unhappy Doug Gilmour to New Jersey and receive, among other things in return, a fast little New Jersey forward named Steve Sullivan who caught Fletcher's eye for his feistiness and scoring ability despite his small size. In the last game of the season, with Steve O'Donnell again driving the Flames' bus in Toronto, the Leafs would once more beat Calgary at Maple Leaf Gardens. Soon after, however, Fletcher himself would be fired as general manager.

After the season, Fleury would take time to renew his passion for golf, even attempting to qualify and just missing the cut for a pro tournament. He made little time to watch the NHL play-offs, it being so much harder to watch at that level than to play. But then came the scary exhilaration and arrival of another son, Beaux, whose birth was timed for the off-season, as pro hockey families know to do if they want the father to be at home for sure. Theo seemed to revel in full-time fatherhood and in the goal of making Canada's Olympic hockey team. Fleury plunged into demanding daily workouts with Rich Hesketh, squeezed in a trip back to Russell to show off the baby and play some base-ball with his brothers, and then concentrated for a full week on training 321 youngsters at his hockey school.

Most of the youngsters naturally plan on having an NHL career. "Hey, guys," Theo would say at centre ice, "listen up. Maybe one of you here today will make a career in the NHL. For everybody else, hockey is going to be a game. And what are games supposed to be?"

"Fun!" the youngsters would cry out. And Theo would show them all how to ride their hockey sticks around the rink like witches.

Back in Manitoba on this dark Tuesday night, Dave Chartier is making some ice alone on the still primitive, still frozen rink inside Binscarth's old metal barn. Both of Dave's knees, blown out at separate times during his stint in the NHL, are hurting now, which usually means more snow soon, though it seems too cold for that. Dave is off from the mine tomorrow. After a day of classes in Linda Baker's school, Nicholas will receive some more lessons from his dad about hockey and life. The seven-year-old boy is learning quickly in his little league; he has thirty-two goals in four games. Who's to say now how far the little guy could go?

As soon as Dave finishes applying this last layer of warm water, he will turn off the rink's lights and walk slowly home through the snow, perhaps to catch some of the game on TV. By midnight, both Dave and Theoren will be inside their homes in their beds, some seven hundred miles apart but together in their fatigue and their thoughts about hockey. The fresh water on both the Saddledome and the Binscarth rinks will be congealing into a glorious, glassy cement awaiting the next day of dreams. Both arenas will be dark and cold and empty inside, enduring another long winter's long night.

In a few hours, however, the whole thing will start all over again, in both places and both lives – and so many others like them.

Acknowledgements

This is my tenth book and this one requires far more acknowledgements than any other. If the subjects of biographies, such as Theoren Fleury, have seen their lives directed, shaped, modified, improved, and otherwise affected by their accumulating experiences and relationships over many years, then the same goes for a project that involves writing about such lives.

Fury may appear to be a book about the game of hockey and one life within it. It is. But in reality on so many other levels, *Fury* is a book about many lives connected by the game of hockey. Connections among humans, even if the links go through a game on ice, are what modern society so surprisingly and sadly lacks – and so badly needs. Despite all of the amazing technological paraphernalia and the invention of new gadgets daily, there is afoot across North America an amazing amount of social and individual isolation. And so, millions of humans seek connections with each other, their teams, and the idea of striving to win through sharing an allegiance to a local team. They show this allegiance by witnessing – and sometimes cheering – the athletic contest in person together, in absentia via the media, or even through wearing identical logos on their clothing.

My connections to others began with my parents, of course, Ralph and Beatrice Malcolm, who played a crucial role instilling in me throughout my upbringing the myriad attitudes, experiences, and sensitivities – especially the curiosity – that formed the mostly adult person I became. My father was a consulting industrial engineer. His job, his passion, was travelling around and deciphering how things worked – or failed to work – the machinery, factories, teams of workers and executives. Then he would report on it. What I spent so long doing travelling around during more than a quarter-century in newspaper journalism was deciphering how society and government worked – or failed to – and then reporting on it.

I can see clearly the hands of individual teachers and coaches, such as Arthur Hughes and Jock Sutherland, on pieces of this book. I suspect many other lessons from them and others who invested time and thought in me over the years have become such an integral part of my personality and thought processes that I no longer recognize the lessons as emanating from the outside. This is good and natural but I still appreciate them.

During some formative times I was fortunate to have a squadron of editors, Gene Roberts, David Jones, John Lee, Joe Lelyveld, Jon Segal, and John LaHoud prime among them, whose questions and suggestions – and patience – added to the ongoing development of my skills and touched my life in personally positive ways, even when they did not realize it.

The New York Times as an institution was also crucial in this respect, supporting and facilitating the development of my professional curiosity and skills and providing a prominent platform for their display. I know of no other publication that would have, for instance, taken seriously some of my more curious story ideas, for instance, following spring north one year to see how a new season affected the lives of four individuals in different regions. But the paper not only allowed me to try to tell large stories through seemingly small tales, it helped make them – and me – better.

The words Theoren Fleury and courage have long been associated with each other in the minds of hockey fans, even the boobirds. But it takes an unusual brand of courage to open the door to a total stranger and, for better or worse, to share your entire life, friends, and family with him. I thank him, and his wife, Veronica, for that willingness and trust, and hope that I lived up to them in terms of accuracy and diligence.

Many people have played crucial and beneficial roles in Theo's life, and thus they played crucial and beneficial roles in the development of this book. There were scores of them, too many to list individually here, although most of their names do appear throughout the book. But I must mention by name a few without whose trust and patient co-operation this book about humanity would not be: Ryan Griffin, Ede and Len Peltz, Ann and Jim Petz, Doug Fowler, Mike Rolling, and Theo's parents, Wally and Donna. This book could not have happened if Ryan had not picked up the phone that first day.

Arthur Pincus played an essential and much-appreciated role in facilitating the book. I have found during this project that the people in the business of hockey, including Arthur and his colleague Gary Meagher, and those in the game of the same business are quite possibly the nicest, most forthcoming group of professionals I have ever met, interviewed, and worked with. And this book about so many lives is the better for it.

They are also, collectively, without a doubt and with a few stunning exceptions the worst group of people I have ever encountered at returning telephone calls. But once I got a hold of them no one could have asked or dreamed for more patience, kindness, assistance, and, if not total understanding, at least acceptance of the no doubt occasionally weird demands of this writer. I am unsure, for instance, how I would have received questions from a basic stranger involving the precise volume of garbage exiting the Saddledome after a hockey game; garbage is, after all, exiting that building because no one wanted to have anything more to do with it.

This special and profound appreciation applies especially to the management and staff of the Calgary Flames Hockey Club, beginning with Brad Andrews in the ticket office and running right on up through George Greenwood and Nancy Cleveland, Libby Raines and Karla Piper, Allan Beesley and many others. When I first called the Flames one autumn afternoon a few years ago, all I wanted was some ticket information, which Brad Andrews readily provided. Two weeks later it was the same Brad Andrews who tracked me down – in another country – with the warning that that particular game was rapidly selling out. He did not want us to be disappointed. And we never were.

The Flames had no control over this book of mine, except that by being so forthcoming, candid, and co-operative, they did enable, I hope, a stranger to better understand and write about their constant efforts to build a winner and their game's explosive growth across North America and beyond. Their ever-present friendliness and patience made this book not only pleasant to do, I believe, but much better. And I thank each one of them for their faith and time from the bottom of my heart, especially Bernie Doenz, Brenda Koyich, Mike Burke, and Rick Skaggs. I must pause a moment to acknowledge as well Jim Utterback, a friend and facilitator, and Harvey the Hound, who did not agree to an interview but did permit Grant Kelba to explain his job.

I also want to express my deepest gratitude to the Flames' president, Ron Bremner, general manager Al Coates, and coach Pierre Page and his staff, especially Kevin Constantine. Their candour and trust were not only essential to this tale but much appreciated and I enjoyed their company immensely.

I am sure some of the players wondered at times what the mustachioed guy was up to, so busily inquiring into and eavesdropping on their lives at home and on the road. But they, too, were patient and allowed me not only to gather the nuggets of information and colour that make these stories come alive but, coincidentally, to live out a longtime fantasy, which I treasure and share within these pages. I did become the Flames' informal arbiter of airborne Scrabble games; I only hope my rulings were fair, if not always popular.

Other contributors I must thank are the numerous individuals related to Fleury or the team and the media who contributed to this story by sharing their lives, their work, and their connection to this game and this player. Almost all of these kind people are mentioned by name in the book. I thank them again here and add the name Kevin Udahl.

On a personal level, I forever appreciate the energies, enthusiasms, and support of our children – Christopher, Spencer, Emily, and Keddy, whose naive juvenile enthusiasm for hockey got us going down this road some years before he mastered his backwards crossovers. Of course, my wife Connie is essential to this process, not only as a longtime friend, debater, sounding board, and bucker-upper when things were not going well but also for her keen professional editing eyes, the first to fall on each day's collection of newly written words. Writing a book is a mental marathon of many months and she was at every turn with encouragement.

I must mention a few friends too. Dino Lucarelli, through his kindness and openness, inadvertently introduced me to the richly detailed goings-on behind the scenes of professional sports. I think those experiences planted the seed for this book many years ago. And I thank him profoundly; this has been a lot of fun. Roger Straus is another friend who became a partner despite his desire for death by kayak and whose company and insights have added richness to my life and accumulating experiences. Eugene Kennedy, as always, was interested, supportive, and offered very useful comments and Ken Dryden's calm and provocative insights helped me down some new lanes of inquiry and thinking.

I want to thank Ann Rittenberg and Doug Gibson for the confidence and enthusiasm they displayed in me and this project and for their patience over some years until we could work together. I must also add a note of appreciation to the colleagues in my day job in the Governor's Office. They no doubt listened to several too many recountings of some passage as I lived it, processed it, and then wrote it. I apologize for that volubility. And I appreciate their ear and friendship.

Last, I want to thank Marc Racicot, who was a friend before he became my boss and our Governor and will be a friend long after he is no longer either. Fortunately, there are no term limits yet on friendship and brotherhood. I have learned countless lessons from witnessing up close his grace, intelligence, patience, and kindness, often like Theo as the target of fame. Sometimes I am successful incorporating Marc's lessons into my life. But always I admire them. Many of those lessons and observations have also seeped into this book; nothing ever seems official in my life until I write it down somewhere. Inspiration is not a word I ever toss loosely about. But it applies here. I thank the Governor for calling me up from the minors and giving me the opportunity to be a starter on his team.

Index

Calgary Flames, 5, 20-21, 60, 63-70, 106, 114-15, 120-23, 133-35, 143, 163-65, 212-15, 215-21, 233, 234-39, 240, 243, 246-47, 252-68, 275-85, 290-97, 301, 307; and entertainment at games, 167-85; marketing and merchandising of, 136, 139-51, 165, 166-67; and the media, 236, 263-66, 270, 276-77; and player training and conditioning, 113, 115-16, 118, 119-20; practice routine of, 68-70; and road trips, 215-21, 252-68, 275-85, 290-97; and scouts, 120-22, 222, 285; and trades, 285-88, 308-10; *see also* Saddledome

Calgary Herald, 179, 254, 263-64, 304

Calgary Hitmen, 51, 58, 237, 247

Calgary Stampeders, 133, 173, 217

Calgary Sun, 243, 263, 267, 276, 304

Campbell, Dean, 185

Carlton, Steve, 82

Carolina Hurricanes, 309

Chartier, Dave, 7-8, 13, 61, 310-11

Chelios, Chris, 304

Cherry, Don, 104-105, 255

Chiasson, Steve, 56, 57, 63-64, 254, 256, 282, 286-87, 291, 307

Chicago Blackhawks, 15, 134, 165, 166, 167, 285, 286, 301, 304

Ciavaglia, Peter, 214

Clark, Wendel, 277

Clarke, Bobby, 195, 214, 241

Cleveland, Nancy, 298-300, 308

Coates, Al, 15, 66-67, 120-23, 140, 145, 174, 216, 217, 219, 252, 255, 258, 259, 266, 267, 270, 281, 284, 285, 285-88, 290, 294, 307, 308, 309

Colorado Avalanche, 56, 133, 139, 143, 165, 166, 258

Colorado Rockies, 105

Constantine, Kevin, 68, 89, 238, 242-43, 253, 254, 258, 262-63, 277, 281, 284, 294, 307

Corkery, Tim, 214

Corrigal, Kim, 278-79

Coulter, Bruce, 44, 103

Crisp, Terry, 57, 221, 223, 224-25, 233, 241, 245, 248-49

Dallas Stars, 267, 284

Davidson, John, 240-41

Deasley, Bryan, 214

Denver Rangers, 234

Derkach, Mike, 44

Deschamps, Dion, 44

Detroit Red Wings, 57, 143, 166, 301

Doenz, Bernie, 236

Domenichelli, Hnat, 286-87

Domi, Tie, 281

Driedger, Irwin, 39

Duben, Mike, 13, 53, 180, 303

Dudley, Rick, 138, 165-66